The Wimp Factor

The Wimp Factor

Gender Gaps, Holy Wars, and the Politics of Anxious Masculinity

Stephen J. Ducat

BEACON
150

Beacon Press, Boston

BEACON PRESS
25 Beacon Street
Boston, Massachusetts 02108-2892
www.beacon.org

Beacon Press books
are published under the auspices of
the Unitarian Universalist Association of Congregations.

07 06 05 8 7 6 5 4 3 2 1

This book is printed on acid-free paper that meets the
uncoated paper ANSI/NISO specifications for permanence as revised in 1992.

Composition by Wilsted & Taylor Publishing Services
Back cover image: Joan Thornton

Library of Congress Cataloging-in-Publication Data
Ducat, Stephen.
    The wimp factor : gender gaps, holy wars, and the politics of anxious masculinity /
Stephen J. Ducat.
        p. cm.
    Includes bibliographical references and index.
    ISBN 0-8070-4345-1 (pb : alk. paper)
    1. Masculinity—Political aspects. 2. Politicians—United States—Psychology.
    3. Sex role—Political aspects—United States. 4. International relations—
Psychological aspects. I. Title.

    HQ1090.D83 2004
    305.31—dc22   2004004809

Credits: p. 107, Mike Thompson cartoon from the *National Forum,* is used by permission of Copley News Service and Mike Thompson. p. 86, OLIPHANT cartoon is used by permission of the Universal Press Syndicate. pp. 11, 106, 132, *The American Spectator* images are used by permission of *The American Spectator.* pp. 154, 164, "American Pathetic" and "Serving His Party!" are used by permission of the Rochester Initiative/ Spotlight Magazine. p. 140, *Spy* magazine cover is used by permission of Sussex Publishers, Inc., © 1995. pp. 104, 151, reprinted by permission of Tom Meyer. p. 234, *Surviving the Feminization of America* cover is used by permission of Rich Zubaty.

Contents

Preface

Observers of contemporary politics, especially those who follow the high drama of presidential campaigns, are plagued by many questions. Most vexing, perhaps, are those concerned with the role of gender in public life. Why is testosterone the coveted elixir of political power? More specifically, what anxieties have made the "wimp factor" one of the most important variables in determining the outcomes of elections? First coined in 1988, this phrase, which denotes a male candidate's deficient manhood, came to haunt the presidency of George Herbert Walker Bush. It is now an issue that dogs most men who run for political office, to such a degree that armies of spin doctors and handlers are hired to inject unseemly quantities of Viagra into their candidate's rhetoric, and stage baroque macho photo opportunities. Even a relatively liberal presidential candidate, John Kerry, in November of 2003 felt compelled to drag reporters and an AP photographer out to a chilly field in Iowa, the first caucus state in the Democratic primary, to watch him blow pheasants away with his twelve-gauge shotgun. Apparently, Mr. Kerry wanted to reassure the male electorate that even though he supports a ban on assault weapon sales, he still likes to kill things.

Do the same anxieties drive the ever-widening gender gap in voting behavior? Many people do not realize that this phenomenon, first observed in 1980, has been marked by men's growing conservatism, not by an increase in liberalism among women. As the 2004 presidential election looms, this disparity between male and female voters is once again on everyone's lips, and has become one of the guiding obsessions of political consultants. "Soccer moms" and "office park dads," and, more currently, "security moms" and "NASCAR dads," are now seen as the demographic groups that decide elections.

There is another demographic influencing politics in the U.S. and around the world—religious fundamentalists. A question many polit-

ical observers have pondered is: Why are fundamentalist men everywhere so concerned about questions of gender? For all the differences
in their respective theologies, holy warriors across the globe, domestic
and foreign, seem to be driven by nearly identical misogynist visions.
This is just as discernible in their idealization of selfless motherhood
and wifely servitude as it is in their fear and hatred of female sexuality.
Politics for these authoritarian priests of patriarchy appears to be largely
a means of achieving with the powers of the state or the dread of terrorist weaponry what they cannot accomplish with the force of their
arguments.

If we are to understand the link between these three seemingly
unrelated phenomena—fear of the wimp factor, the gender gap in political attitudes, and the holy wars of fundamentalists—we must understand the powerful role that unconscious fears and fantasies play in
politics; we must turn to psychology. But focusing on men's inner world
does not diminish the importance of their outer world. Economics,
class conflict, cultural traditions, and the historical residues of white
supremacy are all powerful determinants of American political behavior. And each of these intersects in complex ways with psychological
motives. My interest here is to focus on dynamics that are typically less
evident than the more obvious socioeconomic factors, and thus rarely,
if ever, get attended to by newscasters and political pundits.

While delimited to the psychological, this study draws on many
kinds of data, including the results of my own research, in which I was
able to demonstrate a direct association between the magnitude of a
man's terror of being feminine (femiphobia) and his tendency to embrace right-wing political opinions. The Wimp Factor also takes a close
look at aspects of popular culture, such as editorial cartoons, political
advertisements, movies, and the slips of the tongue made by public figures. The book shows how these apparently disparate elements reveal
much about the effects of femiphobia in politics. And, because men's
fear of the feminine has been a powerful motive force in political struggles for centuries, the book includes in-depth case studies from various
historical periods.

Chief among the more current events examined here will be the recent war in Iraq. I will show how the rhetoric and diplomatic posturing on the part of right-wing politicians and pundits leading up to, during, and after the invasion have exemplified the anxious preoccupation with affirming manhood that is described throughout the book. Also analyzed will be the striking gender gap in public opinion on the war, which has been even greater than it was during the Vietnam War, with 45 percent of men having "strongly" supported the military assault on Iraq, as compared with 21 percent of women (according to a Zogby International poll). The postwar events in Iraq are still unfolding (if indeed one can regard the daily carnage as postwar), and the long-term political aftermath cannot be predicted at this point. Nevertheless, the domestic and global consequences of the current administration's swaggering unilateralism are already making themselves apparent, and are examined through a psychological lens in the final chapter.

While the book looks squarely at the psychological dynamics behind a number of deeply disturbing political phenomena, such as war, fundamentalist terrorism, environmental devastation, homophobia, and racism, it may be reassuring for both genders nevertheless, for different reasons. Women are profoundly affected by the way men defend themselves against their insecurities, in politics as well as personal relationships. An understanding of the rationale behind their thinking and behaviors may be illuminating, as well as heartening. As for men, the extent to which they are conscious of their fear of being feminine varies. No man, however, is completely unaffected. In addition, most men have no idea why they suffer from femiphobia and, as I have observed in many of my male patients, are likely to regard their anxieties as a personal weakness. Understanding the cultural, historical, and developmental origins of an insecure sense of masculinity may not only be reassuring; it may enable men to challenge notions of manhood that seem to animate so much political iniquity in the world.

Fear and the Phallus
An Introduction

The Fear

The rumor was that he sat on his mother's lap until going off to college.[1] "I used to tell her that she is raising him as a girl, and that I have three girls, but she never stopped pampering him," Mohamed al-Amir Atta's father recalled in an interview after learning that his son had been named as the mastermind behind the September 11 terrorist attacks.[2] The younger Mr. Atta, as it turned out, shared his father's sense that the borders of manhood had to be vigilantly guarded against the perils of feminine pollution. He not only refused to shake hands with women, but, in a statement found after his death, insisted that women be barred from his funeral.[3] Mr. Atta's final instructions went on to elaborate, "I don't want a pregnant woman or a person who is not clean to come and say goodbye to me."[4]

This is a book about fear—a particular fear that has composed the very foundation of male selfhood from antiquity to the modern era, from the peasant villages of Afghanistan to the west wing of the American White House. It is the fear of being feminized. For many men, masculinity is a hard-won, yet precarious and brittle psychological achievement that must be constantly proven and defended. While the *external* factors may appear to be that which is most threatening—gay men in military shower rooms, feminist women in civilian bedrooms, or audible female footsteps in the Taliban-era marketplace—the actual threat that many men experience is an unconscious, *internal* one: the sense that they are not "real" men. The book will show how this fantasy of being under constant siege by a multitude of *external* feminizing forces is really an unconscious defense that is employed to keep out of mind something even more disturbing—an *identification* with women.

The Phallus

Somewhere in his angst-ridden oeuvre, Woody Allen catalogues the various mortifications he endured at that developmental station of the cross known as adolescence. Recalling the many torments of high-school gym class, Mr. Allen speculates that he was the only boy in the locker room to suffer from penis envy. What he probably did not realize, embedded as he was in his own private humiliation, was that he was not alone. That is because what Mr. Allen envied, and every man envies, is not the penis but the phallus.

While all anatomically intact males have a penis, no one has a phallus—the mythic, permanently erect archetypal monolith of masculine omnipotence that signifies untrammeled growth, invulnerability, and freedom from all dependency. One who appears to possess the phallus is seen as lacking nothing and no one. He seems to wield a talisman that protects against all feminine danger, especially that which arises from within. The penis, on the other hand, even when tumescent, is vulnerable. It is easily and inevitably deflated. An erection might stand for the phallus, but the reverse is not true.[5] After all, only the phallus is always standing, while the penis is usually at rest. Real men, sad to say, come up short. This is why campaign consultants will never be out of work. There are few places where appearing phallic matters more than on the stage of political life, at least for male candidates. A line from the Tom Waits song "Step Right Up" captures with bracing poetic economy what an effective campaign does: "It gives you an erection. It wins the election."

The Politics of Anxious Masculinity

As the next national election approaches, the gender gap in political attitudes and voting behavior is once more a central preoccupation of media pundits and campaign managers. As mentioned earlier, "soccer moms" and "NASCAR dads" are some of the sociological euphemisms du jour coined by pollsters to denote liberal women and conservative men, groups whose support is coveted by all campaigns because they can swing elections. But no one has been able to explain how this gender difference has come about. This book, along with the research that informs it, is an attempt to offer answers to that question.

Many authors have explored the impact that men's socialization has on the intimate details of private life. In the following chapters I will try to show how male anxiety has also come to shape *political* discourse and behavior, often in profound and surprising ways. More specifically, I will attempt to explain what has puzzled many pundits and ordinary citizens alike—how seemingly disparate issues, such as welfare, the environment, gay and lesbian civil rights, military intervention abroad, separation of church and state, and government regulation of corporate behavior, have become gendered, with the end result that men, more than women, tend to be drawn to ultraconservative ideas and actions.

The book uses many types of data to explore the perplexing gulf between men's and women's political passions, whether they are expressed in electoral politics or by the behavior of fundamentalists. It integrates historical accounts from ancient Greece to nineteenth-century America, the findings of empirical attitude-survey research (mine and that of others), current thinking on how we develop a gender identity, clinical case material derived from my psychotherapy practice, and theocratic screeds issued by fundamentalists of all persuasions. In addition, the book examines specimens of popular culture taken from political cartoons, campaign speeches, comedy monologues, and the feverish polemics of increasingly popular right-wing radio talk show hosts. While these widely divergent sources of data may appear to be all over the map, the map is a holographic one; in each part one can view the whole. In other words, the complex dynamics of anxious male politics are visible in each of its varied manifestations.

Because the aim of the book is to illuminate the gender subtext of political behavior in its *unconscious* as well as conscious aspects—especially the role of internal conflict—cultural data are viewed through the same psychological lens that has helped bring into sharp relief the anguished inner lives of my male patients. What I attend to when trying to understand the minds of individuals in psychotherapy is not just the key events and people of their past and present lives. Equally important are the ways patients *represent* those events or persons—the metaphors, analogies, and slips of the tongue through which they convey the psychological meanings of their experience.

Likewise, in trying to understand the psychology of a culture, it is not enough to know the salient social and political events that have transpired in the life of a people. One must listen to how these events are *spoken of* by politicians, journalists, celebrities, and ordinary citizens. Only by attuning to this usually unconscious aspect of cultural discourse can one appreciate the deeper meanings of events. That is why this book, which is a psychological analysis of political developments in American culture, must at the same time be a kind of ethnography. Movies, newspaper articles, and political speeches are viewed as *folklore* that reveals the values, anxieties, wishes, and fantasies of the culture that produced them.

For this reason, several of the chapters focus on the behavior of various politicians, their public statements, unconscious slips, tortured metaphors, domestic and foreign policies, political and sexual scandals, and image crises—not as entertaining journalistic fluff (although many of these anecdotes are quite amusing), but as cultural data. As part of a history to which we have all been privy, these phenomena make ideal case studies to illustrate the dynamics of male femiphobia (fear of the feminine) in politics. Their inclusion is also guided by the assumption that the politicians who get elected or nominated reflect something about those of us who vote for them, just as our folklore, described previously, mirrors our deepest concerns. In other words, this is a book just as interested in the people who cast ballots as it is in those who jockey for political office.

Along with writing, researching, and teaching about the political psychology of masculinity, I also treat men in psychotherapy. Much of the mental suffering of my male patients seems to derive from a deep fear of women, as well as a paralyzing dread of the "feminine" within themselves. These anxieties have been particularly evident in their denial of dependency needs, their inability to sustain intimate ties with women or other men, their preoccupation with holding positions of dominance and control in relationships, and their various sexual dysfunctions. Paradoxically, but perhaps not unexpectedly, it has been the men who are the most macho in appearance and behavior who have manifested the greatest fear of being feminine.

It is not that there is something pathological about being male. Rather, the problem is the psychological cost of developing a male identity in a culture that disparages the feminine and insists that the boundaries between masculine and feminine remain unambiguous and impermeable. In fact, it may be the latter imperative that compels some transgender individuals to seek surgical alteration to make their bodies conform to their identities. Unlike those cultures in which gender is not bound to anatomy,[6] the West, especially America, accords a feminine man much less tolerance than a "woman" convincingly constructed by the scalpel.

In order to understand the gender conflicts seen in my male patients, I have had to consider more than their individual developmental histories, and look at the larger context of the greater American culture. For example, many of the most vivid expressions of men's fears can be found in the colorful vernacular of everyday macho invective: sissy, bitch, pussy-whipped, mama's boy, wimp, girly-man, pansy. These terms of hypermasculine derision attest to the narrow and rigid boundaries in which our prevailing notions of maleness are confined. Such words also tell us much about the shame that results from the failure to remain within these constricting borders. Even terms of praise in the lexicon of conventional masculinity reveal some of our culture's deepest fears and assumptions about manhood. The term "he-man," for example, is a curious redundancy. One wonders why it is necessary to say it twice. It suggests that being biologically male is not sufficient to confer or sustain masculinity. Instead, it must be asserted through repetition, in words and in actions. The everyday vocabulary and common-sense notions of gender remind us that in the majority of patriarchal cultures, the most important thing about being a man is *not being a woman*. The eighteenth-century French anatomist Jacques-Louis Moreau must have sensed the tenuous and constructed nature of masculinity when he said, "The male is only male at certain moments, but ... the female is female all her life."[7]

There are few places where men's fear of the feminine has been manifested more dramatically than in political rhetoric and behavior, from the conservative redefinition of the word "liberal," to the rise in the 1990s of private armies of angry, paranoid, and government-hating men, to the misogynist decrees of the now-defeated Taliban regime of Afghanistan. Since the U.S. national election of 1980, right-wing political propagandists have relentlessly, and with great success, linked liberalism to weakness, dependency, and helplessness—qualities seen by most male-dominant societies as feminine. As a corollary to the "L-word"—a label that has become so politically profane it requires abbreviation—we have seen the emergence of the feminizing maternal menace of the welfare state, conjured by Ronald Reagan as "Big Government." In 1982, he implored us to "wean ourselves from the long misery of overtaxing, overspending, and the great myth that our national nanny knows best."[8] Certainly no "real man" would want to become a mama's boy to such a state, hence the long and continuing jihad against welfare and other social programs. Right-wing militias, though their memberships have dwindled somewhat over the years, are still present in nearly every state in America. In the 1990s they carried this holy war on government to its logical, if psychotic, extreme. The bombing of the Oklahoma City Federal Building, which targeted, among various government agencies, a day-care center, was a very lethal as well as bluntly symbolic assault on the "nanny state."

From the Ancient Greek Polis to the American White House

Anxious masculinity has been a discernible subtext in politics throughout the entire history of Western culture, visible in phenomena as diverse as the political campaigns of ancient Greece, the editorial cartoon depictions of George Bush Sr., the demonization of Hillary Clinton, and the psychosexual fallout from the Monica Lewinsky scandal. For example, according to classics scholar John Winkler, the most insulting and politically damaging label for ancient Greek citizens was that of a *binoumenos,* a "fucked male." This may seem puzzling to those who have assumed the ubiquity and widespread acceptance of homosexuality among Athenian men of antiquity. However, their homoeroticism existed in an elaborate matrix of gender and class codes that regulated who could have sex with whom, and in what way. Greek men experienced gender as a terrifyingly mutable trait. All that was required for an adult male citizen soldier—the crème de la crème of the class hierarchy—to be reduced to the social equivalent of a woman (or a slave) was to be seen as servile, especially if that meant being the receptive, penetrated partner in sexual relations. Such a feminizing metamorphosis was the ultimate "character issue" for Athenian politicians and, hence, the most effective means of slandering one's opponent. A similar strategy of political emasculation was directed at foreign enemies, as well. One way to commemorate military successes was to produce pottery on which were painted images of victorious soldiers with erect penises getting ready to rape the losers. For the ancient Greeks, the phallus was an essential image in the iconography of conquest—a meaning, this book argues, that still lingers in the shared political unconscious of the modern West.⁹

George Bush Sr., in his 1988 presidential campaign, faced the twentieth-century version of the struggle that confronted scandalized Athenian politicians, a battle against enemies who sought to feminize him. Like so many campaigns, the one in 1988 was fundamentally a contest between images, not a debate over issues. Popular jokes played on the double meaning of Bush having "served under Ronald Reagan." Some of his opponents widely distributed feminizing bumper stickers that read "Lick Bush." Then, the cover of *Newsweek* blared, with unflattering concision, "Fighting the Wimp Factor." Mr. Bush had failed to counter the popular view of himself as a pampered patrician, a man of effete and precious sensibilities whose road through life had always been smoothed by inherited wealth and nepotistic advantage—all qualities that have been coded feminine in American political culture for centuries.[10] His handlers tried hypermasculine photo ops. But posing in nuclear bombers, conspicuously chowing down on pork rinds, and various attempts at impersonating a two-fisted cowpoke did not do the trick. In the popular imagination he was still unable to shed the milky, uncalloused skin of Eastern privilege. Ironically, the intervention of a female speechwriter, Peggy Noonan, was required. She successfully, if only temporarily, resuscitated his manhood with massive infusions of rhetorical steroids in a convention speech bulging with combat metaphors, which significantly boosted his support among men.[11] It was not long after his inauguration, however, that numerous editorial cartoons began to appear depicting Bush as a woman, or wearing women's clothing. This imagery, which was irrelevant to the cartoons' political point, continued to appear throughout the four years of his presidency. Eventually, even fellow Republican George Will would accuse his party's leader of "intellectual and moral flaccidity."[12] The president's Sisyphean struggle to prove his masculinity was clearly not over. In fact, he would find it the most bruising and humiliating struggle of his political career, which would leave him badly hobbled.

The invasion of Panama, however, was an effective, if evanescent, anodyne against the stinging attributions of "wimp" long endured by Bush. In some quarters, the gender subtext lacked all subtlety. A front-page headline in the *New York Times* declared the war a "Presidential Rite of Passage." The article pointed out that American presidents must "demonstrate their willingness to shed blood" and that "the American political culture required them to show the world they carried big sticks." In going after Noriega, the *Times* observed, President Bush was "showing his steel."[13] The next day an Associated Press article appeared with a headline that proclaimed, "Read His Lips: He's Not Kind. Face Analyst Detects a Macho Man in Bush's Features." The article then proceeded to take phrenology to new heights of scientific precision by providing the definitive proof of Mr. Bush's masculinity: "It's right there in the semicircular knob on his prominent, square-jawed chin."[14] When the U.S. went to war with Iraq, the entire nation seemed to notice that manly semicircular knob on our president's chin, if his popularity rating was any indicator. While the missiles, it turns out, often did not make their targets, the missives from the Pentagon press conferences hit their mark with many men, resulting in a twenty-five-point gender gap in approval of the war.[15] Ultimately, however, vanquishing petty despots with technically proficient ardor and presiding over victory parades would not save George Bush's presidency; he remained the repository of many American men's anxieties about their own gender constancy and feared "feminine" aspects.

Women Who Think Too Much and the Wandering Phallus

In addition to the specter of feminized men, there is another terror that haunts the patriarchal unconscious: "castrating" women. A female need only be powerful and self-authorizing to be construed as a threat to the testicular security of some males. Thus, Hillary Clinton, who had been an unapologetically confident and exuberantly independent partner alongside her husband Bill (at least early on in her reign as first lady), evoked a degree of misogynist dread and revulsion unprecedented in American political history.

While stories of her attempting to channel the spirit of a similarly strong and nearly as reviled predecessor, Eleanor Roosevelt, were doubtless apocryphal, Ms. Clinton did succeed in invoking the ghosts of Eleanor's male critics. Suggesting that Ms. Clinton was a woman who didn't know her place, Patrick Buchanan at the 1992 Republican convention referred to the Clinton-Gore campaign as the "Clinton-Clinton ticket."[16]

GOP National Chairman Rich Bond sounded a similar alarm when he claimed that the Democratic candidate's spouse "advised Clinton on every move."[17] On the facing page, the *American Spectator* referred to her as "boy Clinton's big mama."[18] A year after President Clinton's election, the *Washington Post* quoted Jack Wheeler of the Freedom Research Foundation: "A year from now she will be the most despised woman in America, and every guy in every bar in the country will be commenting derisively to the fellow next to him about how 'pussy-whipped' her husband is."[19]

Around the same time, rumors were circulated that Ms. Clinton was tossing lamps, books, and other objects at the president during arguments. Denials by the Secret Service did little to diminish them.[20] Conservative columnists Rowland Evans and Robert Novak seemed to perceive a phallic quality in the object of their anxiety when they decried "the thrust for power of Hillary Rodham Clinton."[21] *Newsweek* expressed its concern by gracing the cover with an unflatteringly blurry in-your-face close-up of the first lady, accompanied by the headline "How Much Clout?"[22] Like the aforementioned Jack Wheeler, the bulk of male political commentators organized their fears around the notion of a castrated Bill Clinton. This was true of comedians as well. Arsenio Hall, for example, noted that the president had not announced a Supreme Court nominee because "Hillary hasn't made up his mind yet."[23] David Letterman revealed that the chief executive's Secret Service code was "Mr. Mom."[24] Ms. Clinton astutely summed up the psychodynamics of her demonization by frightened male pundits when she said to *Esquire Magazine*, "I'm a Rorschach test."[25]

It is interesting that after the revelations of the Monica Lewinsky scandal, Bill Clinton's image went from that of the neutered househusband of an emasculating harridan to that of a swaggering stud-muffin whose untrammeled lust for sexual conquest imperiled all females in his orbit. Behind the tongue-clucking disapprobation of some male commentators was a thinly disguised envy. San Francisco-based right-wing talk jock Michael Savage (whose last name, prior to his media remasculinization, was Weiner—pronounced *whiner*), warned American men to hold on to "their" women because "Clinton suffers from priapism."[26] A. M. Rosenthal of the *New York Times* bemoaned the jour-

Hillary Clinton as engulfing mother

nalistic preoccupation with "the President's penis," and called upon citizens to "gag at the spectacle of America devoting more attention to oral
sex than to Iraqi biological weapons."[27] The real story behind this outrage is that the formerly feminized president had been resurrected as a
phallic leader, to the open admiration of some. All of this points to an
important psycho-cultural truth: the phallus can move around. Until
the Lewinsky scandal, it was possessed (in the conservative male public imagination) by Hillary. It is notable that after Bill Clinton got it
back, his job approval rating achieved a new level of tumescence.[28]

Anxious Masculinity and the Gender Gap: Welfare, the Environment, War, and Homophobia

The gender gap in political opinion and candidate preference is a phenomenon that first caught my eye during the 1980 presidential election. After becoming a clinical psychologist, I found myself wondering whether the conservative political attitudes and rhetoric that were becoming more typical of men were, at least in part, defensive expressions of the same gender anxiety that was so striking in some of my male patients. This led to the research I conducted on the psychological correlates of the gender gap. The study involved administering questionnaires and psychological tests to 294 male and female undergraduate students at colleges in Portland, Oregon, and the San Francisco Bay Area. As it turned out, men who had more conservative, hypermasculine political attitudes tended to adhere more rigidly to conventional gender role expectations, and they were more conflicted about them. These men had a greater fear of femininity than did males who held liberal, gender-atypical opinions.

While these results might not be completely unexpected, this was the first time any research had empirically demonstrated the relationship between men's political attitudes and an insecure sense of masculinity. It is unlikely that the findings are attributable to some unchangeable biological or spiritual difference between men and women. It is not sex hormones or transhistorical archetypes that drive the gendering of politics, but the deeply conflicted nature of some men's masculine identity—a conflict that chapter 1 will show is rooted in familial and cultural influences. In other words, it is not these men's masculinity, but their fear of losing it, that seems to motivate their embrace of right-wing politics.

Among a number of issues, this research sheds light on the nature of the anxieties implicit in the conservative rhetoric about welfare. I found that men, much more than women, tend to disapprove of and be disturbed by certain caregiving functions of the state, such as subsidized childcare and food stamps. They are not disturbed by the expenditures so much as they are, following Reagan's previously quoted metaphor, by the association they make between "welfare programs" and dependency. We have heard these same concerns expressed over the years by politicians as diverse as David Duke, Bill Clinton, and George W. Bush, and it is a view that also seems to be shared by the American population in general. While not broken down by gender, a 1992 *Time/CNN* poll showed that 93 percent of those advocating welfare cuts cited dependency as their main concern. Only 3 percent mentioned cost cutting as the central issue.[29]

The three other areas where I found a significant gender gap were in attitudes toward the environment, support for war, and homophobia. Not only were men less likely than women to support environmental protection legislation, but they tended to feel less of a connection with nonhuman nature as well. This should not be too surprising, since (mother) nature has been gendered female for at least the last five hundred years.[30] Perhaps it is this association that has prompted some right-wing commentators to refer to environmentalists as "tree-hugging wimps," or that compelled Montana Congressional candidate Ron Marlenee to call his green opponents "prairie fairies."[31]

It is popularly assumed that men are always more likely than women to support war, which is often attributed to some biological imperative such as "testosterone poisoning" or the supposedly pugnacious Y chromosome. What the psychological research literature shows, however, is that women and men do not so much differ in their likelihood of favoring military intervention, as they do in their reasons for supporting it. (This illustrates a familiar truism of social science research: How you ask the question determines the answer.) Women, it turns out, are more likely than men to back a military action if members of their family or community are involved. Men, on the other hand, are more likely to cheer on a war effort for reasons of abstract principle, such as "freedom," "defending the New World Order," "fighting the infidels," or "defeating the evil-doers."[32] My research has uncovered another motive for supporting warfare that is divided along gender lines. Men, it turns out, are more likely to experience a vicarious boost in their own sense of power and potency when American military forces attack, and especially when they defeat, an enemy.

In light of these findings, it has been interesting to hear the devastation visited upon Iraq during the 1991 Gulf War proclaimed as the definitive cure for the "Vietnam Syndrome." The American defeat in Vietnam seemed to induce a culture-wide malaise of wounded masculinity that was to be only partially remedied by the spate of revisionist Vietnam War films, such as *Rambo*. In these movies, hypermasculine *Übermenschen* won fierce battles against enormous odds, which enabled the mostly male audiences to momentarily forget about the real war's final outcome. Unfortunately, the salutary effects of these vengeance fantasies were only transient. It took a series of real-life "pump-you-up" military adventures—Grenada, Panama, and the Gulf War—to provide enduring, if not permanent, gratification.

It remains to be seen how the current war on terrorism, and what looks to be the interminable aftermath of the war in Iraq, will shape gendered anxieties and opinion. Already there have been a number of interesting developments. While there may be a gender gap in support of the present war on terrorism, most women favor it, although in all likelihood for somewhat different reasons than men do, as previously suggested. So far there is a more notable gap in gendered opinion of some of the policies *derived* from the war. An NPR-Kaiser Foundation poll found that, by a margin of 8 percent, men were more likely than women to support military tribunals and other curtailments of civil liberties for noncitizens suspected of terrorist activities.[33]

Ever the guardians of gender boundaries, some on the Christian right have attributed the cause of terrorist mass murder to modern society's violation of the divinely ordained structure of heterosexual male domination. Within days of the 9/11 attacks, American holy warriors and Republican spiritual advisors Jerry Falwell and Pat Robertson were quick to illustrate their many points of agreement with Osama bin Laden by asserting that Americans had it coming. Blame, they insisted, could be laid at the feet of feminists, gay rights advocates, and other liberal servants of Satan. God, they explained, withdrew his protection from the United States because of the putative prominence of these groups in American public life. [34]

In the year following the attacks on the World Trade Center and the Pentagon, both terrorist enemies and domestic critics of Bush's policies became the objects of feminizing attributions. And it didn't take long. The lead article in the October 2, 2001, issue of *The Globe*—one of the country's most dependable sources of information about celebrity love children, alien abductions, and Elvis sightings—scooped the rest of the media with a revealing analysis of Osama bin Laden. "What emerges is a startling picture of a mentally ill, drug-addicted fanatic with an inner rage caused by sexual inadequacy," asserts the author on page 8. He goes on to describe bin Laden's "underdeveloped sexual organs," which led his American girlfriend to humiliate him. The editors were apparently counting on their readers' short historical memory. During the Gulf War, another tabloid, published by the same company, printed a virtually identical article about Saddam Hussein, in which his genital insufficiencies and cross-dressing proclivities were mocked by an American female sex slave. [35]

From a different corner of the American *Zeitgeist*, specifically a right-wing talk radio program in Houston, came another echo of Gulf-War-era femiphobia, in this case anal rape fantasies concerning the Al Qaeda leader. Friends of one of the talk show hosts performed a song that caught on across the nation, "Bend Over, bin Laden," sung to the tune of "Roll Over Beethoven." [36] Along similar lines, Navy crewmen personalized missiles intended for Afghanistan by painting the message "hijack this, fags" [37] on them, thereby evincing an ironic similarity with their Taliban targets, who were known for raping their male, as well as female, enemies.

Mohamed Atta, the reputed coordinator of the September attacks, whose last wishes were described at the beginning of this introduction, was dubbed by one male journalist "Mama's Boy Mo." *Time* magazine noted he lived in a pink house. *The National Enquirer* was less subtle: "World Trade Center terrorist Mohamed Atta and several of his bloody henchmen led secret gay lives for years." [38]

Perhaps the most notorious episode that demonstrated the need on the part of many Americans to see the hijackers as unmanly was the outrage that ensued after Bill Maher made the obvious point on his popular ABC television show, *Politically Incorrect*, that the terrorists, contrary to the claim of President Bush, were anything but cowardly. While they may have been repellent, delusional, and misogynistic mass murderers, the suicidal jihadis were willing to *die* for their beliefs. But, in the prevailing gendered demonology, such behavior must not be considered brave—because brave is masculine, and masculine is good. A bad man, on the other hand, must be viewed as weak, cowardly, and thus feminine. Maher's "politically incorrect" observation cost him sponsors and ultimately his show. As of this writing, he remains exiled from network television.

Finally, the issue that showed the most extreme gender gap in my research was homophobia; men exhibited a striking revulsion toward homosexuality. One of the most revealing and amusing cultural case studies in the psychodynamics of political homophobia was the Republican campaign of 1992. The convention was a spectacle that seemed largely in the hands of religious fundamentalists. Among the stone tablets carried off the mountain by the Christian Right after their special audience with God in Houston was one that read, "Thou Shalt Not Tolerate Homosexuals." Some pundits dismissed the homophobic sermons emanating from the pulpit at the Republican convention as the crackpot ranting of a few monomaniacal holy warriors. In fact, they represented the sentiments of more Americans, especially men, than we might imagine. Just prior to the convention, a national survey of college students found that 53 percent of men and 32 percent of women thought homosexual relationships should be made illegal.[39] Perhaps it was this large gender gap in homophobia that explains the aversion many men at the time had to even having personal or emotional conversations with other men. In one study conducted during that period, it was found that 60 percent of women but only 27 percent of men had same-sex conversations that were psychologically revealing.[40]

Prior to the 1992 campaign, even George Bush Sr. seemed concerned about the homoerotic implications of psychological transparency. During one interview he anxiously pleaded with reporters, "Don't stretch me out on the couch."[41] It was as if he viewed the penetration of his interior by the journalistic gaze as a kind of invasive and feminizing sexual aggression. While this may seem to be interpretive overreaching, even the statements of his most loyal defenders reflected this theme. Talk show host Rush Limbaugh once sympathetically proclaimed about Mr. Bush, "Ever since the day he was nominated, the liberal special interests have been probing every orifice of his body."[42] Buffeting reporters' attempts to gain a window into the psyche of George Bush, the president's campaign spokesperson, Torie Clarke, insisted, "Real men don't get on the couch."[43]

There was a moment of subtle but delicious irony when, midway through the 1992 Republican convention, as George Bush briefly took the podium, the theme music to the Broadway play *La Cage Aux Folles* resounded through the Astrodome.[44] Vibrating the tight tympanic membranes of the homophobic Republican faithful was the music to a play that celebrates the joyous and tender relationship between two older gay men. While it would be tempting to interpret this as an unconscious slip of the tune, presidential spokesman Marlin Fitzwater hastened to assure Americans, "It was just a coincidence."[45]

Just as homophobic politicians and pundits are very anxious to distance themselves from anything that might be even remotely suggestive of homosexuality, they eagerly project homophilic qualities onto their opponents. Noting the closure of New York bordellos prior to the Democratic convention, R. Emmett Tyrrell speculated that "the convention is going to be pretty dreary for the handful of heterosexual men who still attend the Democratic assemblage."[46] In another article, Mr. Tyrrell moved from homophobia to calling into question the very gender constancy of liberals, who "put one in mind of nothing so much as a commune of transsexuals who, halfway through their surgical refurbishment, had a change of heart."[47]

These last two quotes, taken together, tell us much about why so many men—and male politicians in particular—find homosexuality so disturbing. When we take a cross-cultural and historical perspective, it becomes clear that the foundation of homophobia is femiphobia. In patriarchal societies as variant as American prisons, the Arab Middle East, and, as described earlier, ancient Greece, male homoerotic practices and identities are only regarded as deviant, shameful, or of low status for the man who is perceived as taking a passive, subordinate, or receptive (and thus feminine) role in relation to another man. The dominant partner manages to avoid much of the feminizing stigma.

Republican strategists of 1992 were apparently counting on male voters to be more frightened by the specter of feminizing hordes of homosexual satyrs than by the reality of the male electorate's own economic vulnerability. Unfortunately, the calculations of the Republican campaign team were all too accurate, since Mr. Bush's post-convention bounce in the polls was due almost entirely to men shifting their support away from Clinton.[48] While bread-and-butter issues ultimately carried more weight in the minds of male voters than the femiphobic hysteria of the "family values" crusaders, it is clear that appealing to men's fears of being feminized can yield considerable political profit.

From Gender Gap to Gender Gulf: The 2000 Election and Its Aftermath

Anxious masculinity and its discourse, along with the resulting gender gap, were powerfully manifested in the campaign for the 2000 presidential election, and seemed to shape the outcome as well. Once the primaries were over, George W. Bush had an unprecedented twenty-one-point advantage among men, whereas women favored Al Gore by six points, according to a national poll.[49] This trend was echoed in the final results.[50] Mr. Gore's attempts to narrow this gulf through a strained and transparent strategy of remasculinization had mixed results. Though groomed by his handlers to appear as an "alpha male," he only earned the appellation of "attack chihuahua" from the press. A *New*

York Times editorial explained, "Mr. Bush is from Mars and Mr. Gore from Venus."[51]

Femiphobic representations of Hillary Clinton also continued, in part as a response to her candidacy for the Senate in New York. In an editorial cartoon from the *Atlanta Constitution,* appropriately titled "Below the Beltway," Ms. Clinton, dressed in a man's suit, is standing at a podium labeled "Hillary 2000." Next to her is a stoop-shouldered Bill Clinton in drag, sporting a coy and girlish countenance, and a purse that covers his crotch. A television reporter in the foreground announces, "Obviously, the President is having difficulty with his role change. His purse doesn't match."[52] This image demonstrated once again the mobility of the phallus as a gendered symbol of dominance.

The theme of the first lady as a castrating *vagina dentata* (vagina with teeth) was also expressed by David Letterman in an opening monologue following his return to the show after bypass surgery. Referring to the interview he conducted with Ms. Clinton just prior to his hospitalization, he said, "I have a whole new respect for President Clinton. I spent a half an hour with Hillary, half an hour, and look what happened to *me.*"[53]

The two Republican front runners in the primary campaign, John McCain and George W. Bush, made sure not to repeat Bill Clinton's mistake of describing his marriage as an egalitarian relationship. Each of *their* spouses eagerly presented herself as a woman who knew her place and who, if her husband were elected, would make a seamless transition to a demure and decorative first lady. Cindy McCain gratified Republican crowds by proclaiming, "I would take my role [as first lady] as a kind of hostess. If that's traditional, I am traditional."[54]

Laura Bush, eschewing any claim to selfhood, and doubtless reassuring George W.'s male constituency, announced, "My life really began when I married my husband. . . . I give my husband some counsel, but I actually think counsel or advice from a spouse ends up being nagging."[55] A year later, under pressure to drum up support for the war in Afghanistan and to close the gender gap in her husband's popularity, the first lady was briefly unmuzzled and allowed to step out from under her political-wife burqa. Taking the president's place during one of his weekly radio addresses, Mrs. Bush, in reborn feminist drag, shed the administration's crocodile tears over the plight of women under the Taliban.[56] This too-little-too-late lacrimation was a response to a condition that only a few months earlier had evoked no discernible outrage on the part of Republicans, who were showering the Taliban with drug-war money for their tepid campaign to curtail opium production. At that time, Mr. Bush and his allies could scarcely summon a yawn when women's organizations lobbied for sanctions against the misogynist Afghan regime.

Once preparations for war were under way, the administration seemed to recall even more vividly that women had voted for Al Gore over George W. Bush by a margin of 11 percent.[57] Because of Bush's retrograde environmental and tax policies, this gap had only widened in the year following the election, in spite of the Republican National Committee's initiative "Winning Women," which was designed to recapture female voters.[58] However, flowers, candy, and empty ungrammatical mumblings about education didn't work. In order to rally women's, as well as men's, support for the massive military deployment, the White House had to change its tune. Enter Mrs. Bush, in a gesture *San Francisco Chronicle* columnist Jon Carroll described as "foxhole feminism."[59] One senator told a *New York Times* reporter, on the condition of anonymity, "I think this is a great chance for them to do a gender gap number without rubbing up against the right wing."[60] Interestingly, among the horrors the first lady admonished the Taliban for perpetrating, she drew particular attention to the Draconian punishments inflicted on women who wore nail polish.[61] It seems that, even while coopting a feminist critique, Mrs. Bush could not hide her June Cleaver soul. Meanwhile, there remains from the Bush administration a deafening silence about Kuwaiti women, who can't initiate divorce proceedings or vote; Saudi women, who must sit in the back seats of the cars they are forbidden to drive; and Pakistani women, who are punished for being raped by men.

Vanquishing the Wimp Factor, Part II:
The 2003 War on Iraq and America's New Global Swagger

Unlike his father, President George W. Bush has had vigilant handlers who have very tightly managed their boss's actions and utterances. One can only speculate about whether he inherited Bush Sr.'s concerns regarding masculinity, along with his name and job. We don't know the psychological consequences of having a paternal role model who was publicly humiliated for his perceived effeminacy. We *do* know that Bush Jr. has been preoccupied with rectifying what many fellow conservatives have viewed as Bush Sr.'s greatest failure of manly determination—leaving Saddam Hussein in power, and worse, doing so at the behest of that decidedly unphallic, collaborative institution, the United Nations.

The virile bombast that emanated from the White House in the buildup to the recent war, especially as manifested in Secretary of Defense Rumsfeld's duels with "old Europe," was of such magnitude that it alarmed even conservative allies of the Bush administration. In a radio interview, American Enterprise Institute fellow Radek Sikorski said, "There is sometimes a little bit too much testosterone in the air in these trans-Atlantic exchanges . . . and sometimes in these matters flirtation and compliments do more good—achieve aims—than, shall we say, a more direct approach."[62] The underlying metaphorical continuum implied here, with seduction at one end and rape at the other, reflects two distinctive modes of hypermasculinity—those, respectively, of the "Ladies' Man" and the "Man's Man," which are discussed in more depth in chapter 1.

As of this writing, the president has remedied that blight on his father's record by launching a unilateral, unprovoked, but militarily successful strike to destroy Mr. Hussein and his regime—and recently by capturing, and then publicly humiliating, the former dictator in an intrusive and globally televised medical exam. That Bush invaded Iraq against the expressed wishes, if not outrage, of the majority of America's UN allies seems likely to have an impact on international relations for many years to come. It is not clear at this point what sort of social and political order will congeal in postwar Iraq, whether the Bush administration will avert its gaze should new tyrannies arise (as it is currently doing in post-Taliban Afghanistan), or what the ultimate economic price tag will be in the event that the U.S. actually sustains its stated commitment to rebuilding Iraq. At this moment, there have already been far more American casualties since Bush declared victory than there were during the war. And, although no evidence has been found of any Iraq-Al Qaeda connection, as postulated by the White House prior to the war, U.S.-occupied Iraq appears to be a global magnet for fundamentalist holy warriors from many nations. It does seem unlikely that many Iraqi civilians will shed any tears of longing for the police-state horrors and genocidal policies of the Hussein regime. However, given the current postwar reality, and the well-known history of betrayal that marked the American treatment of Iraqi Arabs and Kurds who were encouraged to rebel against Saddam during the first Gulf War, it seems that any celebration of a new democratic Iraq may be a bit premature. In addition, the U.S. government's concern for human rights and civil liberties has been only one of many shifting rationalizations for the war. The future remains as murky as the motives for invading Iraq in the first place.

The hypermasculine posturing and triumphalist chest beating on the part of the Republicans toward the end of the war—what *New York Times* columnist Maureen Dowd referred to as "red meat moments"[63] (witness George W. Bush's infamous aircraft carrier victory strut)— have certainly made evident the importance of affirming manhood on the part of the most ardent advocates for, and the greatest political beneficiaries of, the Iraq invasion. Dowd captured well the underlying urge for phallic domination that drives current Bush foreign policy when she said that a better title for the American bombing campaign might have been "Operation Who's Your Daddy?"[64] As one British official who worked closely with Bush administration hawks in planning for the war said, "Everyone wants to go to Baghdad. Real men want to go to Tehran."[65] And Damascus and Pyongyang. One can only guess as to whether Paris has been added to the list. The concluding chapter will take up in much more depth the gendered politics associated with the recent war in Iraq, and its most profound sequela—the phallic unilateralism that has come to characterize American global military, economic, and environmental policy.

Until the gender subtext of contemporary politics is understood as an unconscious as well as a conscious phenomenon, and debated openly and widely, men's fear of the feminine will continue to be central among the various motives that drive electoral campaigns. If femiphobia goes unexamined, it will also remain an invisible force guiding both the tone and content of U.S. foreign policy objectives, and ultimately impair our capacity to combat such *real* threats as the incendiary nihilism of fundamentalist terror. For men to be inoculated against appeals to their gender insecurities, we as a society will need to challenge the notion that masculinity must be based on domination, whether over women or over other men. This will require far more than an intellectual debate, however; nothing short of a thoroughgoing transformation in the way boys grow into men will be needed. This will be the focus of the next chapter—the developmental process by which our society produces men hobbled by the quixotic and futile compulsion to prove their masculinity, and how it can be changed.

1

From Mama's Boy to He-Man

Developmental and Cultural
Paths to Anxious Masculinity

There are many questions that bedevil those who contemplate men's ceaseless and anxious efforts to prove and defend their manhood, especially when those efforts are played out in the political arena. While little boys in the schoolyard may flee from the lethal contamination carried by girl "cooties," male politicians run with equal terror from the feminizing attributions directed by their opponents. Why are men so terrified of being like women? Why do they perceive so many social forces—such as gay men, strong and independent women, social welfare programs, and regulatory restraints on corporate predation—as threatening? Why is masculinity so unstable an aspect of identity that men must constantly prove it? This chapter addresses these fundamental psychological questions by taking a close look at the developmental crucibles, both outside and inside the family, in which gendered identities are forged.

Prevailing models for understanding how we develop a sense of self as male or female are profoundly limited, especially those that attempt to explain masculinity and femininity in primarily biological terms. The much-touted but minor distinctions between male and female brains do not by themselves explain anything. Biology and culture interact in ways that are far more complex than determinists of any stripe can imagine. While brains and hormones certainly influence social behavior, it is also true that experience in the world, such as socialization and status, changes brains and hormone levels.[1] Moreover, it is virtually impossible to study a living brain unaffected by social experience. The same can be said of the putative tyranny of genetics. Although genes play a central role in predisposing us to certain behaviors, our physical and social environments significantly affect which genes will be expressed and which will remain dormant.[2] Men and women may be from Mars and Venus, respectively, but that is largely because from the moment their genitals are identified at birth, boys and girls are exiled to separate planets, complete with color-coded diapers. It is not surprising, then, that in adult politics, an ideological apartheid of pink and blue—the gender gap—continues to reign supreme.

Femiphobia: Does It Exist?

Before offering an account of its origins, or using the notion to understand aspects of political behavior, it must first be established that men's fear of the feminine is a conscious or unconscious psychological reality for a significant plurality of males. Evidence for this phenomenon can be found in multiple locations—from our everyday experience and language, to the laboratories of experimental psychologists who study gender, to ethnographic studies of other male-dominant cultures, to the consulting rooms of clinical psychologists, to historical writings on ancient societies. In this chapter, I will be focusing largely on the first three areas—the everyday, the laboratory, and the fieldwork of anthropologists who study gender.[3]

The introduction described the commonplace but revealing vocabulary of American folk speech regarding masculinity and femininity. There are two sets of phrases that condense much of the culture's values and taboos surrounding gender: *sissy* and *tomboy*, and *mama's boy* and *daddy's little girl*. At first glance, we can see symmetry between these expressions. "Sissy" and "tomboy" both refer to cross-gender behavior. Both "mama's boy" and "daddy's little girl" describe a special closeness with the other-sex parent. Nevertheless, "sissy" and "mama's boy," which apply exclusively to males, are clearly pejorative, and in many cases, viewed as grievous insults. "Tomboy" and "daddy's little girl," which refer only to girls, are far more neutral—and in some circumstances are even used as endearments.

To be labeled a sissy is to endure shame and humiliation and, not infrequently, physical assault. Because of their treatment by peers and adults, such boys tend to have much lower degrees of self-acceptance and confidence, impairments that endure well into adolescence and beyond. On the other hand, girls seen as tomboys may be the subject of some disapproval, but even in culturally conservative settings, the view is often expressed that such female children will "grow out" of their predilection for rough-and-tumble play. Researchers have confirmed what most readers probably know from life experience—that sissies are viewed far more negatively than tomboys.[4] In many settings, being a tomboy can even elevate a girl's status by placing her on par with boys, especially in athletic activities and other endeavors valued in the playground patriarchy. In marked contrast to non-tomboy girls, as well as gender-atypical boys, studies have found that tomboys tend to have significantly higher self-esteem, and seldom seek or are brought to psychotherapy.[5]

A mama's boy is seen as embedded in a shamefully close and dependent relationship with his mother, one that imperils his masculinity and invites the derision of others. A daddy's little girl, on the other hand, is seen as expressing a sweet, quasi-romantic affection and idealization of her father, which often elicits a chorus of approval from friends and family. Of course, the fact that this intimate tie with father is embraced by the culture does not mean it is completely benign. To be a daddy's little girl is, after all, only an opportunity to *admire* the father, not to be *like* him or to take his place in the world of male power and privilege. In fact, in many situations, this romanticized subordination to the father is seen as a rehearsal for the later subordination to a husband. While we may not notice its symbolism, we all know about the point in the standard marriage ceremony at which the bride is "given away" by the father to the groom. Rarely do we see the transfer of property enacted with such tenderness.

Given the complex meanings conveyed by these deceptively commonplace phrases, I don't think it underestimates the damage done to girls and women under the regime of patriarchal gender norms to say that males suffer certain constraints and conflicts from which females, with a few notable exceptions, are largely exempt. Specifically, boys from early on learn that cross-gender behavior is a taboo often enforced with predictable ferocity by family, peers, and the larger society. For example, unlike girls, boys who do play with toys of the other sex often try to hide it from others.[6]

In addition, it doesn't take long before young males are able to read the social message from peers, as well as adults, that dependency on and especially identification with their mother is a shameful thing. In the preponderant American cultural view (one shared by many male-dominant societies), masculinity requires "cutting the apron strings"— the mental umbilicus that keeps a boy tied to what is seen as the blissful but emasculating world of maternal nurturance. Sadly, this adamant renunciation of dependency often carries forward into adult relationships, and even into the world of politics, as later chapters will show.

Striking evidence of male femiphobia has also emerged from the laboratories of research psychologists. Investigators from Florida Atlantic University created a series of novel experimental designs to examine differences in the emotional responses of men and women to being asked cross-gender questions, and to a request to perform cross-gender tasks. In one study, male and female subjects were first given two psychological tests. One assessed their degree of traditional gender-typing—how much they embraced conventional, binary notions of masculinity and femininity. The other measure evaluated the extent to which subjects endorsed gender equality. They were then asked three types of questions: (1) "neutral" or non-gender-related ("Is this April?"), (2) "same-sex" (Do you think you are a real man/women?"), and (3) "cross-sex" ("Would you rather be a woman/man?"). While answering these questions, all the subjects were hooked up to polygraphs. Just as when they are employed as lie detectors, polygraphs measure the physiological indicators of anxiety—respiration, blood pressure, heart rate, and the electrical conductance of skin. When the researchers examined the results, they found that egalitarian, nontraditionally gender-typed females were the *least* anxious in moving from answering same-sex to cross-sex questions, a finding consistent with the studies of tomboys described earlier. On the other hand, nonegalitarian, traditionally gender-typed males were the *most* anxious when contemplating cross-gender questions. Furthermore, men as a group, regardless of their scores of the two tests, were much more anxious facing cross-gender questions than were women as a group.[7]

In a second study, similar results were obtained using different measures. Male and female subjects were asked to perform same-gender and cross-gender tasks. The "male" task consisted of doing part of an automotive tune-up, with tools and parts provided. The "female" task involved a variety of infant-care activities, such as diapering, bathing, feeding, and dressing, using a baby doll and all the necessary materials. Anxiety was assessed using a written self-report test. Once again, men were found to be more anxious than women when transgressing the conventional gender divide. Whether that transgression is in thought or deed, these studies provide empirical support for the validity of the concept of male femiphobia.[8]

As compelling as this research is, it doesn't really tell us *why* men are plagued by this anxiety. One clue is provided by a fascinating experiment in which men and women were once again hooked up to polygraphs. The subjects were monitored as they viewed a videotape of a crying baby. The researchers asked them if they were disturbed by it. Males on the whole denied being troubled by the sounds of the distressed infant, whereas most women said they were made quite uneasy by it. When the polygraph measures were examined, however, they revealed no difference in the physiological responses of men and women. Contrary to the claims of those biological reductionists who would assert a causal association between ovaries and empathy, men were no less affected than women by the anguished wails of an infant.[9] What is most important here is that men felt compelled to deny what they and the larger culture would designate as a female emotion. In other words, their similarity to women had to be disavowed.

This brings us one step closer to understanding the mysterious conflict that forms the psychological foundation of femiphobia. Male femininity is clearly a taboo in a male-dominant culture, in part because women and all things feminine are of lower status. But to really understand the taboo against displaying or even feeling any similarity to women, we have to reflect on the fact that taboos exist only against those things people want to do. For example, unlike incest, cross-dressing, or exhibitionism, there is no taboo against having sex with cheese. Those whose passion for parmesan is more than culinary are just too few in number to elicit a cultural prohibition. When it comes to femiphobia, as we will see, what energizes the taboo against male femininity is that deep down, out of their awareness, so many men want to violate it. Participation in the enforcement of the taboo helps men keep hidden from themselves, as well as others, their largely unconscious sense that they *are* in fact, or *want to be,* like women. It would be akin to a conflicted pyromaniac managing his disturbing impulses by becoming a fire-fighter. Of course, there are men who are conscious of and embrace those aspects of themselves construed as feminine. But these men are a tiny minority relative to those males who express more mainstream—what sociologist Bob Connell calls "hegemonic"—versions of masculinity. For this latter group of men, the "regular guys," who are the subject of this book, achieving manhood requires the repudiation of any part of themselves experienced as feminine. This still does not tell us how our hegemonic he-men get that way. To more fully comprehend men's identification with women, as well as their need to defend against it, we need to look at the world of childhood, where boys and girls first acquire a sense of what it means to be gendered.

Becoming a Boy

From very early on, children come to see themselves as being like those who nurture them. This nurture includes more than feeding, bathing, and holding. It also involves the empathic attunement with which that care is given. A responsive parent must eventually learn the subtle language of infant crying, so as to distinguish a clamor for food from one seeking relief from a wet diaper, or one that communicates a longing to be touched. Given the division of parenting labor in most patriarchal cultures, this kind of care—at least for the first few years of a child's life—is provided almost exclusively by women. Fathers, being relatively remote from early caregiving, physically and psychologically, are less likely to provide children with this kind of empathic responsiveness. According to some writers on child development, one consequence of this scenario is that boys as well as girls incorporate into their initial sense of self an identification with the mother. This does not mean that boys, especially by the time they are eighteen to thirty-six months old, do not know that they are male. After all, children get assigned a gender as soon as their anatomy is identified in the first seconds of life, and that label is reinforced by everyone in their world on a daily basis. Yet, this early gender identity is remarkably inclusive. At three years, they do not yet identify objects, such as toys, as "appropriate" to their sex. The young boy, for example, reasons, "Yes I have a penis and I'm a boy, but I can also have a baby just like mommy." In addition, prior to age four, gender is seen as mutable—not something permanent, like one's anatomy. Children at this phase could believe that a change of hairstyle or clothing could turn a boy into a girl, or vice versa. In other words, they lack gender *constancy*, the term used by developmental psychologists to denote the sense that one remains the same gender regardless of superficial modifications, something that does not get firmly established for most children until about six or seven years of age. This brings us to a question of central concern in this chapter: How do the absence of fathers from early childcare and their relative emotional distance in later childhood affect the nature of boys' masculine identity and the constancy of that identity?

Because girls will grow up to become women—thus, they will become like the mother—most of them experience continuity in the inclusiveness of their gender identity. While they may eventually, and perhaps with some reluctance, give up any fantasies of having both a male and female body, the larger culture, as I've described earlier, has much greater tolerance for cross-gender behavior in girls and women than in boys and men. Also, unlike men, most women are generally unburdened by the need to constantly prove their gender, which suggests that the constancy of their femaleness is more solidly established.

For boys, on the other hand, who must become men, gender identity and constancy are much more difficult achievements. An inclusive, consolidated, and secure sense of a masculine self requires a secure attachment to and intimate relationship with a father (or salient male caregiver) as well as a mother. The problem for many boys is that their fathers are often emotionally or physically unavailable. Of course, the extent of this unavailability varies within and between cultures. Regardless of these variations, fathers are almost always far less present than mothers. (Some remarkable exceptions to this pattern will be described later in the chapter.) In addition, there is often a powerful imperative, both from within and outside the family, for the boy to stop identifying with the mother, to prematurely separate from her, and to repudiate any aspect of himself that might be construed as feminine. Thus, his male gender identity goes from being greedily *inclusive* to being anxiously *exclusive*. The result can be an unstable sense of maleness constructed out of the culture's readily available caricatures of manhood, so exaggerated and inflated that it is punctured by the most innocuous of threats. The painful irony here is that fathers who view being a nurturing and sensitive parent as too feminine often end up raising sons who are insecure about their manhood and who, when they grow up, repeat the generational cycle of defensive hypermasculinity by becoming distant fathers themselves.

The developmental scenario laid out here is more than fanciful speculation. Social scientists from various disciplines have come to similar conclusions—linking the father's absence and men's insecure sense of masculinity with a wide range of compensatory macho behaviors. Psychologist Robert Munroe, for example, found that men whose fathers were remote or distant from childcare were more likely to swear, drink alcohol to excess, and gamble. In contrast to subjects whose fathers were more involved, father-absent men also scored higher on measures of unconscious feminine gender identity.[10] A cross-cultural study of these dynamics was conducted by sociologist Scott Coltrane. In a survey of ninety-three societies around the world, he found a very significant correlation between distant father-child relationships and the likelihood that men will boast of their strength and sexual prowess, engage in frequent warfare, and demand the submissiveness of women.[11]

From Womb Envy to Machismo: The Paradoxical Journey to Manhood

So far, I have sketched out the broad outlines of how femiphobia develops. But to really understand what makes this such a powerful motive force in public, as well as private, life, we must take a closer, more textured look at the process of becoming a man. The place to start a deeper examination is at the beginning of this developmental story, in the world of the mother-infant dyad. Although the process is long, complicated, changeable, and subject to multiple influences, this is where notions of gender begin to take shape. As mentioned earlier, within the first two and a half years of life most children can correctly label themselves and others as boys or girls, but they don't really know what that means, nor do they yet have a sense that biological sex is an enduring attribute. So, up to a certain age it is not only secondary qualities of gender, such as hair, that are mutable; even enduring anatomical traits and limitations are subject to magical transformation.

In one study, researchers asked three-to-eight-year-old boys and girls, from working- and middle-class backgrounds, whether they wanted to be mothers or fathers when they grew up. Not surprisingly, the children four years and older aspired to emulate the same-sex parent. It was the findings for the three-year-old groups that proved to be the most interesting. As the researchers anticipated, most of the girls wanted to be mothers one day. Quite unexpectedly, so did the majority of boys.[12] This study illustrates more than the role of the mother as the primary object of early identification for both sexes; it gives us a sense of an expectation that will go, for males, sadly unfulfilled. A logical assumption for a boy who experiences himself as like his mother, in spite of knowing his label, is that one day he will assume for himself the won-

drous female power to bear and nurse children. Eventually, the boy dis-
covers that not only will his wish never come to pass, but that the wish
itself must be reviled and disavowed if he is to inherit the powers and
privileges accorded his gender. He confronts two painful realizations:
(1) The limitations of anatomical reality are non-negotiable—he will
not be able to get pregnant, deliver a baby, or suckle a newborn. (2) Cultural reality can be nearly as inflexible—women are designated as beings of inferior status, and feminine wishes or behavior in males are
despised.

The thwarting of the boy's maternal identification, along with related wishes, by both biology and culture can be experienced as what
psychologists call a profound narcissistic wound—a shameful sense of
one's inadequacy and deficiency, and thus a powerful blow to one's self-
esteem. Unfortunately, because these fantasies, as well as the pain of
their hopelessness, must be denied and relegated to the unconscious,
there is little cultural space in which to mourn the loss, or otherwise
come to terms with it. Out of this conflict, and the seeming impossibil-
ity of its resolution, there develops in the boy an abiding but unconscious envy of the mother, which many scholars have described more
specifically as *womb envy*, and which later in life gets extended to women
in general. Following the example of others who have studied this phenomenon, I am subsuming under this concept men's envy of women's
ability to breast-feed, as well as their birth giving potential. In addition,
the notion refers not simply to the functions of women's unique body
parts—uterus and lactating breasts—but to the psychological and re-
lational capacities symbolized by those body parts. Because those capacities are culturally relegated to the devalued feminine, men must
foreswear any longing to possess them.

The problem with envy, as the child psychoanalyst Melanie Klein
has pointed out, is that it is an emotion that involves hatred for that
which one covets, and a desire to ruin the very object that is the source
of one's gratification.[13] One can envy a capacity that is lacking in oneself, like the ability to bear children, or a resource one cannot provide
for oneself, such as breast milk or other forms of nurturance. In either

case, envy sets up an intolerable conflict between one's longing for the riches of another and a powerful desire to destroy those riches as reminders of one's deficiencies and dependency.

What's a boy to do? How is he to manage such an agonizing predicament? One strategy is to keep the whole thing out of mind. In her writings on envy, Klein outlines a number of ways that children and adults defend themselves against the conflictual emotions associated with envy. Feminist scholar Eva Feder Kittay, in a nuanced and thorough exploration of the phenomenon of womb envy, adapts Klein's ideas to explain the ways men defend themselves against their envy of women.[14] I will be drawing on and modifying her scheme, as well as the work of others, to show the link between womb envy and femiphobia.

There are five common defensive strategies men unconsciously employ to cope with their envy of women's capacities to generate and nurture life: *idealization, appropriation, provoking envy in others, devaluation of the object,* and *transforming love and longing into hate and fear.* These defenses are not mutually exclusive, and often operate in concert. *Idealization* is at play whenever a woman is "put on a pedestal." This enables a man to appreciate her virtues, which are imagined to be unsullied by any flaws. It also keeps her at an unattainable distance, free from the contaminating impurities of her unworthy devotee. The man's lust is redirected at devalued "bad" women, "whores," who function as libidinous and psychic toilets that can safely carry away unbearable longings fused with hatred. Sometimes mythic women, such as the Virgin Mary, are revered, and their desexualizaton and heavenly repose provide the distancing pedestal. Every form of fundamentalist theology has as a central feature a romanticized view of motherhood, a Hallmark-card version that is purged of all ambivalence. As we know from the conduct of authoritarian thumpers of holy books around the world, the idealization of *some* women is ironically but not surprisingly accompanied by contempt for and persecution of *other* women. But we also know that the adoration felt for idealized women can readily function as a prison, a kind of patriarchal protective custody. In a variety of fundamentalist cultures and subcultures around the world, it is not uncommon for upper-class, "privileged" housewives to live under virtual house arrest and have far less freedom than underclass women, or even prostitutes. *Appropriation* by men of women's life-giving and nurturing capacities is perhaps the most visible defense against womb envy. Among the Black Carib of Belize there are men who experience a baffling array of physical and emotional symptoms: backaches, leg cramps, strange food cravings, nausea, and mood swings, among other complaints. While no conscious connection is made by the men experiencing these problems, their symptoms just happen to coincide with their wives' pregnancies. From a Western perspective these men suffer from a disorder called "couvade syndrome."[15] The term "couvade" is derived from the French verb *couver,* which means "to hatch or brood." It denotes a cluster of male "pregnancy" symptoms and is seen in many cultures around the world, including the U.S. (Later in this chapter, I'll describe the findings of an astonishing study of American men suffering from this condition.) Anthropologists who studied the Carib found that men who experience the couvade syndrome, when compared with nonsymptomatic males, scored higher on measures of unconscious feminine identity, and tended to exhibit more overtly macho behaviors, like fighting and cursing.[16]

This syndrome differs from a ritual form of couvade seen in some cultures, and also practiced among the Carib, whereby men *consciously* identify with their pregnant wives, observe food and exercise prohibitions, and, when their wives prepare for imminent delivery, take to bed in a ceremonial imitation of the birthing process, complete with wails of ersatz labor pains and devoted attendants mopping up their sweaty brows. In the various cultures in which these rituals are enacted, it is asserted that the father's couvade practices are as vital to the well-being of the fetus as is the pregnant mother's conduct. It is not uncommon in these circumstances for the postpartum mother to return to her usual activities, while the father continues to convalesce from his symbolic ordeal for months thereafter, nursed back to health by his wife and other family members. The fact that it is only the father who is allowed a period of recuperation suggests that men seek not only to imitate women but to deny their role in childbearing altogether, a theme I will return to shortly.[17]

Male birth fantasies and womb envy have been no less present in Western cultures, and can be traced all the way back to ancient Greece. The Athenian males of antiquity were among the most misogynist in recorded history. Disparaging and fearful of all things feminine, especially if manifested in men, they were nevertheless embedded in a mythological system in which male gods enacted various female functions. For example, Zeus, the ruler of heaven, took from the burning body of Semele, who was conveniently immolated by her lover, the three-month-old fetus of Dionysus and sewed it up in his own thigh. Carrying it to term, Zeus gave birth to the young god six months later. In another story, Zeus swallowed one of his wives, Metis—*literally* appropriating a woman—in order to give birth to Athena from his own head.[18]

The ancient playwright Aeschylus, in his complex trilogy *The Eumenides*, tells the story of Orestes, who murders his mother, Clytemnestra, as vengeance for her murder of his father, Agamemnon. He goes on trial before the gods for the serious crime of parricide, the murder of a parent. The defense Orestes makes is an ingenious one; he pleads not guilty on the grounds that mothers are not really parents. Here is Apollo speaking on behalf of Orestes:

> The mother is not the begetter of the child begotten, as they call it—merely the nurse of the new-sown embryo. The male who mounts is the begetter. The woman keeps the offspring as a hostess for a guest, if no god harms it. I shall show you positive proof of this argument. There could be a father without a mother. Beside us Athena, daughter of Zeus, is a present witness, not reared at all by a nurse in the dark of the womb, an offspring that no goddess could give birth to.[19]

This notion of conception as the exclusive fruit of fathers was even echoed in the ideas of seventeenth-century scientists, such as William Harvey, whose most renowned contribution to medicine was the discovery of the circulation of the blood. With one foot in medieval embryology and the other in the modern era, these writers argued for the homunculus theory of human development. This was the idea that the child existed preformed in the man's sperm cell. The value of the womb was simply as an incubator for the male seed. A few discerning researchers even claimed to detect the homunculus in spermatozoa under microscopic examination, showing that a scientific instrument can function just as effectively for a Rorschach test as an ink blot can.[20]

Of course many of the founding myths of the Judeo-Christian tradition are expressions of male womb envy. In Genesis, after giving birth to heaven and earth, God the father places Adam, a preformed man, in the Garden of Eden, and in another move of male birthing, fashions a woman, Eve, from Adam's rib. As folklorist Alan Dundes has so astutely observed, on the seventh day, following the completion of his labors, this otherwise omnipotent God felt the need to rest, just like the mortal fathers in couvade rituals.[21] The erasure of mothers from the patriarchal lineage of the Old Testament continues the theme of denying the female role in reproduction. Couvade is also at the center of the New Testament's organizing folktale—the virgin birth of Jesus. Here we have the male God's seed, which contains the Christ homunculus, placed in Mary for incubation.

Prefiguring the "born again" metaphor of contemporary Christian fundamentalists, a curious ritual emerged around the early 1700s in the Moravian community of appropriately named Bethlehem, Pennsylvania. The famous wound in the side of the crucified Christ was regarded as a womb by the local minister, Ludwig von Zinzendorf. From this premise he developed a bizarre but inventive baptismal rite. He commanded the town's carpenters to build an opening in a wall of the community's church and line it with a red cloth so that it would resemble the sacred wound. Referring to it as the "birthplace" from which "all souls were dug or born," he would pass baptized infants through the wall's sanguinary canal and say they were being "born again." A local poet, enamored of the minister's good work, wrote:

I am at the lips before speech,
at life's labia.

Her crack of a door opening,
her cunt a wound now
the gash in His side
from which monthly blood flows.
So Zinzendorf saw
All maidens bear Christ's sign with them.[22]

Part of what such a baptismal practice suggests is that to be born again is to be reborn from a male. This is the explicit meaning of certain other rites of passage, especially male initiation rituals in which even the repudiation of maternity is stated openly. There are few places where this is more starkly in evidence than among certain cultures of New Guinea.

Perhaps the most compelling illustration of the developmental and cultural roots of male womb envy, appropriation, and femiphobia can be found in anthropologist Gilbert Herdt's remarkable study of an isolated tribe of warrior-hunters and horticulturalists in the Eastern Highlands of New Guinea, the Sambia.[23] Warfare is the central organizing force of Sambian culture. All men are raised to be fierce combatants. Their battles with neighboring tribes are not mediated by the sophisticated and emotionally remote weaponry familiar to many Westerners, in which the enemy is represented as a blip on a radar screen. The Sambia engage their opponents in a much more intimately brutal warfare, reliant on physical strength and crude weapons, such as clubs and spears. Males dominate society in most respects; kinship is patrilineal, and married couples live with the husband's family. Marriages occur by prearrangement within the various hamlets or by abducting women from other groups. Needless to say, romantic courtship is not a central feature of Sambian relationships. Mutual attraction appears to play no role in their couplings. The men are enmeshed in what would seem to most Westerners to be a profoundly misogynist belief system that sees women as polluting, untrustworthy, and dangerous. There is very little physical contact between the sexes. Eating utensils for husbands and wives are kept separate, and even pathways through the forest are des-

ignated "male" and "female." All emanations from women—their bodily fluids, their smells, their gazes—are regarded as potentially lethal
contaminations. From illness to failures in hunting, all manner of mis-
fortunes are blamed on wives. As a result, it is not uncommon for them
to be beaten by the husbands, sometimes to death. Women have not
simply accepted their role in this cultural system; Sambian female suicides outnumber male suicides three to one.

There is one area of Sambian life almost completely dominated by
women: childrearing. Because of fears of female pollution, there are not
only postpartum sex taboos between mother and father, but the man
cannot even see the baby for many months after birth. The mother, on
the other hand, has constant physical contact, twenty-four hours a day,
with her child, for the first few years of life. Their intensely symbiotic
relationship is only gradually attenuated in later childhood, when the
father has somewhat more contact with his children. Boys begin to sleep
farther away from the mother, but must still avoid the "male space" in
the house, which is occupied by the father. Then, at between seven and
ten years of age, boys are abruptly and sometimes violently taken from
the mother, often against her screaming protest, and forced to undergo
a series of painful and terrifying initiation rituals, lasting from ten to
fifteen years, which are designed to make them into men.[24] The Sambia believe that while girls will naturally develop into women, boys require extraordinary intervention to make them men. What is needed
is a special elixir, one that only men can provide—seminal fluid. The
Sambia are convinced that if boys fail to get semen from an outside
source, they won't mature physically or be capable of sexual reproduction. Maleness, in their view, is *made*, not born. To accomplish this
difficult task, ritual fellatio of the adult men is an important part of the
initiation process. In addition, the boys are forbidden, on pain of death,
any contact with females, including their own mothers, for the entire
period of the initiation. After years of exclusively homoerotic relationships and warnings about the severe dangers posed by women, the
young men, now with full warrior status, are expected to take wives and
father children. Not surprisingly, this is done with great trepidation.

Because sexual contact with women is so polluting and loss of semen threatens the loss of manhood itself, men regularly but secretly imbibe a white, milky tree sap in the forest. The sap is thought to replenish the semen absorbed by the woman and to revitalize the man. Interestingly, this sap is only ingested after heterosexual intercourse, not after donating semen to an initiate. Also, in order to diminish the considerable anxiety that accompanies sex with such a dangerous and feminizing creature, young men will often require their wives to dress as boys for the first ten years of marriage.

At first glance, the beliefs, rituals, and practices of the Sambia may seem strange and exotic, if not wholly irrelevant to understanding gender relations in modern Western society. But, further reflection may make it apparent that in some ways the Sambia present merely a much starker version of our own world. In their culture as well as ours, fathers tend to be physically and psychologically remote from childcare, and thereby contribute to their sons' experience of masculinity as fragile and threatened. Among the Sambia, as in the West, anxious males rely on a variety of hypermasculine actions—including the subordination of women and the military domination of other men—to shore up their precarious manhood.

The similarities extend even deeper. Sambian men echo their Western counterparts in the way they respond to the traumatic rupture of their maternal cocoon, and the ensuing demand to repudiate the feminine in all its forms. As fearful as they are of being feminized, and as much as they claim to revile all that emanates from women, there are indications of an unacknowledged, if not unconscious, identification with and envy of a number of female functions, which are managed by appropriation. They refer to semen as "male milk," and, as I have described earlier, believe that without it boys will not grow into men. After intercourse, according to Sambian physiology, semen travels to the woman's breasts, where it is transformed into milk for babies. During initiations and following sex with women, the men will insert razor-sharp leaves into their nostrils until they bleed profusely. This process, which is also done each month when their wives menstruate, is employed to get rid of dangerous female contaminants that the men have somehow absorbed. While no explicit connection to women's periods is made by the Sambia, other New Guinea tribes refer to this ritual as "male menstruation." Again and again the same pattern repeats itself— what men consciously disparage they end up unconsciously mimicking. I will conclude this discussion of appropriation with a striking example from a decidedly less exotic setting, Boston, Massachusetts.

The late Ruth H. Munroe, a renowned expert on cross-cultural child development, had long been intrigued by the couvade phenomenon in non-Western cultures, and had been one of the principal investigators, along with her husband, Robert, on the study of the Black Carib, mentioned earlier. She wondered whether similar dynamics were at play among American men. While anecdotal reports abounded of expectant fathers with inexplicable physical symptoms, Dr. Munroe was curious whether such reports could be confirmed by a controlled study using a rigorous empirical methodology. In the early 1960s, she managed to find a pool of subjects through the maternity clinic of the Boston Lying-in Hospital (now the Brigham and Women's Hospital). The final sample consisted of thirty-one males with severe pregnancy-like symptoms and a control group of twenty-five demographically matched men who experienced no symptoms. All the subjects were interviewed and given an extensive battery of psychological tests. Dr. Munroe found that the men in the symptomatic group differed in a number of significant ways from those in the control group. Symptomatic men were much more likely to have fathers who were entirely absent or, if present in an intact home, tended to be neglectful and emotionally cold. In spite of this, the men who suffered from couvade symptoms were more consciously identified with their fathers and with the traditional male role in general. They also tended to be less egalitarian in the sharing of stereotypically female household chores. These more *conscious* hypermasculine qualities were belied by their scores on two other measures, which were designed to assess *unconscious* gender identity. On both of these tests, the symptomatic men scored high on "feminine identity." (To be consistent in terminology, we can take this as shorthand to mean that these men had an unconscious aspect of their male gender identity that was inclusive of "feminine" elements. On the other hand, their conscious sense of masculinity was based on the exclusion of anything deemed feminine.) So, here in one study on men's appropriation of women's reproductive capacities, we find all the factors I've named showing up and highly correlated with one another: a history of emotional or physical father absence, various indicators of unconscious feminine gender identity, an aversion to "feminine" activities, conscious hypermasculine identity and attitudes, and womb envy.[25]

Provoking envy in others can be another way for men to defend against the psychic pain of envying women's ability to birth and nurture. One way to think about this strategy is as a version of what psychoanalysts refer to as *projective identification*. This is a complicated defense mechanism that involves two or more people. One person does more than project unwanted thoughts or emotions onto another; he or she behaves in such a way as to get the second person to identify with that disavowed part, to experience it as if it were his or her own. This whole process is, of course, largely unconscious. So, in the case of womb envy, this would involve men individually or as a group doing something that could stir up in women envy of something that is the exclusive prerogative of males. Two familiar examples of this defense are the theory of penis envy, and male privilege in general.

Freud's notion of penis envy is a curious irony in psychoanalytic theory. It is ironic in that it represents a failure of Freud to think psychoanalytically. He assumes that women want penises because they are such cool appendages to have; they are just inherently superior to women's genitalia, and so any woman would naturally want one. Rather than viewing the penis symbolically—as the *phallus* described in the Introduction, a signifier of male power and dominance—he regards it as a naturally enviable feature of male bodies. No explanation is necessary, and no history need be explored. In other words, he suspends the psychoanalytic method by seeing penis envy as self-evident.[26] This is not to say that penis envy does not show up in the inner worlds of women. It has certainly made itself manifestly evident in the dreams of several of my female patients—but only as the phallus, a talismanic symbol of autonomy and agency. Herein lies an important difference between penis envy and womb envy. The special features of the actual penis are the abilities to swell and get hard, to urinate easily while standing, and to ejaculate semen. The womb, on the other hand, gestates and gives birth to another life, and lactating breasts sustain that life throughout infancy—astonishing capacities that are more than symbolic. It is not surprising then that Alan Dundes has found that penis envy seldom shows up in folklore narratives, whereas womb envy is a pervasive theme.[27]

While male privilege cannot be explained as simply an attempt to induce envy in women, it can often serve that function. The complete or partial exclusion of women from male domains of power and influence, while gradually waning in American culture, is nevertheless still with us. All-male social clubs, the absence of women from the top two positions in the White House, the glass ceiling in corporations, and the wage gap in the labor market all provide opportunities to transfer envy from men to women.

Devaluation of the object is an especially common and sometimes effective defense against envy. If what you have is worthless, I could not possibly envy it. In its broadest form this involves the devaluation of all things associated with women—their work, their artistic or literary creations, their philosophical contributions, their athletic achievements, and their scientific accomplishments. Much of the devaluation of women is directed more specifically at their childbearing and nurturing capacities. Nothing produces a more deafening silence at a cocktail party than a woman responding to a question about her occupation by answering "mother." Welfare mothers are regarded as lazy and unproductive because they are "only" raising children. "Pro-life" Christian conservatives agonize about the plight of fertilized eggs and unwanted fetuses, but remain remarkably unperturbed by children left home alone because their mothers are off fulfilling the minimum-wage work requirement mandated by welfare "reform." The devaluation also extends to those who perform maternal functions for hire, as the notoriously low wages of childcare workers can attest. Teaching, a female-dominated profession that many in the culture see as somewhat derivative of mothering, is another activity that is famously devalued and underpaid—political campaign rhetoric to the contrary.

Sometimes devaluation is an ineffective method of coping with envy. In this case, a strategy more radical, more destructive of the envied object, is called for. *Transforming love and longing into hate and fear* may be necessary to defend against the unbearable feelings of dependency, weakness, and lack associated with male womb envy. It could be viewed as a special case of what psychoanalysts have called *reaction formation*. This is an especially deceptive defense mechanism because it involves a person displaying behavior and asserting attitudes that are the very opposite of what he or she unconsciously thinks and feels.

One pleasurable experience associated with the mother-infant relationship that males later revile and fear is that of penetration. Psychoanalyst Diane Elise has written several thoughtful and original studies of this phenomenon.[28] Nursing, Elise points out, is the first and most primitive act of intercourse, in which the infant is pleasurably penetrated by the nipple. In some ways, the breast with its erectile nipple is the first "phallus" in the life of the unconscious. In other words, it is the first symbol of omnipotent, bountiful, seemingly self-sufficient penetrating power. (As described earlier, the Sambia make the same symbolic equation in their notion of semen as male milk.) And by identifying with the mother, the child can in fantasy become a powerful penetrator. Anyone who has ever taken care of or observed older babies has surely noticed how they often try to put fingers, pacifiers, and milk bottles into their mother's or other caregiver's mouth. But nothing in this should be taken to mean that being penetrated is necessarily a passive experience. Obviously, whether in breast-feeding or sexual intercourse, the recipient often actively and hungrily seizes the penetrating object. It is only in the femiphobic imagination that being penetrated renders one passive and thereby feminized.

More importantly, this is not just about breast-feeding. Elise notes that infants are penetrated by more than the mother's nipple and its nu-

tritive white fluid—the mother's care of her child's body, and her empathic attunement also constitute a kind of pleasurable penetration, a
comforting sense that mother knows and responds to the infant's interior states. Unfortunately for boys, who become aware early on of the
cultural imperative to disavow attachment to mothers, the joys of maternal penetration must also be repudiated. In fact, impenetrability
soon becomes one of the defining features of what it means to be male.
(As the reader may recall from the Introduction, that *was* the defining criterion for ancient Greek masculinity.) Females, on the other
hand, come to be viewed as fundamentally permeable, as objects to be
penetrated. Sons imagine their fathers, and later themselves, to be impenetrable penetrators of others, who can enter women without being
engulfed, controlled, or perhaps even affected. Ultimately, the pleasures
of penetration are not merely repressed, but defensively transformed
into dread. With the obvious exception of gay and bisexual men (at least
on a physical level), the joy of permeable boundaries is a domain of experience where there is perhaps the greatest psychological gap between
men and women.[29]

Frank misogyny may be the most common expression of this transformation of love into hate. Raw, primitive hatred of women, however
complicated with other emotions, has animated a wide variety of
patriarchal cultures, from ancient Greece to some of the theocratic
regimes and social movements of the contemporary Middle East and
Africa. Such sentiments are also close to the hearts of male perpetrators
of domestic violence, rapists, and misogynist serial killers across the
globe. It was a central motive for the witch-hunt holocaust of early modern Europe, and continues to fuel much of the antifeminist backlash in
the United States. This is particularly notable among some of the more
histrionic right-wing male talk-show demagogues, like Michael Savage, whose most noxious paranoid vitriol is directed at the "sheocracy"
—that cabal of uppity, castrating women who supposedly dominate
American public life. The sense of women as contemptible and threatening is often condensed and symbolized in the most common fantasy
of female monstrosity, the *vagina dentata*. This image, pervasive across

all male-dominant cultures, has been a central theme in the conservative campaign against Hillary Rodham Clinton. It has been such a striking feature of political discourse over the last decade that it will be the focus of an entire section of this book, chapter 4. Rather than repeat that analysis here, I would direct the reader to that chapter. What is worth noting at this point is the elegant logic of this defense: the body parts that are coveted and envied—women's reproductive organs—are transformed into detestable and malevolent entities.

A somewhat more displaced expression of defensive misogyny is the valorizing of destruction over creation. Unable to embrace the longing to bring life into this world, one worships the means for wielding death. Exterminationist weaponry is revered. A culture of permanent war becomes a society's perverse raison d'être. The nihilist partisans of Al Qaeda seem to have met their doppelgangers in an American regime eagerly pursuing the development of more pragmatic ("low yield") nuclear war technologies.[30] While the incineration of civilians is the direct aim of the former, it is regarded as untroubling collateral damage by the latter.

The criminal justice system has become another site where killing, in the form of the death penalty, has become a virtual sacrament, complete with priests, solemn attendants, and authoritative pronouncements. The prisoner, diapered in preparation for the inevitable incontinence, and swaddled in white, is placed in his cradle of death— gas chamber, electric chair, or crucifix-like lethal injection table—and delivered from this life in a rite that suggests a kind of couvade in reverse. Support for the death penalty is now an article of faith that must be endorsed by any politician who hopes to draw male voters. The rare male candidate who fails to enthuse over state-sanctioned killing has his phallic credentials questioned, is seen as "soft" on crime, and bears the taint of effeminacy. This concern about feminine sensibilities in a man brings us back to femiphobia, the organizing concept underlying all the case studies in the later chapters, and which we can now see as one of a number of defensive responses to womb envy.

One way to think about male femiphobia is as an inner-directed expression of misogyny, an unconscious hatred for and dread of a part of the self experienced as feminine. To understand how this emerges we have to return to the beginning of this discussion of womb envy. The reader may recall that the whole process begins in the first years of life, the period when the mother becomes the primary object of identification for both boys and girls. Eventually, the fantasy of being like the mother, with all her life-giving and life-sustaining powers, cannot be consciously sustained by boys, who must now "cut the apron strings" and construct a masculine identity based on the repudiation of anything within him that might be deemed feminine.

Like all forms of paranoia, femiphobia is a response to an unwanted part of the self that is projected out into the world and then experienced as a persecutory threat. The feminizing danger may seem to come from multiple sources—gay or transgender men and women, a maternally construed "big government" or "nanny state," advocates of national health insurance, environmentalists seeking to increase regulatory constraints of corporate activities, or peace activists. Throughout the rest of the book, the focus will be on how political issues get gendered and then incorporated into the femiphobic imagination. But here I want to say something about the impact of femiphobia on private life, effects which in subtle and not-so-subtle ways spill over into politics.

Men's Terror of the Feminine
in Personal Life and Relationships

Unfortunately, intimate relationships provide no haven from femiphobia, and for some men, they can be a site of their greatest anxiety. As we have seen, boys from early on are pressed to eschew the comforts of maternal nurturance, to renounce the wish to bear children, and to break out of the cocoon of dependency—all vital to the achievement of a conventional masculine identity. As boys grow into men, these concerns are carried forward into their adult relationships.

Sexual orientation plays a central role in all this. There are certainly gay men who struggle with femiphobia. After all, while they had no concept of homosexual *identity*, Sambian and ancient Greek men did show that homoerotic desire was perfectly compatible with femiphobia. And, anyone who has read the butch rhapsodies to hypermasculinity by gay conservative Andrew Sullivan knows that gay identity is no impediment to femiphobia or the politics that flow from it. For straight men, however, an intimate relationship with a woman provides a unique challenge. Gender studies scholar Judith Butler puts the dilemma succinctly: "A man wants the women he would never be caught being."[31] Part of not being the woman involves getting her to experience those aspects of himself he would like to be rid of, especially dependency longings and feelings of vulnerability. If she unconsciously agrees to take this up, and in turn projects her "unfeminine" autonomy and agency onto him, then the man is free to be attracted to the very qualities he would revile in a man like himself. In this way, heterosexuality can actually make femiphobia a more workable defense.

One can see this scenario enacted on the large stage of popular culture, as well as in the small theater of personal life. Men are often portrayed in film, television, and literary narratives as independent and self-made free spirits—lonesome cowboys/cops/superheroes who pass *through* women but never stay. It is women who are the dependent, clingy ones, the ones who "love too much." While men in these stories are constantly scheming to "get laid" (note the impulse indifferent to its object in this common phrase), women are always hatching elaborate plots to snare a man into a committed relationship, to turn a lover into a husband. But, to their credit, some of these narratives—especially the derisively labeled "chick flicks"—do not always take men's defenses against attachment at face value. There is the inevitable plot turn in which the clueless male protagonist loses the girl, which is followed by the belated realization of the good thing he'd had all along, and finally the desperate battle to win her back.

The different consequences of being single for men and women belie the fantasy of male emotional independence. While marriage benefits the physical health both of men and women, the advantage for men is much greater. Twenty-three percent of single men between forty-five and fifty-four will die within ten years—as compared to 11 percent of married men, 7.7 percent of single women, and 4 percent of married women.[32] In my clinical experience working with separating couples, the psychological impact of impending divorce has been notably more severe for men. This has been especially so when couples have inflexibly assumed traditional gender roles—in particular, when there is an unspoken, and often unconscious, agreement that the woman will act needy and helpless but discretely provide emotional sustenance (as well as clean and cook) for the man, and that he will act like the stalwart provider for and protector of those who, unlike him, are too weak to fend for themselves. When the marriage collapses, so does the man's fantasy of self-sufficiency, a defense he desperately needed in order to get taken care of without feeling feminized.

One way to think about the psychological consequences of femiphobia for the private lives of men is a typology developed by psychiatrist Leonard L. Glass.[33] While no classification can fully capture the complexities of mental life for any particular person, Glass's model has considerable heuristic value. He divides defensive hypermasculinity into two predominant motifs, the *Man's Man* and the *Ladies' Man*. These types can differentiate one man from another, or they can be understood as different modes of hypermasculinity within a single man— one or the other being called up as needed in different circumstances. Both strategies are designed to manage the perils posed by unconscious feminine identification.

A Man's Man is the prototypical cowboy or jock—the Marlboro Man—who presents as rugged, strong, reliable, and rigidly moralistic. He seeks primarily the company and admiration of other men, but has a consuming hatred of male homosexuals. His motto is "I am unlike women," and thus his central impairment in heterosexual relationships is an inability to empathize with partners. In fact, he wears his clueless-ness about what women want or how they think as a badge of honor, as a confirmation of his dissimilarity to them. His unconscious stance toward women is a kind of revulsion at their "castrated" condition.

The Ladies' Man, on the other hand, is personified by the riverboat gambler of American frontier lore or the various versions of the Casanova archetype. He comes off as nimble, slick, charming, and a bit sociopathic, and pursues mostly the company and admiration of women. His motto is "I can satisfy (control) women," yet his unconscious attitude toward women is one of triumphant contempt. Because this capacity for eroticized dominance must be constantly proven, his main impairment in heterosexual relationships is a tendency toward compulsive promiscuity, and thus an inability to sustain any commitment. This pattern enables him to compromise between the two poles of an unconscious conflict—between a desire to be close to women and a need to push them away. The Ladies' Man mode of hypermasculinity is a particularly important defense because it is precisely in the seemingly most "studly" of endeavors—heterosexual erotic intimacy—that straight men are potentially the most vulnerable to a variety of "feminine" experiences, such as tenderness, dependency, mutuality, and, at times, the pleasures of surrender.

Of course, a man need not fit into one of these sharply defined categories to share similar concerns with either the Man's Man or the Ladies' Man. As I have been arguing, the repudiation of dependency seems to be one of the key dynamics that link all men struggling with femiphobic anxieties. It is so central that it even appears to drive much of both the domestic and stranger violence perpetrated by men against women.

Subordinating the Feminine through Violence

At the risk of belaboring the obvious, it should be pointed out that while men may mobilize in countless ways against the emotional dangers associated with closeness to women, it has been *women* who for many thousands of years under patriarchal rule have faced real physical peril as a result of their relations with men. FBI studies of homicide report that nationally one-third of female murder victims are killed by their male domestic partners.[34] In San Francisco, which some might regard as the global epicenter of feminism, the figure is nearly 60 percent.[35] More women are injured by domestic violence than by muggings, stranger rape, and car accidents combined. According to the AMA, a third of women's visits to medical emergency rooms are attributable to spousal abuse.[36] What is particularly notable is that, according to a Justice Department study, women who actually flee their abusive partners are six times more likely to be violently assaulted than those who remain in the home.[37] This strongly suggests that when a woman refuses to stay with a man, it becomes humiliatingly obvious to him that she isn't the only needy one. His dependency on her becomes unbearably evident and must be violently denied.

The movement from emotional vulnerability to misogynist mayhem can occur so rapidly it is easy to lose sight of just how complex the process is. To understand this we must first appreciate the extent to which dependency in adult intimate relationships is not just an imagined danger, an irrational, anachronistic relic of the infantile imagination. When we allow our lover to become vitally important—a fundamental source of emotional nurturance, a lubricious fount of sexual ecstasy, and a compelling object of desire without whom life would seem much emptier—we are not only reexperiencing the early psychological centrality of the mother. Our lover is also a person in the real world, in the here and now, whom we could indeed lose. Such is the dangerous but exhilarating adventure of adult romance.[38] The problem for men, as I have pointed out, is that this vulnerability is a deeply gender-coded experience. For some men it betokens a shameful feminization. They experience this as an assault on their entire self-worth. Since they project the source of the threat onto women, it produces a retaliatory attack driven by what the late psychoanalyst Helen Block Lewis referred to as "humiliated fury."[39] This is the paradoxical alchemy that transmutes love into hate.

Male violence, like so many other behaviors, cannot be reduced to one cause. As important as shame-fueled rage is in the complex of emotions that motivates assaults against women, we must not overlook the imperative some men feel to assert dominance. Often the apparent aim, and certainly the effect, of physical abuse is to induce docility and compliance. As described in the Introduction, patriarchal societies since the time of ancient Greece have defined masculinity first and foremost in terms of dominance. Athenian manhood, the reader may recall, had nothing to do with the gender of one's sexual partner. Rather, manliness was determined by the position one occupied in relation to that partner. Real men were dominators, which meant being a rear-entry penetrator of men or women. This cultural and psychological link between masculinity and domination has been expressed in a multitude of ways across the centuries. This may be why rape has not only been used as a *metaphor* for military conquest but has often been employed literally as a strategy of physical, psychological, and genetic invasion. Some of the prominent examples from twentieth-century history include Japanese soldiers' systematic rape of Korean women during World War II and, more recently in former Yugoslavia, the highly organized rape by Serbian soldiers of more than twenty thousand Muslim women.[40] As part of the Serbian strategy of "ethnic cleansing," the rapes were designed to shame the women (many of whom feel they have been defiled and thereby rendered worthless), humiliate the men by befouling their "property," and shatter Muslim cultural identity by forcing the women to bear Serbian babies. Muslim men have been raped as well, which suggests another important psychological aim: to feminize Serbia's perceived enemies.

Even within national boundaries, sexual assault is used as a technique of asserting dominance over political opponents and instilling the terror upon which totalitarian states thrive. In pre-war Iraq, certain military personnel were designated official state rapists and ordered to assault female dissidents, who were then perceived by themselves and others to be ruined for marriage. In the 1990s, human rights organizations released reports on similar actions in Haiti.[41] Government soldiers organized gang rapes against politically active women who were opponents of the regime. Mothers, wives, and daughters of male critics of the government were targeted as well. It becomes readily apparent from these accounts of the political use of rape that, in addition to being a direct assault on women, it is intended to be a vicarious attack on and feminizing humiliation of the men in their lives. This has roots that go all the way back to the ancient Babylonian code of Hammurabi in 1800 B.C.E., in which the rape of a wife or daughter was seen as a property crime committed against a man.[42] As recently as 1976, in the U.S., no husband could be charged with raping his wife, due to marital rape exemption laws. The reasoning seemed to have been unchanged since Hammurabi: since a woman belonged to her husband, he should be able to rape her without legal consequence.[43]

As researchers have long established, rape is not a crime of passion, but a sadistic assertion of male dominance. It will continue to be a strategic atrocity of military conquest and a private horror of personal life as long as masculinity is defined in terms of domination, and men are able to dissociate from any feeling of empathy toward women. One way to think about rape is as an attempt to vanquish the feminine—*internally*, within males, by enabling them to overcome the feeling that they are not "real" (dominant) men, and *externally*, by subduing and sexually assaulting women. In other words, men who feel that the "feminine" parts of themselves are bad, frightening, and destructive of their manliness will project them onto women or enemy males and unconsciously fantasize that, by overpowering and destroying the women or men, they are subjugating and annihilating the unwanted aspects of themselves. As chapter 4 will illustrate, similar dynamics operate on the rhetorical battlefield as well.

The Gendering of Safety and Risk: How Femiphobia Imperils Men

Closely linked with men's denial of dependency is a cluster of familiar self-destructive tendencies: an aversion to seeking help of various kinds, inattentiveness to health, ambivalence toward comfort and security, and an often compulsive pursuit of high-risk, even life-threatening endeavors. Male reluctance to ask for directions is an infamous, if trivial, example of avoiding help. Far more lethal is men's disinclination to get medical or psychotherapeutic care unless or until a disorder profoundly impairs their ability to function. Studies of the influences of gender on the defense mechanisms people employ to manage disturbing emotions have found that men are more likely to deny distress than are women.[44] The fact that male emotional pain must become a crisis before it is discernible may explain why more men *commit* suicide, though more women *attempt* it. It may also explain why in the case of the potentially deadly skin cancer melanoma, 66 percent of afflicted women detect their own lesions, in contrast with only 42 percent of men.[45]

When businesses want to interest men in products related to health or preventive care, the message must come marinated in testosterone. For example, a chain of Mexican health food restaurants in Oregon, in an apparent effort to defeminize the notion of healthy eating, named their business "Macheezmo Mouse, Healthy Mexican Food."[46] Closer to home, amid the daily tonnage of junk mail I receive, was a promotional letter for *Men's Health* magazine. It begins by reassuring the potential subscriber that, "Whether you're a lumberjack or a hard-driving CEO, today's man really does care about his health, his good looks, his waistline, his emotional well-being, and his sexuality—just as much as the women in his life care about theirs—*if not more so.*" The accompanying brochure goes on to describe tantalizing future articles such as "Macho Minerals that Fortify Male Sexuality," "Strong Arm Tactics" (about biceps exercises), and "What's Your 'Erectile Quotient'" (presumably a take-home exam). Vitamins are given martial appellations, like "disease fighters" and "white knights." And, as if it needed to be more phallocentric, two of the magazine's four regular feature sections include "Men's Shorts" ("brief" articles about health) and "Dr. Private Parts" (the oddly priggish title for their regular urology column).[47]

The irresistible attraction some men have to high-risk, life-threatening activities reveals another paradox of hypermasculinity: the most frightening danger is seen in safety. Men's curious aversion to safety can be seen in the statistics on seat-belt use; males, it turns out, are less likely to use them than females.[48] This, combined with the greater proclivity of young men to speed and drive recklessly, leaves little doubt as to why so many males die in automobile accidents. Studies conducted by the Harvard Center for Risk Analysis, as reported in their journal, *Risk Analysis,* found that "men tend to judge risks as smaller and less problematic than do women."[49] Risk-taking behavior has become so intimately associated with masculinity, questions are seldom asked about its psychological basis. Arguments that attribute these characteristics to male biology dominate the media, because they suggest the reassuring (to some) inevitability of gender-role behavior (especially male dominance), and because they are more conducive to sound bites. Nevertheless, an intriguing study of Israeli soldiers provides surprising confirmation of the theory that runs through the course of this chapter, and one that illustrates the social and developmental construction of male risk taking.

Two cross-cultural researchers, John Snavey and Linda Son, were interested in the fact that more than 25 percent of the male soldiers killed in the Six-Day War of 1967, the Yom Kippur War of 1973, and subsequent conflicts in Lebanon, grew up on kibbutzim, even though kibbutzniks constitute less than 4 percent of the Jewish population. It turned out that kibbutz-born men volunteered for the most dangerous, high-violence combat units. In the course of unraveling this mystery, the researchers found that kibbutz childrearing, though collectivized, was dominated exclusively by female caregivers. They also observed that in spite of an egalitarian gender-role ideology, labor was highly stratified by sex, with men doing the high-status "productive" work and women performing the low-status "service" tasks. Snavey and Son suspected that these conditions set up an intense conflict within kibbutz males between an unconscious feminine sense of self that resulted from being nurtured solely by women, and a desire to be recognized by and feel themselves to be higher-status males. Their results showed that on a measure of unconscious gender identity, only a minority of the city-born control group of males (45 percent) had feminine scores, whereas a majority of the kibbutz-born men (70 percent) showed responses more typical of women.[50, 51] Snavey and Son quote from a revealing interview with a kibbutz-born soldier that was conducted by another researcher:

> Even though I said all along, together with everyone else, that I hoped there would be no war, somewhere inside—and I say this in all frankness—I wanted it to happen. . . . I smelt the smell of war and it was a sweet smell. It is not a question of a man acting in a certain way knowing that if he doesn't then the Jewish people will be annihilated. . . . It seems to me that when it comes to the moment of truth, when he has to stand up and advance, then all that motivates him is, quite simply, this issue of self-respect. My father used to tell me that until a man had been through a war, he wasn't a man. He was right; I know now. It's like part of a man's education.

Because the first and most prolonged experience of comfort, security, and safety for most boys is in the early relationship with a mother or other female caregiver, it becomes clear why risk taking would be utilized by men struggling with unconscious gender identity conflicts. By defying concerns for safety, such men are avoiding the feminization they associate with being secure and protected. The paradoxical threat posed by safety, along with every other bizarre feature of the femiphobic world-view described up to this point, does not prevail everywhere and is not an inevitable consequence of our biology. There are cultures that organize gender, and especially the division of labor around parenting, in starkly different ways from our own.

Marriage, Parenting, and Masculinity in Egalitarian Cultures

In this exploration of the developmental and cultural origins of femiphobia, it would be a baneful misunderstanding to conclude that there is something fundamentally toxic or emasculating about either the love a mother feels for her boy or his deep attachment to and identification with her. The problem, in cultural environments where women are demeaned and subordinate, is not the proximity to the mother, but the distance from the father. The solution, then, is not for the boy to stop identifying with the mother, but to grow up in a developmental matrix in which a secure attachment to and identification with both mother and father (or other salient male caregiver) are possible. In other words, we must stop insisting that young boys precipitously cut the apron strings to mothers. Rather, from the moment of a child's birth, we must allow those strings of attachment to be extended, and to adhere just as tenaciously, to fathers.

Of course, approaches to parenting don't arise simply from the intentions of individual mothers and fathers. The values of the larger culture are powerful determinants of how women and men go about caring for children. While not large in number, the few egalitarian societies in the world can teach us much about other ways human beings can structure families. Anthropologist Karen Endicott considers a culture to be egalitarian if "adults of both sexes are free to decide their own movements, activities, and relationships" and if "among adults no individual holds authority over others; and neither sex group has power through economic, religious, or social advantage."[52] Endicott studied the Batek, a nomadic group of hunter-gatherers in the rain forest of Malaysia. One of the most prominent features of this world in which men and women treat one another as equal partners is the extensive involvement of fathers in the primary care of their children—feeding, bathing, and providing physical comfort.[53] In Endicott's observations, the Batek treat their boys and girls equally, such that she could not determine the sex of an infant by watching how adults interacted with it.[54] Parenthood is central to the identity of fathers, as well as mothers. For example, the birth of a baby leads not only to the naming of the infant but to the renaming of parents. The man is thereafter known as "Father of So-and-so"; the woman becomes "Mother of So-and-so."[55]

The Aka Pygmies, whose population of fifty-two thousand is spread across several nations of central Africa's tropical forest, are hunter-gatherers and traders. Barry Hewlett, an anthropologist who has conducted extensive research among the Aka, describes them as "fiercely egalitarian."[56] Sharing of resources and labor, cooperation in most tasks, and nonviolence are among their central values. Married couples are extraordinarily close, and in quite literal ways. Husbands and wives are within sight of one another almost half of the time during the workday. And, of course, at night they sleep together.[57] Like the Batek men, Aka fathers are intimately engaged with the care of infant children. In fact, when babies in their charge indicate a need to nurse, and mothers are unavailable, fathers will offer their own nipples as a pacifier.[58] While this could be read as a kind of breast envy, there is no indication that men imagine that they are providing a substitute for a lactating mother, or that they disparage their wives' contributions. Since fathers are involved in holding, carrying, kissing, and cleaning infants, they are not just immersed in symbolic activities designed to enact a fantasy—unlike the fathers in cultures that practice couvade rituals. Although Aka men may very well harbor childbearing wishes, it seems that their involvement in such a high degree of nurturance may provide a very healthy (for all concerned) sublimation of those wishes. Based on a comparison of a number of Aka families, Hewlett found that as a husband and wife increase the time they spend together, the father's participation in childcare also increases. While this may not be a very surprising finding, it is nonetheless an important one. It tells us that cooperative, intimate, and equal relationships between men and women lead to greater likelihood that fathers will take on what we might see as more maternal caregiving tasks. It also seems likely, given all the research previously cited, as well as Hewlett's work, that boys who grow up in these circumstances are less destructively envious of mothers and other women, more able to embrace identification with both mothers and fathers, less fearful and disparaging of women and the "feminine" in themselves, and less inclined to engage in hypermasculine acting out in adulthood. Unfortunately, these conditions do not prevail in most cultures. As we will see in the next chapter, the world of nineteenth-century America was one in which circumstances were ripe for the emergence of a deep and malignant femiphobia that in many ways set the stage for the gendered political struggles of our own era.

2

The Miss Nancy Man in Nineteenth-century America
Historical Roots of Anxious Male Politics

The notion of manhood is a cultural invention, and it has a history. The nineteenth century was a particularly tumultuous period for American masculinity. Transformations in the nature of work and the composition of the labor market led to upheavals in education, family structure, and parenting roles. This chapter examines how these changes led to a thoroughgoing shift in the way manhood was defined and achieved, and in the forces perceived as threats to it. Women's equality, men's overcivility, and the swarthy hoards of nonwhite males around the world who were outbreeding Anglo-Saxon Americans were just some of the imagined perils. Also highlighted are the various nineteenth-century battles to rescue masculinity from these dangers. Some fronts in this war were spiritual. For example, many religious authorities sought to erase the image of Jesus as a turn-the-other-cheek pacifist wuss. Others took Christianity to the gym, where bodybuilding and boxing were the sacraments of choice. During this period we also see the rise and extensive popularity of male fraternal orders (whose main function consisted of defeminizing initiation rituals), the creation of the Boy Scouts of America (to ensure that boys will indeed turn into men), and the disappearance of male romantic friendship (a tradition of intense affectionate bonds between heterosexual young men). Other topics explored in the chapter are the invention of football (an unconsciously, but transparently, homoerotic game of territorial conquest in which an important goal is to "penetrate the opponent's end zone"), the femiphobic discourse that surrounded and fueled the Spanish-

American war, and, perhaps central to all the above, the appearance in the cultural lexicon of the "Miss Nancy Man," a new and reviled category of man into which men's disavowed feminine identification could be projected.

Absent Fathers, "Mother Banks," and the Politics of Women's Virtue

While this was certainly a unique period in the history of gender relations, in many ways it prefigured our own contemporary crisis of masculinity. Looking at the diaries, newspaper accounts, political rhetoric, editorial cartoons, and other cultural artifacts of the last century evokes an eerie familiarity, not unlike the haunting experience of recognizing in old family portraits of generations ago the countenances of one's own immediate circle of relations.

One of the most frequently invoked specters in the gendered political demonology of modern neoconservatives is "Big Government," an entity spoken of in explicitly feminine terms. The "National Nanny," as Ronald Reagan and so many of his disciples have often referred to the federal government (when Republicans are not controlling it), is seen as making Americans weak, fat, and dependent on her bounty. This appellation has been attached to targets as varied as Welfare, the Federal Trade Commission, the office of Surgeon General, and the government of France.[1]

In 1828 Martin Van Buren's rhetorical assault on national banking seems to have been driven by similar anxieties. "National banking threatened to produce throughout society a chain of dependence; to nourish, in preference to the manly virtues that give dignity to human nature, a craving for luxurious enjoyment and sudden wealth, which renders those who seek them dependent on those who supply them; to substitute for republican simplicity and economical habits a sickly appetite for effeminate indulgence."[2]

Echoing his colleague, Andrew Jackson used the term "mother

bank" to evoke the engulfing and controlling threat such an institution posed to masculine autonomy.[3]

Of course, the Jacksonians had no monopoly on femiphobic rhetoric. In the 1840 presidential campaign between William Henry Harrison and Martin Van Buren, the latter was referred to as "a man who wore corsets, put cologne on his whiskers, slept on French beds, rode in a British coach, and ate with golden spoons from silver plates when he sat to dine at the White House."[4] This attack on Van Buren's masculine credentials illustrates the link nineteenth-century men made between effeminacy and indulgence in the comforts of civilization, especially those associated with aristocratic privilege. The gendering of upper-class luxury and preciousness would later come to motivate Theodore Roosevelt in the late 1880s and George Herbert Walker Bush one hundred years later to battle their own versions of the "wimp factor."

Early industrialization had transformed fathers and husbands into wage laborers, and facilitated a national male migration from family farms and artisanal workshops to factories and offices. No longer were fathers a vivid, if authoritarian, presence in the lives of young boys. Colonial-era parenting—in which fathers were the targeted readership for childrearing manuals, and were routinely given custody in cases of divorce[5]—was by now giving way to a new set of values and gender norms. Women, who were left behind as the sole guardians of domesticity, took over much of what had been men's responsibilities, such as the education and moral training of children. There developed, partially in response to these changes, a gendering—male and female, respectively—of "rugged" public life and "soft" private life.

These and other socioeconomic developments introduced an anxious instability in nineteenth-century manhood, especially when women began to join the paid workforce. This female intrusion in what had been an exclusively male sphere led to certain minor but salient changes, such as the disappearance of the spittoon from offices and the appearance of particular accoutrements of domestic life, such as carpets and artwork.[6] Popular magazines were replete with cartoon images of emasculated husbands cleaning kitchens and feeding infants, while their wives, wearing men's suits, smoked cigars and negotiated business deals.[7] More central to male concern were the command and obedience structures of hierarchical work environments, the dependency, and even the relative security jobs provided, which sharply conflicted with the freedom, autonomy, and risk taking that had been traditionally associated with the masculine sphere. Such changes also reflected another blow to middle-class manliness—the radical decline in male self-employment, which went from 67 percent in 1870 to 37 percent in 1910.[8] In addition, many thousands of bankruptcies resulting from a series of depressions between 1873 and 1896 made it abundantly clear to even the most secure small business owner that the "invisible hand" of the market, as posited by Adam Smith, could on occasion deliver a devastating sucker punch to manly self-sufficiency.[9]

Although many yet-to-be-married women entered the work force, neither single nor married females had any rights of political citizenship. Women were not only excluded from politics but also from the mythologies generated about the two frontiers that constituted the testing ground of nineteenth-century masculinity—the wilderness of the West and Wall Street in the East, locations united in a common ethos involving the rapacious conquest and exploitation of land, resources, and people.[10] Thus was born a curious psychological division of labor between self-interested men and virtuous women. Americans believed that the only thing that could prevent society from being destroyed by the predatory individualism of men would be to have women act as the steadfast guardians of moral rectitude. As wives and mothers, they not only had to nurture their families and make them happy, women had to make them *good*.[11] Of course, implicit in women's task of constraining men's lust, selfishness, and aggression was the imperative to repudiate these qualities in themselves. And, since politics was seen as the domestic equivalent of war—a site for manly contestation[12]—women were most suited to the roles of political muses and moral cheerleaders for male politicians. In fact, female virtue was used by one opponent of women's suffrage to argue against their having the vote: "It is a grand position, that of standing outside of strife and using moral power alone, keeping alive patriotism, inspiring valor, holding up the highest aims, animating sons, husbands, fathers, and breathing an atmosphere of pity and heroism, aloof from the perils of camp life. This is a noble sort of disfranchisement."[13]

Behind this kind of paternalistic rationalization we might suspect there lay other, more troubling motives. This was made explicit by naval historian Alfred Thayer Mahan, who saw American manhood endangered by Gilded Age luxury, softened by the absence of war, and at risk of degenerating altogether in the face of women's suffrage. If women had the vote, in Mahan's view, gender differentiation itself would be threatened. The "line of demarcation" between "the respective spheres of men and women" would disappear and annihilate the "constant practice of the past ages by which to men are assigned the outdoor rough action of life and to women that indoor sphere which we call the family."[14]

While women's suffrage and their "natural" virtue would remain mutually exclusive until the next century, there were unintended and ironic consequences of delegating the role of cultural superego to women. Namely, it allowed them a powerful voice in certain political causes, such as temperance and the abolition of slavery. It also legitimated women's domination of the teaching profession, church groups, and philanthropic organizations. Thus, confining women to those tasks related to their special role in private life paradoxically opened up areas for their participation in the male public sphere. The new link between women's goodness and the issues of charity, education, and social reform led to an unprecedented gendering of political issues, and, correspondingly, to florid expressions of femiphobia. For example, men who openly favored voting rights for women could expect to have their manhood publicly called into question.

George William Curtis, the late-nineteenth-century editor of *Harpers Weekly,* was not only a reformer but a supporter of women's suffrage. Critics threatened by his efforts referred to Curtis and his comrades as "political hermaphrodites . . . namby-pamby, goody-goody gentlemen, who sip cold tea." Such reformers "forget that [political] parties are not built by deportment, or by ladies' magazines, or by gush..." Men seeking social change were a "third sex," bellowed Kansas senator John Ingalls, and they "have two functions. They sing falsetto and they are usually selected as the guardians of the seraglios of Oriental despots."[15] Male members of the Populist Party were dismissed as "she-men."[16] From the perspective of nineteenth-century male femiphobes, crossing a political "line of demarcation" was equivalent to crossing the all-too-porous barrier of gender.

From "Manliness" to "Masculinity": The Cultural Renovation of American Manhood

Until the late nineteenth century, the ideal middle-class man resembled in some ways the ancient Greek prototype of optimal manhood.[17] He was self-restrained, honorable in business affairs, not given to extravagant spending, a reliable caretaker of his family, a master of all his appetites—sexual, aggressive, and culinary—and he exhibited unimpeachable civic comportment. In other words, such a man was the embodiment of the victory of "civilized" self-control over "savage" impulsivity.[18] However, many social forces gradually eroded this moral version of manhood that historian Gail Bederman calls "manliness."[19] First and foremost, women's growing monopoly on the domain of virtue threatened to dedifferentiate moral manliness from feminine goodness. As mentioned earlier, some of the other destabilizing forces included a series of economic depressions, a rash of bankruptcies, and women joining the labor force. In addition, immigrant workers were challenging native middle-class men for political control of cities, and working-class men in general were making their power felt through the thirty-seven thousand strikes that took place between 1881 and 1905.[20] Another major cultural and economic upheaval was under way— the shift from an abstemious, Calvinist capitalism that emphasized productivity, saving, self-denial, and delayed gratification, to a more impulse-dominated capitalism that valorized consumption, leisure, and the pursuit of pleasure. This change provided the cultural oxygen in which the seductive propaganda of advertising could thrive, which in turn further fueled the appetite for consumer goods.[21] Also shaking the foundation of manliness was a new mental disorder that began to spread across the continent, "neurasthenia," also called "American nervousness."

The term was coined by its physician "discoverer," George M. Beard. The condition was understood as a pathological depletion of one's "nerve force," something present in finite quantities and subject to loss resulting from profligate expenditure, a failure to invest it properly, or overstimulation. As may be evident, this disease of the body's energy economy was conceived largely in capitalist metaphors, and was regarded as a malady unique to the modern era. "American nervousness is the product of American civilization," proclaimed Beard in 1881.[22] In fact, it was almost diagnostic of one's refinement and civility. Beard saw neurasthenia as an affliction that vexed only the "advanced" races and religious adherents, Anglo-Saxon Protestants in particular. And, only members of the middle class and the professions—because they used their brains, unlike laborers—were vulnerable to nervous disease,[23] a view that was retained well into the next century. A medical textbook published in 1918 noted that "neurasthenic states" were most often found in "persons actively engaged in business or taxed with responsibility of the household."[24] Symptomatically, neurasthenia was a kind of catch-all diagnosis that could include fatigue, hypochondriasis, irritability, poor concentration, headaches, muscle spasms, anxiety, or sexual dysfunctions. What was particularly striking about the medical approach to this condition was the gender-specific treatments. While their symptoms might be the same, men and women were counseled to seek very different cures. Male sufferers were prescribed exercise, rugged outdoor activity, and travel, whereas female neurasthenics were given the rest cure and told to remain in bed or otherwise inactive.[25] Thus, by treating this disorder, doctors were returning men and women to their "proper" places in society, the public and private spheres, respectively. Such "treatments" thereby helped to remedy the larger and intersecting

social disorders of men's overcivilized refinement and women's growing presence in public life.

The common view of female neurasthenia was that it was a condition in which women were simply being women, but to a pathological
extreme. But when men exhibited such a syndrome, nature was in a
state of serious disorder. In fact, Beard was particularly concerned for
the fate of neurasthenic males, and wrote about a troubling paradox.
Only white Anglo-Saxon males had the capacity to control their passions, and only they were evolved enough to build a glorious civilization based on reason and intellect. The dilemma was that the comforts,
technological achievements, mastery of impulses and emotions, and
cultural refinements that were so characteristic of America's superior
civilization were the very hazards that led to neurasthenic symptoms
and imperiled American manhood by making men soft and delicate.[26]
In fact, according to Beard, even the structure of neurasthenic bodies
was characteristic of "women more than of men," with "a muscular system comparatively small and feeble."[27] Neurasthenics also had "fine soft
hair, delicate skin, [and] nicely chiseled features."[28] To put the paradox
most starkly, what marked white males as superior—their manly civility—threatened to atrophy their rugged masculinity.

Turn-of-the-century psychologist and educator G. Stanley Hall had
his own inspired solution. Boys were, from his perspective, naturally
savages and exhibited the sort of primitive masculinity that characterized adult men of the "lower" races. This normal virile barbarism of
white male childhood should be encouraged as a way of immunizing
boys against the feminizing influences of our advanced civilization, and
thus against neurasthenia as well. Once out of adolescence, males could
be socialized into manly gentility. Facilitating the childhood recapitu-
lation of the evolution of the races could allow white males to grow up
capable of both savage masculinity and civilized manliness. So, in Hall's
framework, the neurasthenic paradox is resolved by creating two developmental stages for manhood.[29]

Of course, for grown men it was too late for their own developmental inoculation against effeminacy à la G. Stanley Hall. By the late

1800s, middle-class men begin to adopt the working-class code of manhood, which was seen as emphasizing violent aggressivity, risk taking, physical strength, and brazen sexuality. They began to attend boxing matches, dance halls, and other venues that had earlier been exclusively proletarian. Even the ideal middle-class male body type changed from the 1860s, when being thin and sinewy was desired, to the 1890s, when men wanted large, muscular frames.[30] Bodybuilding promoters, such as Bernarr McFadden, got rich pushing their own schemes for achieving manly bulk.[31] And, as will be discussed later in this chapter, football became a spectacle in which one could affirm one's virility, either directly as a player or vicariously as a fan.

Boy Scouts, Odd Fellows, and Other Remedies for Masculinity in Jeopardy

If gentility, comfort, good manners, caregiving, organized altruism, and peace were now the province of women, then masculinity would have to be defined as crude, danger-seeking, impolite, self-interested, and primitively violent. Rowdy, defiant behavior that in earlier times would not have been tolerated in teenage boys was now admired in adult men. As we have seen, "good" had shifted its meaning from *virtuous* to *feminine*. "Bad" was no longer merely sinful but connoted manliness. G. Stanley Hall, mentioned earlier, insisted that an adolescent male "whom the lady teacher and the fond mother call a perfect gentleman must have something wrong with him."[32] Even male criminals were portrayed in some quarters as more manly than average. An 1892 book on physiognomy (the fine art of divining character traits through physical appearance) described features of the typical "sneak thief," and warned readers to look for "the mean and sneaky expression of the whole face" and "the peeping half-shut eye." Most notable was "a large development of the organ of human nature."[33] Of course, unless such a scoundrel was also a flasher, this last identifying trait may not have provided a sufficient tip-off for intended victims.

A plethora of organizations emerged for the express purpose of

countering the feared feminizing effect on boys of being nurtured, socialized, and educated by women. These included groups such as the
Knights of King Arthur, the Sons of Daniel Boone, the Woodcraft
Indians, the YMCA, and most famously, the Boy Scouts of America.
Their activities were designed to transform soft, sensitive boys cosseted
by mothers and female teachers into hard, aggressive "manly boys"
through strenuous and competitive pursuits such as sports and wilderness exploration.[34]

It was in the fraternal orders of adult men, however, that the most
organized and thoroughgoing efforts at defeminization took place. In
1897 it was estimated that nearly one out of every five American men
belonged to a fraternal lodge.[35] The names of some of these groups,
such as the Odd Fellows and the Free Masons, are probably familiar to
contemporary readers. Others are more obscure, such as the Improved
Order of Red Men, the Grand Army of the Republic, and the Supreme
Tribe of Ben Hur. The latter group, which took its name from the famous Biblical-era novel by Lew Wallace, actually held chariot races.
Originally they had designated themselves the *Knights* of Ben Hur, until
Wallace gently informed them that there were, in fact, no knights
among the ancients.[36] The Ku Klux Klan, the infamous white racist organization, actually began as a fraternal order in 1866.[37] Even though the
ostensible purpose of each of these organizations varied considerably—
from providing mutual insurance, to curbing immigration, to promoting temperance, to reinstating white supremacy—the central
preoccupation of each of them was ritual initiation. This did not simply involve induction into the organization but, more importantly, induction into manhood. Using music, special effects, and elaborate
costumes, the lodge elders created baroque symbolic dramas that had
the generic theme of killing off the feminine within each initiate, destroying his bond and identification with his mother, and facilitating
his rebirth from men. It was common for bastardized versions of Native American rituals to be employed. One typical plot sequence (vastly
simplified here) involved the elders accusing the initiate of being a
"squaw" who "could not bear the torture."[38] This would be followed by

mock sadistic violence, execution, and burial. The initiate would then be reborn into the "bosom" of the "tribe," which would confirm his status as a real man. Interestingly, members would often refer to their fraternal order using feminine pronouns and maternal metaphors. One Masonic leader described the order as "a divinity whose alluring graces beckon men to the grotto, where she shrouds herself in symbols to be seen by eyes, and understood by hearts. Her robe is the mantle with which we clothe ourselves."[39] Another fraternal elder said the lodge members have been "cradled in [Free Masonry's] lap, have nursed at the fountain of her wisdom, have listened to her sweet songs of love, her gentle admonitions, her prayers."[40] This quote, which was quite typical, brings into sharp relief the obvious irony of ritualized defeminization, in which feminine metaphors such as giving birth and nursing are used to accomplish initiation into manhood. It also reveals the way in which such initiations function as a kind of couvade ritual—a practice, reminiscent of the Sambia described in chapter 1, that is driven not just by a need to purge the feminine, but also by a wish to appropriate it.

Another way to understand these initiation rituals is as an attempt to reappropriate from the fantasized savage those qualities that white men had wanted to disavow in themselves and therefore had attributed to native men. This would include a cunning facility with masculine violence, a primitive and rapacious sexuality, an unyielding domination of women, and a capacity for the merciless annihilation of enemies. A common psychological consequence of this sort of projection is envy of that which one believes the despised other possesses. This seems to operate with any form of bigotry. Some men, as we have seen in chapter 1, tend to envy the life-giving and nurturing capacities they can only see in women. Anti-Semites envy the intelligence and special ability to accumulate wealth they attribute to Jews. White racists envy the sexual potency, athleticism, and natural rhythm they project onto African-Americans. Middle-class white New Agers envy the special closeness to nature and greater spiritual wisdom they locate in "primitive" peoples. And so it was with the nineteenth-century fraternal orders, who not only pilfered native traditions for rituals and costumes in their competition for members but believed that in so doing they could take on the traits they had imagined and coveted in their vision of the hypermasculine savage. It was as if Indian men were totem animals whose cultural skin, once seized, could confer their qualities on the hunter. The white male initiates sought more than to don the mantle of primitive masculinity. Placing it on the shoulders of those who embodied the evolutionary endpoint of civilized manliness allowed these lodge brothers to imagine they had it all—hence the name of an aforementioned fraternal organization, The *Improved* Order of Red Men.

Beyond the lodges, there were other cultural responses to men's fear of feminization, which ranged from the entrepreneurial to the literary. A panoply of quack medical devices was marketed, promising to restore to men their lost manhood. Most were simply ridiculous, like the "Wimpus," a metal splint presumably designed to keep a man erect even in the absence of desire. Others were quite dangerous, such as the "Testone Radium Energizer." This conveniently portable jockstrap nuke claimed to be "a scientific means of applying the ENERGIZING GAMMA RAYS to the male gonada or testes—those fountainhead[s] of Manly Courage and Vigor [original capitalization]." The user was assured that "the Radium Pad comes into direct contact with the testes and completely envelops them." For those men concerned about losing their "vital bodily fluids" through nocturnal emission (and many were), there was a grisly little device called "The Timely Warning," which functioned as a kind of erectile iron maiden, a ring of tiny metal spikes that alerted the aroused dreamer to impending manly fluid loss.[41]

Literature was another front in the battle to rescue an imperiled masculinity. A new muscular aesthetic emerged that expressed itself, for example, in a whole genre of heroic male biographies. Early Calvinist values of parsimony and religiosity, now seen as too passive, gave way to a focus on vitality, aggression, and dominance. Even writings about Jesus Christ evinced this literary remasculinization. Religious leaders sought to erase the image of Jesus as a "pale, feminine, wishy-washy . . .

other worldly Christ."[42] The new, improved savior would not turn the other cheek, for as one author at the time wrote, Jesus was "the Supremely Manly Man" and "no Prince of Peace-at-any-price."[43]

Linked to the new defeminized Christ, boxing and bodybuilding, as mentioned earlier, became enormously popular, and were both seen as pathways to moral and spiritual development. Bloody fights between males had been viewed at the beginning of the century as a failure of the sort of self-control that defined manhood. Within eighty to ninety years, such combat was valorized as a noble expression of masculine animality, and prescribed as an antidote to the feminization ushered in by the demands of bourgeois civility.[44] But nothing held more promise to make men out of boys than warfare itself.

Fighting for Masculinity: From the Gridiron to the Imperial Battlefield

Actual military combat was seen as the terrain in which male primitivity could be most fully realized. Even though the American Civil War, in its immediate aftermath, induced widespread revulsion at the unprecedented and pointless slaughter and mutilation of young men, it took only fifteen to twenty years for the societal nausea to settle and the collective memory to fade, especially for those men who were too young to have fought in that conflagration. The older generation, the Civil War cohort, had a more restrained and ironically less martial idea of manhood.[45] Among younger men, the same demographic that had flocked to fraternal orders, there developed a curious nostalgic fantasy of a glorious moment when, through bravery, struggle, and the eschewing of the comforts of civilized life, men could prove their mettle. Warfare for nineteenth-century men was not simply imagined as a proving ground for manhood, it became an organizing metaphor for life itself. A spokesman for the Knights of Pythias explained why the members of this fraternal order donned military uniforms: "Human life is not a playground but a battlefield, in which individuals may make their lives sublime."[46] William James hoped to infuse peacetime civic activities with the "tonic air of battlefields." He recommended inducting young men into battalions of laborers who would engage in all manner of vigorous work, from building roads to extracting coal from the earth. This aggregation would constitute "an army against nature."[47] The reasoning here, however unconscious, seems to have been that by vanquishing the feminine in nature these men could do the same for themselves.

By the 1890s competitive sports became a centerpiece of American life. Combat metaphors became fused with the language of the playing field, the new arena in which, as the president of Princeton put it, "the gentlemanly contests for supremacy" could be enacted.[48] Football became the most popular of American sports, perhaps because it most closely resembled the conquest and acquisitiveness of imperial warfare, as well as the command structure of military social relations. Walter Camp, the founder of American football, noted in 1896 the "remarkable and interesting likeness between theories which underlie great battles and the miniature conquests of the gridiron."[49] It must be remembered, though, that the battle so many men were waging was not just against opponents on the football field. Given women's perceived encroachment on what had been exclusive bastions of male privilege—not to mention their troubling centrality in the inner lives of boys and men—the playing field was, as one newspaper put it, "the only place where male supremacy is incontestable."[50]

A closer reading of football's vernacular reveals another dynamic which, while probably unconscious in the game's participants, can tell us much about what has made the sport such a compelling spectacle, now as well as then. Folklorist Alan Dundes has done a provocative and thoughtful analysis of the symbolism in the folk speech of those who play and follow the game. It is most likely that for the majority of readers football is simply an engaging pastime, and an interpretation of its psychosexual subtext could easily seem like absurd intellectual overreaching. In that light, it would be good to keep in mind that the language being analyzed was invented by the game's participants, not by Dundes or me. As he notes, there are two groups of men trying to "penetrate" one another's "end zones" in order to "score." To accomplish this, a ball carrier may attempt to "go through a hole" in the defensive line. Of course, in order to avoid such a vulnerable position, both teams strive to keep their "holes closed."[51] Based on its own discourse, it is hard to avoid the impression that football is a form of ritual combat, unconsciously symbolized as homoerotic rape intended to feminize the loser, who is commonly described as having gotten "creamed." Dundes has also studied the language surrounding analogous competitive male sports, especially some of the schoolyard games boys are fond of playing that are not officially sanctioned by school administrators. While these twentieth-century games, unlike football, have no direct link to the sports of the late 1800s, their structure and language are close enough to be regarded as derivative of the gridiron. Most striking about these games is how explicitly they refer to homoerotic combat, with names like "Smear the Queer," "Cream the Queen," "Bag the Fag," "Tag the Fag," and "Smear Butt."[52] Although this folk speech expresses a derision of homosexuals, there also seems to be a pleasure involved in being the object of threatened feminization,[53] as well as in attacking the manhood of others. These games are, after all, largely played for fun. It may be, then, that the rise and popularity of football in the late nineteenth century was not only attributable to the opportunity it provided players (and fans vicariously) to prove their masculinity, but also related to the unconscious and forbidden pleasure of being coveted as a "feminine" object of desire. The game allowed the wish and the defense against it to be elegantly condensed in the same act. Unfortunately, however, the men of Victorian America would not be content with the gridiron as the sole arena for affirming manhood and enacting mental conflicts; many felt a pull to enter actual battlefields.

In 1890 the American frontier was declared closed; the masculine conquest of feminine nature and her children (as Jacksonians had viewed Indians[54]) was largely concluded.[55] The locomotive, a technological personification of unstoppable phallic conquest, had penetrated the deepest recesses of "virgin forest." But through wars of imperial expansion, such as those that took place throughout America's Pacific and Caribbean "spheres of influence," the American frontier and its opportunities for affirming manhood could be extended. Jingoists in the U.S. had been campaigning throughout the 1890s for some kind of military intervention in various conflicts in South America. Among those clamoring to defend the "nation's honor" was Republican senator William M. Stewart, who insisted, "I want American manhood asserted."[56] The explosion and sinking of the *Maine* on February 15, 1898, in Havana harbor was the gasoline that turned the already incendiary calls for war *somewhere* into a focused rhetorical firestorm against Spain. President William McKinley, on the other hand, an actual veteran of the Civil War, knew the decidedly unromantic carnage of real combat. But his caution and attempts at thoughtful diplomacy with Spain (whose responsibility for sinking the *Maine* was never proven) drew scorn and femiphobic vitriol from the jingoist press in the spring of 1898 for moving too slowly to declare war. The *Atlanta Constitution* declared, "At this moment there is a great need of a man in the White House," instead of that "goody-goody" McKinley. Another issue called for a "declaration of American virility."[57] The president's stance toward Cuba was, in the view of the *Chicago Tribune*, "a weak, ineffectual, pusillanimous policy."

The peace activists of the day, the arbitrationists, were viewed by themselves as well as their critics as taking a feminine position. In fact, arbitration as portrayed in editorial cartoons was often personified as a woman. In one example, she is dressed in a flowing robe, standing tall upon the Earth and holding in one hand a declaration that reads "The Glad Tidings of the New Era. Peace, Good Will." Below, at her feet, and only a fraction of her height, stand the American and Spanish parties to the conflict, with welcoming arms outstretched. Her size is obviously intended to represent her towering moral authority, as if she were a mother containing a squabble among contentious children.[58] As might be expected, opponents of arbitration saw in the maternal imposition of civility something more threatening than warfare. "The new danger will be peace rot," proclaimed one magazine.[59] To be civilized, to have one's martial instincts arbitrated into quiescence, was to be feminized and, thus, to have one's manhood degenerate. Moreover, those unvirile men who advocated a diplomatic solution were, in the view of some critics, "deluded by sentimental gabble and persuaded to advocate the theories of gush."[60]

After the war was eventually declared, fought, and won, and foreign territory seized, the empire envy of the jingoists was at least momentarily satisfied. Nevertheless, there were scores to settle with the arbitrationists who had sought peaceful solutions to various international conflicts.

In 1899, following the Spanish-American War, Teddy Roosevelt railed against those men who had opposed the war and America's colonial ambitions:

> I have scant patience with those who fear to undertake the task of governing the Philippines...who make a pretense of humanitarianism to hide and cover their timidity, and who cant about "liberty" and the "consent of the governed" in order to excuse themselves from their unwillingness to play the part of men. Their doctrines, if carried out, would have made it incumbent upon us to... decline to interfere in a single Indian reservation. Their doctrines condemn your forefathers and mine from ever having settled in these United States.[61]

Roosevelt's femiphobic distemper would endure long past the McKinley era. Years later he would denounce President Woodrow Wilson for hesitating to leap into World War I, claiming Wilson had "done more to emasculate American manhood...than anyone else I can think of."[62] Impugning Wilson's own masculinity, Roosevelt called him a "white-handy Miss Nancy."[63] Perhaps Roosevelt was also a tad bitter about losing to Wilson in the 1912 election. Nevertheless, in spite of his electoral defeat, he retained many ardent admirers. One of them, novelist, newspaper editor, and Progressive Party founder William Allen White, speculated in a letter to Roosevelt that a large number of those who *did* vote for him were: "Teddy votes—votes of men who had confidence in you personally without having any particular intelligent reason to give why; except that you were a masculine sort of a person with extremely masculine virtues and probably masculine faults."[64]

White, we can assume, was including himself among these Teddy votes. When he was fourteen years old, his father died, and his mother —a stern, demanding, highly cultured, and hands-on parent driven by a deep sense of Puritan rectitude—was well prepared to take over his care. From then on he was never able to move out of her orbit. When he left home to attend the University of Kansas, she followed him. Upon his marriage, she moved into his home and remained for years. White eventually bought her a house next to his, where she lived until her death at ninety-four. A major theme of his book of short stories for boys, *The Court of Boyville*, published in 1898, was the importance for boys of leading a rugged, independent life, in which their wild masculine instincts could be expressed outside the surveillance of maternal authority, and without constraint by feminine civility. As with so many reformers of his day, he was very concerned about education. But the issue that most animated him was the remasculinization of the classroom, bringing many more male teachers into public schools. The only way to prepare boys to function in the larger world of manly business and politics was for them to experience the early influence of a craggy, muscled schoolmaster. White seems to have suffered a profound father hunger that got played out in his writings, as well as his social activism, all of which occurred in the larger cultural context of anxious masculinity. He seemed to view Roosevelt as the embodiment of his paternal ideal, perhaps someone who could make up for White's terrible loss at fourteen. His description of his first meeting with the famous Rough Rider in 1897 does convey a sense of something powerful being evoked: "He sounded in my heart the first trumpet call of the new time that was to be." White was awestruck with "such visions, such ideals, such hopes, such a new attitude toward life and patriotism and the meaning of things." He was taken by the "splendor" of Roosevelt's character, and admired his manly physique.[65] In light of White's history and concerns, the redundant praise of Roosevelt's masculinity in White's post-election letter to his candidate seems understandable, and may even have been an accurate assessment of Roosevelt's base of support. There were, as we have seen, many men in nineteenth-century American society who shared White's anxieties. Chief among these, it turns out, was his own mentor, Theodore Roosevelt.

Teddy's Wimp Factor and Other Precursors of Today's Political Femiphobia

"Punkin-Lily," "weakling," and "Jane-Dandy" were only some of the unmanly monikers daily newspapers had given to the upper-class twenty-three-year-old New York state assemblyman after his election in 1882.[66] Derogated for his aristocratic couture, he was referred to as "the exquisite Mr. Roosevelt," "Oscar Wilde," and a man who was "given to sucking the knob of an ivory cane."[67] Ever the shrewd manager of his public image, Theodore Roosevelt knew that nothing could ensure political doom more than to be seen as a prissy fop raised in the lap of class privilege. He embarked on a program of masculinization that would remain a central preoccupation his entire life—reflected as much in his artfully constructed mythos as in his political rhetoric and positions. By the time he became a candidate for the New York City mayoral election, Roosevelt had bestowed upon himself a more swaggering sobriquet— "Cowboy of the Dakotas."[68]

In 1883, TR decided that a Western cattle ranch was a manlier provenance for his new persona.[69] He spent forty thousand dollars on a property in the Badlands of South Dakota, which turned out to be the location of choice for becoming a rugged bad boy. Now hailing from "Cowboy Land,"[70] as he called it, Roosevelt was more electable in New York than he would have been had he remained there. Riding his ranch and shooting buffalo was the fulfillment of a fantasy that dated all the way back to his sickly, asthmatic childhood.[71] Trading in his patrician duds for buckskin finally enabled him to don the long-coveted mantle of primitive masculinity. In 1884, TR debuted his new cowboy identity in a *New York Tribune* interview:

It would electrify some of my friends who have accused me of representing the kid-glove element in politics if they could see me galloping over the plains, day in and day out, clad in a buckskin shirt and leather chaparajos, with a big sombrero on my head. For good healthy exercise I would strongly recommend some of our gilded youth go West and try a short course of riding bucking ponies, and assist at the branding of Texas steers.[72]

Needless to say, Roosevelt knew better than anyone that in American politics, it was a short step from seeming gilded to looking gelded.

As described earlier, both modes of nineteenth-century manhood—"civilized manliness" and "primitive masculinity"—were cast in racial terms. The former was white, the latter nonwhite. Like so many of his contemporaries, TR agonized about "a certain softness of fibre in civilized nations."[73] (This had an explicitly gendered meaning, as he personified nations as male.[74]) American imperial expansion, in his view, was the remedy. By accepting the "white man's burden"[75] to colonize those nations made up of people of inferior races, men of the "American race"[76] could not only appropriate foreign lands, labor, and resources, but also usurp and inhabit the primitive masculinity of the vanquished, thereby winning the global Darwinian battle for racial superiority.[77] Roosevelt viewed with disgust anyone who opposed these imperial ambitions, and regarded them as "beings whose cult is non-virility."[78]

TR's dual concern about the fragility of American (and, implicitly, *his own*) manhood and the threatened global viability of the white race was fused in the nationwide anxiety over "race suicide" that gripped the country at the turn of the century. This was the term coined by sociologist Edward A. Ross in 1901 to denote the reproductive peril posed by the contradictions of American manliness, discussed earlier in this chapter. In other words, the very qualities that marked Americans as the most advanced "race"—civility and the capacity to inhibit impulses—were leading to a lower birthrate relative to the inferior but more fecund races around the world. Roosevelt regarded this as a "warfare of the cradle" in which "good breeders" were as important as "good fighters."[79] Everywhere he went across the country, he praised as heroes those citizens who took it upon themselves to produce large families, and thus do their patriotic duty to prevent "race suicide."[80] From this point on, American manliness no longer required male sexuality to be subject to rigid self-control, and procreative sexuality was elevated to a kind of national service. From the bedroom to the battlefield, thanks to the leadership of Colonel Roosevelt (as TR was known after his fleeting but renowned Rough Rider exploits in the Spanish American War), there was no longer any perceived conflict between civilized manliness and primitive masculinity. And white guys could imagine they had it all.

Whether men's defensive hypermasculinity was enacted in warfare, sports, business, or politics, the legacy of the nineteenth-century crisis in male gender identity continues to influence political discourse to the present day. For example, as a consequence of women's preeminence in the last century's efforts to aid the poor, charity and social welfare have been gendered female. Thus, in the 1960s, Lyndon Johnson's attempts to expand opportunities for and elevate the standard of living of underclass Americans had to be defeminized, and thereby legitimated, by being labeled a *War* on Poverty. Since the 1980s, however, right-wing male politicians have made great efforts to undermine the social legislation of the Johnson era. Beginning with the election of Ronald Reagan in 1980, and gaining particular momentum after the 1994 conservative restoration in Congress, politicians such as Newt Gingrich, nostalgic for the Dickensian "tough love" of unregulated laissez-faire capitalism, have even sought to undo the minimal social safety net of Franklin Roosevelt's "New Deal." In fact, as of this writing, an exquisitely fitting symbolic coup is under way by Congressional Republicans who are seeking to replace the image of FDR on the dime with the likeness of Ronald Reagan.[81] Where the right wing hasn't actually succeeded in abolishing programs, they have been able to control the terms of debate, such that even many partisans of social programs now speak about the importance of ending the *dependency* (that most dreaded and despised of "feminine" conditions) of the poor on any sort of government help. This thereby strengthens a political discourse that fuses morality with a subtle femiphobia, which needless to say turns a blind eye to taxpayer-funded corporate subsidies and bailouts.

Contemporary political manifestations of homophobia, such as the widespread effort to curtail the civil rights of nonheterosexuals of all varieties, can be traced back to the late 1800s. Whereas, in the early nineteenth century, male politicians derided their opponents by saying they were *like* women, by the 1850s they were accused of *being* women. "Miss Nancy Man" was the most common denunciation, as we saw with TR's attack on Wilson, but "Mary Jane" and "old maid" were also used. "Sissy," formerly a colloquial term for "little sister," was first used in the 1890s to denote a feminized man.[82] Gradually, these terms came to be applied to male homosexuals, who, until the late nineteenth century, were not seen as a different kind of person, even though their actions may have been regarded as sinful. As homosexuals became more visible in large cities, social scientists and physicians grew increasingly preoccupied with finding out why some people became "inverts." This labeling, in turn, helped create a sense of distinct identity among gays and lesbians themselves, who began to form self-conscious communities in major urban areas. As is true today, those who sought to study and regulate homosexuals were more concerned about male "degenerates" than lesbians, and a man was designated homosexual if he appeared or acted effeminate.[83]

Outrage over "perverse" sex acts was secondary to the concern over the feminine tendencies that supposedly animated male homoeroticism. No longer understood as a simple moral lapse but as an expression of one's nature, homosexuality could be a hidden feature of any man's character. Thus was born a new reason for individual and cultural vigilance. Affection among males became increasingly suspect. Men engaged in aesthetic or creative pursuits felt compelled to assume a hypermasculine pose. Boys were closely monitored for any behaviors that might mark them as "fairies," and were anxiously pushed into athletic activities to inoculate them against effeminacy. There had been a tradition among middle-class males of romantic friendship, in which, prior

to marriage, heterosexual men would develop extremely close relationships with one another. These could include, if the friends were
separated, the exchange of flowery, sentimental letters replete with
declarations of undying love, or, if they were together, nights spent
cuddling in the same bed.[84] The construction of the new homosexual
identity rendered such tenderness between males too disturbing to be
tolerated. At the same time, this new social category served an important reassuring and thus defensive function. The "pervert" could be, in
the mind of the homophobic male, a container for feared and disavowed
"feminine impulses," which might then be "treated," punished, attacked, or otherwise eradicated. Then, as now, the foundation of homophobia was femiphobia.

The current gender gap in attitudes toward environmental protection was foreshadowed by the frontier mentality of nineteenth-century
men, which was described earlier. This, in turn, was the logical expression of an older Enlightenment construction of nature as a feminine
entity to be conquered, controlled, and exploited. Thomas Sprat, a
founding member of the Royal Society of London for the Advancement
of Science, which was established in 1662, excitedly described his hopes
for the future of scientific inquiry: "The beautiful bosom of nature will
be exposed to our view. We shall enter its garden and taste of its fruits,
and satisfy ourselves with its plenty."[85] One hundred years earlier, in a
well-known drawing dating about 1575, the artist Jan van der Straet portrayed the "discovery" of America as a sexual encounter between the
Italian explorer Amerigo Vespucci and the land mass of America, represented as a naked and inviting woman. He is depicted as a stout and
towering figure with a phallic flag pole in one hand that looms even
taller than he. His gaze and posture convey a sense of dominance and
impending ravishment.[86] Discovery, whether as knowledge in Sprat's
imagination or as imperial adventure in van der Straet's vision, was seen
as a journey of masculine conquest over feminine nature—an attitude
that continues to influence, as unconscious subtext, contemporary debates over environmental policy.

The implicitly gendered aspects of current controversies concerning Welfare, homosexuality, ecology, and other political issues will be plumbed more deeply in chapter 6. But only by understanding the profound and enduring impact of the nineteenth-century crisis of masculinity can we fully appreciate how debates over these issues in the present day have become so starkly divided along gender lines. In the next chapter, we will explore a particular continuity with the era of Theodore Roosevelt—namely the efforts of another Republican, George Herbert Walker Bush, to rebuff insulting feminine attributions concerning *his* patrician origins and manners, and the ensuing efforts by his handlers to give Mr. Bush an extreme masculine makeover—one that, sadly for him, was not nearly as successful as that which propelled Teddy onto the craggy cliffs of Mt. Rushmore.

3

The Wimp Factor
Performing Masculinity in the Presidential Career of George Herbert Walker Bush

"There you go with that fucking hand again. You look like a fucking pansy!" media advisor Roger Ailes bellowed at his client, the Republican presidential aspirant in 1988.[1]

Unfortunately for then vice president George Herbert Walker Bush, political pundits and other opinion makers of the 1980s, like those of the 1880s, did not take kindly to aristocratic manners, generally seeing them as feminine. Even a patrician bearing as ungainly and spastic as Mr. Bush's incurred femiphobic derision. However, the gestures so disconcerting to Roger Ailes did not get nearly as much bad press as did his client's high-pitched adenoidal bleating, audible in contentious exchanges with reporters and opponents. Worst of all was the media response to George Bush's unfortunate turns of phrase, which he deployed in settings almost calculated for maximum humiliation, such as his request for "a splash more coffee" at a New Hampshire truck stop.[2] The vice president's own attempts to don the rough-hewn rawhide of a Texas good ol' boy produced only cringing embarrassment in his handlers, such as when he declared after the 1984 vice presidential debate with Geraldine Ferarro, "We kicked a little ass."[3] By the time George Bush was selected in 1988 to carry the torch of the Reagan counterrevolution, the masculinization of his image was in the hands of more vigilant and competent, if not always successful, managers.

Carefully crafted photo opportunities were provided for television and print reporters that featured the Republican candidate chomping on pork rinds while tossing horseshoes with the guys, a scene often accompanied by a country music soundtrack. However, the Bush campaign managers had their work cut out for them—not so much because of their client's gracelessly flamboyant gesticulations or his infamously fractured syntax—but because of the longstanding popular interpretation of their candidate's passive, obedient, and affiliative character as feminine.[4] At the very moment that Bush announced his candidacy for president in October of 1987, the cover of *Newsweek* featured the now famous headline, "Fighting the Wimp Factor," a phrase that would later turn out to be a succinct summary of the central preoccupation of his remaining political career. This was a perception held as much—if not more—by Republicans as by Democrats. Alexander Haig, Ronald Reagan's close friend Senator Paul Laxalt, and even Reagan himself regarded Bush as effete and unmanly.[5] Newspaper articles appeared describing his life as one devoted to pleasing others.[6] Conservative columnist George Will dismissed Bush as a "lap dog" with "a thin tinny arf."[7] Someone close to the Bush family summed up the Republican candidate's dilemma: "You could make a case that the worst possible training for the presidency is seven years as Vice President. Seven years of perfecting the habit of never making decisions or speaking up—something has to atrophy."[8] Unfortunately for George Bush, there was widespread consensus, at least in the early phases of the campaign, as to just which organ had atrophied.

Bush did not help himself with one particularly embarrassing slip of the tongue. Summarizing his longstanding relationship with Reagan, Bush said, "For seven and a half years I've worked alongside him, and I'm proud to be his partner. We've had triumphs; we've made mistakes, we've had sex." He hastened to correct himself, "Setbacks. We've had setbacks." As if dimly aware of the disturbing anal-receptive meaning his misstatement might have, Bush added: "I feel like the javelin competitor who won the toss and elected to receive."[9]

The Bush team's initial response to the aspersions cast upon their candidate's manhood was to highlight Bush's war record, hoping that having been shot down in World War Two would elevate his poll numbers in the current battle. Another interesting strategy developed by the vice president's media consultants for the first debate of the Republican

'I ADORE THE BUSH STYLE, BUT I THINK IT LOOKS BETTER ON BARBARA.'

George H. W. Bush before his macho makeover

primary campaign was to have Bush attribute to his opponent, chemical heir Pierre Samuel Du Pont IV, the very qualities Bush was struggling so hard to cleave from his own image. Du Pont, whose preppy pedigree extends from Harvard Law School back to Princeton and all the way back to Exeter, was the perfect target for the projection of Bush's unwanted identity as patrician wimp. As with all candidates for public office, Du Pont tried to cultivate the unvarnished patina of "regular guy," and thus insisted on being called "Pete." Bush, however, appreciating its effete connotations, stubbornly referred to him as "Pierre."[10] Bush spin doctors performed a clever feat of plastic surgery on another aspect of the vice president's image. They transformed their candidate's years of servility to Reagan, which had been seen as a feminine lack of courage and autonomy, into a masculine and noble fidelity to one's comrade. As Bush said, in an effort to reframe his uncritical obeisance to Reagan, "In our family, loyalty is not a character flaw."[11]

It was under the vigilant watch of the notorious pit bulls of political consulting, Roger Ailes (now working as "fair and balanced" Fox News Chief) and Lee Atwater, that George Bush underwent his most thorough de-wimping. No longer the pallid preppy who uttered exclamations like "darn," "heck," and "dippity do,"[12] he was made into George the Impaler, who was to take no prisoners as he vanquished political enemies. The most decisive battle was a highly contentious exchange with CBS news anchorman Dan Rather. An informant inside the network had warned Ailes that Rather was planning to confront Bush on his role in the Iran-Contra scandal in an upcoming interview. This allowed time for Ailes and Atwater to orchestrate Bush's counterattack in advance. Also, since Rather was directing the interview from CBS studios in New York, and Bush was responding from his Washington office, Ailes was able to stand behind the network technicians, hold up cue cards, and choreograph the vice president's bristling outrage for maximum effect. Of course, it wasn't the content of Bush's rebuttal that mattered; it was in any event rather feeble and infantile. ("It's not fair to judge my whole career by a rehash on Iran. How would you like it if I judged your whole career by those seven minutes when you walked off the set in New York?") It was the display of manly attitude—angry defiance, in particular—that made this contest politically useful for Bush. "The bastard didn't lay a glove on me," the candidate gloated from his corner after the fight. While this testy proclamation into a live microphone wasn't broadcast, it was later printed in newspaper accounts of the exchange. Lee Atwater summed up the significance of Bush's performance: "I think it was the most important event of the entire primary campaign. It was stronger than grits in the South. . . . It solidified our base."[13]

In spite of this success, as well as others, there were times when, out of his handlers' control, Bush would briefly slip out of his role as snarling cowboy pugilist from Texas, and back into his own less marketable character and origins. After a poor showing in an Iowa straw poll, he explained, "A lot of people that support me—they were off at the air show, they were at their daughter's coming-out party, or they were off teeing up on the golf course for that all-important last round."[14] But George Bush's difficulties were not due simply to his occasional reversion to type. He had a hard time pulling off the contradiction that Ronald Reagan had managed so well, which was to embody the images of *Übermensch* and Everyman simultaneously. In other words, try as he might, Bush was unable to seem both omnipotent and ordinary at the same time. In spite of posing with all manner of lethal weaponry and delivering studied performances of working class manliness, he was unable to project either image. Straining to be tepid, the preconvention George Bush set no hearts ablaze. Then came The Speech. Chief among the amusing ironies of his peroration was that it supposedly established the vice president as "his own man"—a speech that was openly acknowledged to have been written by someone else, and not just anyone else but one of Reagan's main speechwriters, and not just any of Reagan's writers but a woman, Peggy Noonan.

A new, more carefully packaged Bush persona was launched onto the candidate market. The Noonanized Bush was a paternal protector. The phrase "I'm not going to let them take it away from you" was repeated at least a dozen times. While Ronald Reagan speeches had conjured a Norman Rockwell fantasy of a mythic America, as a distraction from the Dickensian reality imposed by his policies, the 1988 nominee took a different approach. As a new, more sensitive Republican, Bush partially acknowledged and decried this reality while simultaneously disclaiming responsibility for it. His "thousand points of light" image was to usher in a new era of compassion. (Unfortunately, the only lights visible to many were the trash can heaters of the homeless, who, for the first time since the Great Depression, were becoming ubiquitous.) To keep this kinder, gentler rhetoric from rendering Bush feminized, combat was used as the unifying metaphor of the speech—the presidency itself being portrayed as a military mission. Afterward, even his wife Barbara got caught up in the martial euphoria. Proclaiming her tender affection for her husband, she declared, "I would lay down on a grenade for him."[15]

As important as Peggy Noonan, Roger Ailes, and Lee Atwater were to the marketing of George Bush, perhaps the single greatest asset to the Republican campaign was the Democratic candidate himself, Michael

Dukakis. Rather than challenge GOP efforts to define the central issues of the campaign (flags and furloughs), as well as determine the very language in which they were to be debated, Dukakis capitulated without a fight. Nowhere was this truer than in the struggle over who should be wearing which political label. Republicans encountered virtually no resistance in their successful attempt to create what Sidney Blumenthal called a "phobic aura" around the term *liberal*.[16] According to the 1988 Unabridged Republican Dictionary, a liberal was someone who had an abiding affection for violent criminals, was in favor of completely disarming the military and surrendering American sovereignty to the whims of any number of rapacious tyrants, wanted public schools not only to require classes in homosexuality but to mandate flag burning as a substitute for the Pledge of Allegiance, and believed the government should raise taxes on the middle class to pay for programs designed to give every drug-addicted Welfare mother a second Cadillac. On a slightly more subtle level, liberalism was associated with dependence, weakness, and effeminacy. Instead of contesting this premise, Dukakis rushed to dissociate himself from the "L-word," and designate himself a "conservative," at least at the beginning of his campaign.[17] He went far beyond dissimulating his liberalism, to the point of promising to continue President Reagan's foreign policy[18] and declaring his gushing enthusiasm for a variety of new weapons systems.[19] Interestingly, Reagan not only rebuffed his new disciple but, as if intuitively sensing the gender dynamics at play, characterized Dukakis's posture of military hawkishness as political transvestism: "We haven't seen such a radical transformation since Dustin Hoffman played 'Tootsie.'"[20] The Democratic candidate's most insipid display of macho military boosterism was his visit to a General Dynamics tank factory. Accessorized with helmet and uniform, Dukakis went on a highly orchestrated joyride in an M1 tank, with the theme music to the movie *Patton* booming in the background. Instead of the formidable battle-hardened leatherneck he wished to present himself as, Dukakis looked more like a frightened four-year-old boy on his first bumper car ride. Since he insisted on having this escapade captured on television, the Republicans were given some of the best campaign footage they could have asked for, which they used to good effect.

The irony of Dukakis's silly reborn conservatism is that it made him seem more weak and ineffectual than if he had passionately argued for liberal positions. This seems to be the implication of a fascinating survey conducted by a Democratic political consultant during the campaign. The poll was framed as a mock presidential election. Two candidates, A and B, were created. While not explicitly linked to Bush and Dukakis, candidates A and B articulated, respectively, traditional Republican and Democratic ideals, as each party would want them portrayed. Candidate A was strong on national defense, embodied "conservative family values," was a robust cheerleader for untrammeled economic growth, and favored a "no-nonsense" punitive approach to crime. Candidate B, on the other hand, was an advocate of universal health care, an explicit ally of working people on a number of issues, and a stalwart protector against foreign competition. (This was obviously before the Democrats had jumped on the NAFTA band wagon.) The contest was held every day up to and including the actual election day. Each time, candidate B won by more than 60 percent. This research suggests that even though the electorate may have recoiled at the liberal *label*, they embraced the *content* of liberalism.[21] Unfortunately, the study, like a lot of the advice he received, apparently did not influence or even interest Dukakis, at least at the time. Only when it was too late, in the last week of the campaign, did Dukakis proclaim in a confessional tone "Yes, I'm a liberal." And even in this he had misunderstood his advisors, who had counseled their candidate to associate himself with the "Dead Democrats"—FDR, Truman, and Kennedy—and leave labels aside.[22] A last-gasp performance as a fiery populist ("George Bush is on their side. I'm on your side.") caused a notable bump in his poll numbers, but it was too little, too late, to affect the election outcome.[23]

The controversy over Dukakis's political label was, in many ways, a clear if coded debate about his masculine credentials. A far less subtle critique of the Democratic candidate's manhood could be read in the Republican discourse surrounding the adroitly constructed and managed Willie Horton scandal. Willie Horton, a black man, was sentenced to life in prison for the 1974 murder of a seventeen-year-old gas station attendant, committed during a robbery in Lawrence, Massachusetts. He left prison on June 6, 1986, for an unsupervised two-day furlough. More furloughs followed. The following April, he was arrested after fleeing in a car stolen from a white Maryland couple. Horton had knifed and pistol-whipped the man, and beaten and raped the woman. This generated outrage throughout Massachusetts over the state's prison furlough program (enacted by the previous governor, a Republican), which granted furloughs to unparolable convicts. When political attack dog Roger Ailes eventually sniffed out this aromatic scandal, he could barely disguise his drooling delight: "The only question is whether we depict Horton with a knife or not."[24]

Thus was born the campaign's most effective series of ads, shamelessly designed to appeal to primitive racial paranoia and its related white male anxiety. The first ad, which began airing September 9, 1988, opens with an image of Dukakis wearing an expression of feckless befuddlement, and is accompanied by the caption "Allowed Murderers to Have Weekend Passes." This is followed by a mug shot of Willie Horton, peering menacingly through half-shut eyes, with his name written below. The next image depicts a tall, Afro-bedecked Willie Horton being led away in handcuffs by a diminutive white policeman, who seems to be at least two feet shorter than his prisoner. This photo appears above the words "Kidnapping Stabbing Raping." The final frame repeats the opening image of the dazed Democratic candidate, along with the caption: "Weekend Prison Passes: Dukakis on Crime." The voice-over narrative refers to Dukakis's opposition to the death penalty and tells a story of Horton's crimes that ends with a reference to Horton having "repeatedly raped [the victim's] girlfriend."[25]

On October 5, 1988, the famous "Revolving Door" ad made its debut on television screens across the country. Willie Horton's name is not mentioned, but there are unmistakable references to his crimes. In place of his image, the ad features a procession of a dozen or so vaguely dark-skinned convicts circling through a prison turnstile labeled "The

Dukakis Furlough Program." To make the threat as unambiguous as possible, the ad appears in black and white and in slow motion. The gruff, compelling voice of the narrator concludes by warning us that "Michael Dukakis says he wants to do for America what he's done for Massachusetts. America can't afford that risk."[26]

The third ad first appeared on October 20, 1988, and featured the images of the now-married Maryland couple, Clifford and Angela Barnes, with voice-over narration by Clifford Barnes and Donna Cuomo (the sister of the slain gas station attendant). Barnes summarizes the key elements of the horror story, by then familiar to many Americans, links the events to the Massachusetts governor, and skewers him with the L-word for good measure: "For twelve hours I was beaten, slashed, and terrorized. My wife, Angie, was brutally raped. When his liberal experiment failed Dukakis simply looked away." Cuomo later repeats the reference to "Governor Dukakis' liberal furlough experiment," reiterates the story of her brother's murder, and reminds us that "Horton went on to rape and torture others."[27]

Deep reflection is not required to discern in these ads a transparent incitement of the white male racist imagination. Here is a story that fuels the old but enduring fantasy that black males are by nature sexual predators, who are after white women in particular. It also confirms the worst fear that femiphobic white men seem to have about the black rapist scenario. He, the white male, will be symbolically emasculated, not only by having his sexual property defiled by the stronger and more potent black man, but by his failure to protect his woman from the assault. This may have been the reason the Bush team chose to tell the Barneses' story from Clifford's point of view, instead of Angela's. He, rather than his raped wife, may have been regarded as the more compelling victim to present to male voters—the demographic to whom Bush most needed to affirm his manhood. While Clifford Barnes was the failed masculine protector in the story, he was also a stand-in for another failed protector, Michael Dukakis. "Elect him," the ads seemed to be saying to the male electorate, "and expect to be visited by armies of furloughed black rapists, who will ravage your wife—while you remain a

helpless emasculated witness, whose terror is exceeded only by humiliation. George Bush, on the other hand, would never let this happen,[28]
and, as we had been told in his convention speech, he will protect us."

A question always arises in any interpretation of an evocative symbolic narrative, such as a political ad: To what extent can we infer in-
tention or a conscious strategy on the part of its creators? While all the
meanings of a message need not be consciously constructed in order to
be communicated and have a powerful impact on the receiver, there are
indications that to some extent the Bush team knew what they were
doing. It was no secret that the central vulnerability for Bush was the
wimp factor. From the foregoing examples it seems his campaign di-
rectors sought to masculinize him in two ways—directly, by packaging
Bush as macho, and indirectly, by casting doubts on Dukakis's manhood. (The very significant gender gap in voting, which will be discussed later in this chapter, certainly suggests they succeeded.) The
Willie Horton scandal was made-to-order for use as part of the indirect
strategy of casting doubt on the testicular qualifications of the Democratic candidate. How conscious were Republican consultants of the
gender subtext underlying their presentation of the furlough issue? A
curious comment by Lee Atwater indicates that the Willie Horton ads
were not designed to present a vague criminal menace to voters, but a
specific emasculation menace to white men. Speaking at a post-election
conference at Harvard's Kennedy School of Government, Atwater described Horton's first crime: "There was a seventeen-year-old kid there
who was trying to work his way through college. The guy stabbed this
kid twenty-four times, cut his sexual organ off, stuck it in his mouth,
cut his arms and legs off, and stuck the guy in a trash can." The genital
and other dismemberments never took place, and were not in the police report.[29] Although this particular embellishment of an already
sufficiently horrific murder was part of the folklore surrounding Willie
Horton, and was not Atwater's invention, it speaks to the prevalence of
white male castration anxiety in the larger culture. Atwater repeated the
fantasy and had the good political sense to cast Horton as the central
villain in Atwater's own campaign ad psychodrama, in which emascu-

lation was symbolic instead of literal, and for which Dukakis was held responsible.

Political advertisements, like the commercial ones on which they are modeled, are focused less on *changing* beliefs or fantasies than on *exploiting* them. The latter requires far less effort. Simply associate the voters' preexisting fears with one's opponent, and link your candidate with whatever the latest polling data show that people find reassuring. Put into story form, this strategy is sometimes referred to as the "get 'em sick/get 'em well" approach.[30] A danger already dreaded is presented and paired with the other party's candidate. The viewer's terror is assuaged by images of hope intimately tied to the politician running the ad. The Willie Horton spots not only put a specific African-American face on white men's inchoate black rapist nightmare, it also effectively associated Dukakis with it. The view of the Democratic candidate as a weak, unmanly, and ineffectual protector of dependent females even came to dominate the presidential debates, especially the second one, which took place on October 13.

The events were more like parallel press conferences than debates, since reciprocal interactions were forbidden, at the insistence of the Bush campaign.[31] The format whereby candidates field questions from reporters was apparently preferred by the Republican team because it was more congenial to the recitation of the canned answers and quips that their less-than-articulate candidates had to rely on. The main concern of Bush pollster Richard Wirthlin was not so much the debate as a whole but "the 25 seconds played of the subsequent news broadcasts."[32] The GOP victory on the format question apparently filled Republican strategist Eddie Mahe with confidence. Mahe noted about his candidate that, "All he has to do is avoid saying or doing anything [that goes] beyond the point of acceptable George Bush stupidity."[33]

As far as Dukakis was concerned, by the time of the second debate he was already badly wounded, having gone from a commanding sixteen-point lead early in the race[34] to being three points behind Bush.[35] When the smoke cleared following the October 13 confrontation, it was apparent that the coup de grace for Dukakis's presidential prospects had not been administered by his opponent, but had resulted from a self-inflicted wound—an inept response to the most important question of his political career, one that would give Richard Wirthlin a twenty-five-second sound bite exceeding his fondest hopes.

"Governor," inquired CNN anchor Bernard Shaw, "if Kitty Dukakis were raped and murdered, would you favor an irrevocable death penalty for the killer?"[36] With this question the gender subtext of the Horton ads was being made more explicit. Was the Democratic candidate a failed masculine protector, as the TV spots had implied? Shaw wanted to know. Of course, since the crime in question had, hypothetically, already occurred, the issue was now whether Dukakis had enough testicular integrity to seek the ultimate vengeance and thereby (as asserted by capital punishment's proponents) protect other vulnerable females. This challenge to Dukakis's manhood, coming, interestingly, from a black reporter, did not evoke anger, the "gender-appropriate" emotion, from the candidate. He neither expressed outrage at the possibility of someone violating and harming "his" woman, nor did he get fiercely indignant at such an intrusive question. Either response would have helped to remasculinize him. Instead, Dukakis offered a bland and rambling monologue on the lack of evidence for the deterrent effect of capital punishment and the dropping crime rate in Massachusetts. Even though his comments were factually correct, Dukakis left the impression of a stolid bureaucrat whose pulse was quickened more by statistical graphs than by a sexual assault on his own wife. After the debate, he was savaged by Republicans and most reporters for failing to summon manly emotions. Even his advisors sensed the gravity of Dukakis's dismal performance. His campaign manager, Susan Estrich, later reflected, "When he answered by talking policy, I knew we had lost the election."[37] Indeed, polls taken immediately after the debate showed Bush's lead jumping ten percentage points.[38]

One response to a debate question would not ordinarily have such an impact. But this event was simply the climax of an electoral battle characterized by its comical but earnest performances of masculinity. While Bush, with much help, had adroitly, if temporarily, countered attributions of effeminacy, Dukakis had not been so successful. The rhetorical assaults on his manhood had ranged from subtle innuendo to grotesque caricature, but the cumulative effect was an enduring image of the Democratic candidate as a feminized man. Nowhere was this portrait more starkly drawn than in a thirty-two-page Republican comic book, *Magical Mike: The Real Story of Mike Dukakis*. It was avidly endorsed by Reverend Jerry Falwell at a "Family Forum" religious convention in New Orleans. He implored his flock to disseminate ten million copies of the pamphlet before the election. It presents Dukakis as "Sheriff Pansy," a soft-on-crime, limp-wristed liberal who wears a dress and pearls. He is not only attacked for supporting the Equal Rights Amendment and the notion of comparable worth, but is accused of having advocated blasphemy, bestiality, and witchcraft. To further establish his castrated condition, his wife is portrayed as a dominant, "take-charge" woman.[39]

Similar attacks emanated from other quarters. Two weeks after the comic book made its debut, Republican senator Orrin Hatch referred to the Democrats as "the party of homosexuals."[40] GOP pamphlets distributed in Texas claimed that Dukakis "wants special privileges for gays and lesbians."[41] Pointing to his deficient, technocratic heterosexuality, James Baker said of Dukakis, "He's the only man I know who could look at the swimsuit issue of *Sports Illustrated* and complain because the bathing suits weren't flame-retardant."[42] Extending the failed masculine protector theme of the Willie Horton ads to global issues, the Republican vice presidential candidate, Dan Quayle, said, "Dukakis' defense and foreign policy positions amount to a litany on retreat."[43]

All these attacks on the Democratic candidate, ineffectively rebutted by him, formed the context that made Dukakis's pallid response to Bernard Shaw's debate question such a salient and fatal mistake. By the third week in October of 1988, Bush's lead over Dukakis had soared to seventeen percent. Interestingly, this was primarily among men, who favored Bush by thirty-four percentage points. Bush led among female voters by only four points, while the gap *between* women and men was sixteen points.[44] The gender gap at election time, while not as robust, was still quite significant. Exit polls showed an overall gender gap of 8 percent. Bush won by thirteen points among men and lost by three points among women.[45] It does appear as if the sometimes subliminal and sometimes overt characterization of Michael Dukakis as a feminized male was far more disturbing to male voters.

Once the election was behind him and men had been reassured of Bush's potency, the President-elect's handlers could afford to drop the macho posturing and fatuous combat metaphors from his rhetoric. This shift was reflected in his January 20 inaugural speech[46]—a bland, self-consciously plain-spoken address that was crafted by Peggy Noonan, and delivered from "democracy's front porch." It seemed designed to lower expectations, defuse Democratic opposition, and create the appearance, however timidly, of a departure from the Reagan ethic of untrammeled greed. In spite of the assertion that a "new breeze is blowing," there was an unmistakable air of familiarity about this speech. More telling than the folksy call for philanthropic volunteerism was the frequent repetition of the phrase "free markets," and Bush's insistence on a "free will unhampered by the state"—Reaganoid euphemisms for removing all regulatory fetters from corporate exploits.

As might be expected of any inaugural speech, this one was also thick with patriotic sentimentality. While calls for unity and nationalist pride constitute the vapid Styrofoam packing of most political addresses, they also serve a specific propagandistic function. Namely, they evoke an image of American society sanitized of conflicting class interests and other inequalities, and encourage the audience to feel part of an abstract, harmonious national community embodied by the speaker. Perhaps the most explicit and cynical expression of this strategy was found in a 1984 memo written by then Assistant White House Chief of Staff (later Bush cabinet member) Richard Darman, during the Republican campaign against Walter Mondale: "Paint Ronald Reagan as the personification of all that is right with or heroized by America. Leave Mondale in a position where an attack on Reagan is tantamount to an attack on America's idealized image of itself—where a vote against Reagan is, in some subliminal sense, a vote against mythic 'America.'"[47] Republican rhetorical strategy, more than that of the Democrats, had been based, especially since 1980, on encouraging the lower and middle classes to identify with the economic elite—a kind of class-based Stockholm syndrome. Reagan's and later Bush's handlers seemed acutely aware that any failure to keep disparities of wealth and privilege invisible might impair this identification and increase the risk that the disenfranchised would demand real rather than vicarious power. In fact, one of the most impassioned denunciations Bush leveled against Dukakis toward the end of the campaign was that he was stirring up "class antagonism." In the next breath, Bush insisted, without pondering the contradiction, that we live in a classless society.

While there were many reasons for Bush and his campaign team to be concerned about this issue, it seems to have been particularly relevant to the task of reassuring his largely male constituency. The visibility of class differences might have rendered femiphobic men (those outside the economic elite) dangerously conscious of the "feminine" (subordinate) position they occupied in relation to other men. After all, most males (as well as an increasing percentage of women) spend most of their days in hierarchical work environments characterized by sadomasochistic command and control power structures.[48] What modern-day conservatives seem most interested in conserving is a social order based on various forms of domination—as long as their class, gender, and ethnic group remain on top. The last thing they want is for subordination to one's "superiors" to become a *political* issue. Attention to class, the economic form of domination, might threaten to destabilize men's psychological defenses against not only the social *fact* of submission but also its prevailing social *meaning*, feminization. While it is unlikely that Bush and other right-wing members of the ruling elite were to any great extent conscious of the dynamics I have outlined here, they had nevertheless evolved an effective strategy to manage the potential femiphobic hazards of class consciousness, which could have easily redounded to their disadvantage. That strategy was (and, in the era of Bush Jr., continues to be) one that involved projecting all authoritarian social control, limitation of freedom, intrusive surveillance, and emasculating demands for submission on to the feminizing monstrosity called "Big Government."[49] Any resistance or disturbing emotions generated by the exercise of corporate power, over both the larger society and companies' own workers, were readily displaced onto this federal bogy. (Moreover, the American people seem to accept this even when the right wing controls all three branches of government, as it does at the present moment.) In later chapters we will trace the logical thread that leads from the antigovernment demonology of the 1980s, to the right-wing militia movement of the 1990s, to that ultimate paroxysm of murderous paranoia, the Oklahoma City bombing in April of 1995, and finally to the current orgy of corporate deregulation, federally subsidized corruption, tax breaks for the wealthy, and rollbacks of environmental protections.

In spite of his electoral triumph, and his inaugural promises to slay the castrating dragon of government regulations, George H. W. Bush's victory over the wimp factor would, like all struggles to prove manhood, turn out to be a short-lived achievement. The president's greatest, if fleeting, moment of masculine glory, the point when his Sisyphean battle against feminine attributions seemed to be over, was the Persian Gulf War of 1991.

Sodomizing Saddam: Flexing Patriotic Muscle in the Persian Gulf War

The invasion of Iraq in 1991, the subsequent expulsion of Saddam Hussein's military from Kuwait, and the defeat and mass extermination of his soldiers within Iraq itself were widely proclaimed as the final cure for a crippling political disorder called the "Vietnam Syndrome." But before we can understand the psychological nature of the remedy, or its impact on George Bush and other American men, we need to look deeper into the affliction itself. The Vietnam Syndrome was Richard Nixon's diagnosis for the malady he saw as enfeebling the American body politic. Its symptoms were shame and guilt about power, a reluctance to use it to "defend national interests," and an unmanly predisposition towards compromise, negotiation, and the pursuit of common agreement.[50] While the obvious cause of this syndrome was the American defeat in the Vietnam War, the condition cannot be fully understood without an appreciation of the cultural meaning of that loss. First and foremost, the routing of Americans came as a severe blow to a military whose elite had viewed themselves as invincible global policemen anointed by God, and who viewed their enemies—at least initially—as diminutive, if inscrutable, primitives in black pajamas, easily exterminated by carpet bombing. The shame of the American defeat was rendered all the more withering by having retreated from foes, from Asian males, whom American racist dogma had long regarded as less masculine. By the time of the U.S. withdrawal, many pro-war males feared America had become, in President Nixon's memorable words, "a pitiful, helpless giant." The experience of national humiliation at the hands of Third World males was recapitulated only four years later, in 1979, when the American embassy in Teheran, along with U.S. hostages, was captured by enemies of the Shah. Every evening Walter Cronkite would close his news broadcast with the hostage day-count, a statistic that increasingly spelled political doom for Jimmy Carter, much as Cronkite's nightly Vietnam War body count hastened Lyndon Johnson's retirement.[51] Carter was widely criticized for his failure to sacrifice the hostages and bomb Iran.[52] One Republican critic questioned the President's phallic competence, asserting that Carter "has engaged in scabbard-rattling in the last couple of weeks, but without anything in [it]."[53] *Time* magazine claimed the crisis was evidence of the nation's masochistic feminization: "Like your wife, America is always around, ready to get a beating."[54] Carter's botched helicopter rescue attempt only solidified these impressions. Not only did he pay a devastating political price for his failure to reduce Iran to a smoldering pile of radioactive embers, but subsequent Democratic presidential candidates have been "Carterized" by GOP image makers. Mondale, Dukakis, and Clinton have all been subtly and not so subtly linked to Carter and accused of the same reluctance to flex military muscle.

In the Introduction, I referred to the 1980s genre of revisionist Vietnam War movies that focused on heroic victories in small battles, as a fantasy compensation for the actual military defeat. These films carried a number of meanings for the larger culture. Most significantly, they signaled a society-wide shift in modes of hypermasculinity (as described in chapter 1) from the "Ladies' Man" to the "Man's Man." The Ladies' Man, as you may recall, seeks to avoid dangerous (feminizing) emotional attachments to women through a compulsive strategy of sexual conquest in which attractive females are viewed as coveted prey, who would cease to be exciting if they expressed interest in an enduring relationship. Being a successful predator requires the cultivation of a smooth and charming persona, along with a stylish and graceful appearance. This masculine ideal was most fully represented in the 1950s and 1960s by Hugh Hefner's "Playboy Philosophy."

While both hypermasculine character types have long coexisted in Western culture (and sometimes in the same person), over the last several decades the Man's Man has gradually become preeminent. The guiding imperative of the Man's Man is to affirm his dissimilarity to women. He must therefore repudiate all attitudes and qualities the larger culture identifies as feminine. Thus, he can be a dependable and protective heterosexual partner, but a cold and unempathic one who must work hard to "not understand" women. His primary emotional attachments and his only friendships are with men, to whom a hard, rough, and crude exterior must be presented. Behind his superficial jocularity with fellow males lies a homophobic avoidance of tenderness and a preoccupation with dominance struggles. With male enemies his sometimes conscious and at other times unconscious metaphor for inducing submission is anal rape. Thus, he threatens "your ass is mine," and in turn fears being "fucked over."

Since the American defeat in Vietnam, male film heroes have more often been Men's Men than Ladies' Men. The protagonist's goal has correspondingly shifted from heterosexual seduction and conquest to homoerotic domination. Valor less often involves "getting the girl," and more frequently means "sticking it to" other men. Women, if they appear at all in male action films, exist only to be mutilated and to thereby

provide the male hero with a motive for violent retribution and an opportunity to display his hard, muscled body to male viewers. Sometimes the significance of women is reduced simply by relegating them
to the role of vapid cheerleaders of manly violence. In these film narratives the feminine is both literally and symbolically eviscerated in order
to inflate the masculine.[55] But nothing succeeded in engorging American muscularity more than real and victorious military interventions,
even if limited to crushing petty tyrants protected by weak, ineffectual
armies.

The *Time* magazine logo for the December 1989 invasion of Panama
and capture of Manual Noriega was a flexed and bulging bicep covered
in stars and stripes.[56] According to then Republican National Committee Chairman Lee Atwater, Bush had, in this latest adventure, "knocked
the question about being timid out of the stadium."[57] While Atwater
may not have hit a home run with this metaphor, he certainly exemplified the longstanding American tradition, discussed in chapter 2, of
symbolically linking sports, warfare, and masculinity. But the really big
pump-up would follow the Persian Gulf War.

Once Saddam Hussein was defeated, George Bush spoke for many
males across the country who had long suffered from that gender-
specific affliction of South East Asian origin, when he excitedly proclaimed, "By God we've kicked the Vietnam syndrome once and for
all."[58] Needless to say, what was curative about the Gulf War was not the
hundreds of thousands of civilian deaths that resulted from the bombings, nor their devastating public health consequences,[59] but the symbolic victory that, along with media censorship,[60] helped to render the
actual suffering invisible.[61] Dramatic footage of American missiles penetrating Iraqi targets demonstrated to those men still hobbled by the
Vietnam Syndrome that our scabbards were not empty. The bombs not
only carried a symbolic payload for the public in general, but for George
Bush in particular. Numerous editorial cartoons labeled images of Bush
and Saddam "Patriot" and "Scud," respectively. Others showed the two
leaders being propelled toward one another in the night sky.[62] There was
much talk by military analysts and commentators in televised briefings

of "Bush punishing Saddam." The personification of nation states as individual male actors, whether in images or words, has always been an
effective rhetorical strategy to generate public support for war.[63] It cre-
ates a simplistic moral narrative in which messy realities such as mutilated and murdered people recede behind the black-and-white drama
of jousting male warriors. Men's support in particular appears to be
more readily mobilized when the aggression of both leaders is represented as a contest for phallic superiority. This dynamic seems to have
been most vividly portrayed in the Gulf War rhetoric and editorial cartoon images of anal rape.

Kneeling on a prayer rug, Saddam Hussein presents his large round
buttocks as the perfect "soft target" for the large American missile poised
for imminent penetration.[64] This cartoon, which was reprinted in a
number of periodicals, was complemented by another that showed a
limp-wristed and perspiring Saddam, his aching posterior cushioned
by a large pillow tied around his waist.[65] The image was apparently
expressing the feminizing consequences of anal rape, which the American missile attack seemed to symbolize for many U.S. males. This was
a theme widely heard in popular discourse about the war, from the
bumper stickers that commanded "Saddam, Bend Over," to the sar-
donic claim made by some American troops that the "USA" emblazoned
on their desert khakis meant "Up Saddam's Ass."[66]

At higher levels of military public relations, the rhetoric of anal rape
was articulated with a bit more subtlety. Throughout the Gulf War there
were myriad Pentagon press conferences during which the media (having largely given up any pretense of critical inquiry in favor of devo-
tional stenography) were treated to gushing encomia to the penetrating
intelligence of American "smart bombs." During one of these performances, Colonel Al Whitley boasted, "You pick precisely which target
you want—the men's room or the ladies' room."[67] Political psychologist
John Broughton, in an astute and playful deconstruction of that statement asks, "How did the bathroom, of all things, come to be selected as
ground zero?"[68] Right away, missiles entering gendered bathrooms may
suggest other invasive penetrations, such as depicted in the aforemen-

Sodomizing Saddam

tioned cartoons. Obviously, Broughton points out, once you get past the soothing euphemisms of military newspeak, it becomes clear that the aim of all weaponry is to penetrate the body, enter its vulnerable interior, and destroy as much tissue as possible.[69] From this perspective, all warfare could be characterized as phallic aggression. Colonel Whitley's missile, however, had a more specific goal. By striking its human targets at their most vulnerable moment, on the toilet with buttocks spread, it sought to deliver maximal humiliation and, in the case of male enemies, emasculating homoerotic domination.

Editorial cartoons and the technophilic musings of military spokesmen were not the only cultural sites where this gendered psychological warfare was waged. On the cover of the supermarket tabloid *National Examiner*, a clumsily doctored photograph depicts Saddam Hussein in a sexy cocktail dress, along with the headline "He Even Wears Dresses... Saddam Hussein's Bizarre Sex Life, Secret CIA Report Reveals."[70] One of the putative informants for the article is quoted as saying, "Oddly, for a man who could be so viciously cruel, he preferred the submissive role in homosexual encounters." Another source, a "tawny-haired Houston housewife" who had fallen under "Hussein's spell" while working for an American oil company based in Baghdad, excitedly anticipated their erotic liaison. However, the bunker rendezvous turned out to be a considerable disappointment. "He took off his clothes, and I couldn't help laughing. 'Well, Saddam,' I muttered to myself, 'I can see you're never going to be a candidate for the centerfold of *Playgirl.*'" Unfortunately, this outburst prompted an eighteen-hour visit to his "torture chamber." While the *National Examiner* used a pseudojournalistic fantasy to feminize Saddam Hussein and assault his phallic status, General Colin Powell promised that, militarily, American forces would be "cutting it off and killing it" (another sports metaphor ready-made for the discourse of homoerotically charged combat).[71] According to the revelations of several CIA agents, George Bush did his bit on the psychological warfare front by intentionally mispronouncing the Iraqi leader's name, by referring to him as Sáddam rather than Saddám. The former means "little boy who cleans out men's shoes" in Egyptian street slang. Taking issue with this claim, one Arab scholar read Bush's mispronunciation as an attempt to link the Iraqi leader to Sodom, the ancient Biblical city of anal copulators destroyed for its wickedness.[72] Whichever interpretation of Bush's "error" seems most compelling, the intent appears to have been to deliver an emasculating insult.

By critiquing the gender subtext of the American psychological warfare strategy, both intended and unconscious, I do not mean to diminish the fact that Saddam Hussein—like so many world leaders, in and out of favor with the American government, elected and unelected—was and remains a sadistic and Machiavellian sociopath. What is of interest here is the way men's anxieties about being feminine were projected and used for propagandistic purposes. And, just as men in general tend to establish their manhood by disavowing "feminine" traits in themselves, and attributing those qualities to women, so George Bush's masculinity was affirmed by contrasting it with Saddam Hussein's feminization.

Clarifying who now wears the overalls in the family

In one editorial cartoon, Bush is depicted in "Before" and "After" images. Under the "Before" heading, we see a cadaverous Bush shrink-wrapped inside a package of "Weenies." Below the "After" label, Bush is now a "Hot Dog," and looking rakish in his desert camouflage, he rests comfortably on a bun.[73] In yet other cartoons, bombs bearing the label "A Thousand Points of Light" explode over Iraq.[74] Thus, a "feminine" sentiment about voluntary charity, first articulated in Bush's 1988 nomination speech to minimize his alienation of female voters, is transformed into a more "masculine" delivery of destructive payload.

The imagery and rhetoric of sports, especially football, which were so heavily deployed in Pentagon press briefings, were also used by editorial cartoonists to represent Bush's remasculinization.[75] On the left side of one such cartoon, Bush, a hulking square-jawed college football hero, is draped by admiring, glassy-eyed females, and followed by men holding up a sign reading "We're #1." To his right, wearing a "Democrat" button, a bookish-looking nerd with a large head and shriveled body stands on a soapbox in front of a sign that reads "A Democrat for Class President." To his audience, which consists entirely of a small dog, he says, "And, furthermore, my opponent is flunking economics, soci-

Driving home the point

ology, ecology..."[76] Although this cartoon appears to be critiquing the fact that issues of substance, such as the economy, social issues, and the environment, were eclipsed by the post-Gulf-War-victory euphoria, it also demonstrates the way the war masculinized Bush and emasculated the Democrats. The latter have only domestic issues on which they can claim superiority. In some ways, the false dichotomy between foreign policy and domestic concerns can be viewed as an extension of the long-standing gendered split between masculine public life and feminine private life. Thus, as this cartoon suggests, Democrats (at least those few willing to designate themselves social policy liberals) have been constructed by Republicans and the conservative male electorate in general as the housewives of politics.

It was not just in editorial cartoons that male Democrats who directly opposed the war were pictured as less manly. For example, the late Minnesota senator Paul Wellstone, who did not support the early use of force in the Persian Gulf, not only received telephone death threats at his home but was confronted by demonstrators chanting "Wimp Wellstone" when he returned to Minnesota to attend his mother's funeral. In words that may have been intended to convey a double meaning, *Newsweek* characterized Wellstone's first address to Congress, which was devoted to explaining his resistance to any precipitous military assault on Iraq, as his "maiden speech."[77]

Considering the political benefits, however transient, that accrued to Bush as a result of the Gulf War victory, we should not be surprised by the public response years later to President Clinton's June 1993 raid on Iraq, supposedly in retaliation for the putative plot against George Bush many months earlier. The attack boosted Clinton's approval ratings by 11 percent[78] and produced editorial cartoons in which he was portrayed as a Schwarzeneggerian Superman. In one of this series, a buffed-up Bill Clinton, under a banner reading "The Last Action Hero," is slaughtering Iraqis with one hand, while with the other he carries to safety damsel-in-distress George Bush, who is resplendent in his finest heels, dress, and pearls.[79] This cartoon also shows just how precarious was the former president's Gulf War remasculinization.

Revenge of the Wimp Factor:
The Presidential Campaign of 1992

"Muscular Conservatism" may sound like a redundancy, especially after examining the steroid-enhanced right-wing rhetoric of the preceding pages. However, as a label for the pugnacious conservative man's man Patrick Buchanan, the phrase—which was coined by fellow Republicans Rowland Evans and Robert Novak in 1991 to designate the political stance of their colleague—has descriptive value.[80] At the 1992 Republican convention, Mr. Buchanan was a take-no-prisoners crusader against Hillary Clinton, immigrants, Welfare recipients (whom he conflated with Los Angeles post-Rodney-King-verdict rioters and referred to as "Vandals and Visigoths"), and demonic liberals, whom he saw as "on the other side" in the "war ... for the soul of America."[81] It may not be surprising, then, that in the primary campaign of 1992, Buchanan's support came largely from men. In fact, there was a larger gender gap in enthusiasm for Buchanan over Bush (13 percent)[82] than there was in the polls measuring support for Bush (11 percent).[83]

Gender seemed to be an even greater factor in the Democratic primary contest. In one poll, men favored Clinton over Tsongas by nearly twenty percentage points, whereas women's preferences went in the other direction by the same margin.[84] This may seem somewhat paradoxical, since Tsongas was markedly more conservative than Clinton (although both of them proudly located themselves in the right wing of the Democratic Party). This particular gender gap might be understood as a triumph of "masculine" image over traditionally "masculine" policy. The moderate but philandering ladies' man, Clinton, was preferred by men to the more conservative but tepid nebbish, Tsongas.

The most explicit and strident expressions of anxious male politics in the 1992 presidential campaign emerged from the Republican convention. In the Introduction, I described some of the homophobic hysteria that characterized that eclectic and colorful gathering of right-wing ideologues. The reader may recall the distress on the part of Torie Clarke, Bush's campaign spokesperson, over attempts by reporters to put the president "on the couch," a place, Clarke insisted, where "real men" didn't belong. The preoccupation with psychological penetration extended to a Bush campaign manager, James Pinkerton, who claimed that the cities chosen by the Democrats and Republicans for their conventions indicated which was the party of real men. New York, the Democratic choice, consisted of guys "on couches talking about their childhood urges." Houston, on the other hand, the site of the Republican gathering, was where you could find men "digging in their backyards for oil."[85] It is not clear from this statement which childhood urges Pinkerton had in mind. Only his analyst knows for sure.

The Bush handlers preferred that their candidate present a reflective surface for the ad-driven projections of others, rather than provide even a narrow window into his psyche. The Democratic campaign, on the other hand, used carefully calibrated self-revelation to neutralize Clinton's negatives. Only those things that might engender empathy, identification, and trust were revealed. Just like many voters, he came from an imperfect family. Like them, he struggled against material and emotional adversity. Like theirs, his marriage had been difficult as well as loving. Through this strategy, Clinton tried to reframe what the Republicans and the media had dubbed "character flaws," transforming them into obstacles overcome. As the redeemed sinner and triumphant victim of early adversity, he hoped to speak with greater moral authority than George Bush, the patrician boy scout with the opaque interior and sanitized life history—and perhaps Clinton even sought to remasculinize self-revelation in the process.

In Houston, there was another femiphobic impulse on prominent display—the urge to suppress strong, independent women. This was evident in two themes articulated at the Republican convention, and in right-wing venues outside the meeting hall: the Draconian anti-choice position of the platform committee, and the bellicose reviling of Hillary Clinton. In declaring a woman's uterus a proper site of state intervention (no problem with "Big Government" here), the GOP—if we are to judge by its platform—did not see a moral dilemma in forcing a victim of rape or incest to carry the fetus to term. The putative basis for their stand against the right to abortion was their deeply felt Christian theology and their abiding love for the unborn. Nevertheless, these same people had been consistent and explicit about their desire to abolish many of the social supports that could allow babies and children to develop healthily. It is difficult to escape the conclusion that, for these earnest "pro-lifers," life began at conception and ended at birth. Thus, the central motive, conscious or not, for these anti-choice activists—especially the men—was apparently the reassertion of men's control over women's bodies. In a statement that could have been uttered by one of the thin-lipped, neofascist patriarchs of Margaret Atwood's dystopian novel *A Handmaid's Tale,* Christian right leader Pat Robertson let Americans know how threatened he was by the prospect of gender equality. The good Reverend insisted during the 1992 election campaign that the proposed Equal Rights Amendment to the Iowa Constitution "encourages women to leave their husbands, kill their children, practice witchcraft, destroy capitalism, and become lesbians."[86] He stopped short of petitioning for the renovation of the old Salem gallows to accommodate modern America's incorrigible handmaids.

Around the same time, however, the call for Puritan justice *was* heard in the classified section of the ultraconservative *American Spectator* magazine, where an ad appeared for mail-order T-shirts that read "Pillory Hillary."[87] This was merely an entrepreneurial echo of the unrelenting scorn heaped on Bill Clinton's wife inside and outside the Republican convention, some of which was described in the Introduction. Rehabilitated elder statesman Richard Nixon got straight to the point with a dire warning: Hillary Clinton's sharp intellect would make the Democratic candidate "look like a wimp."[88] Here he illustrates something that will be explored further in chapter 4—the tendency of femiphobes to locate the uppity woman's phallus in her mind. When Marilyn Quayle addressed the convention, she seemed to be drawing a contrast with Hillary when she said, "Most women do not wish to be liberated."[89] Interestingly, the male star of TV's *Major Dad* (doubtless an appealing designation for advocates of authoritarian family values) was selected to introduce Mrs. Quayle.

In spite of the florid femiphobic rhetoric of the right, the failed economy ultimately trumped all other factors in deciding the outcome of the election. Yet, however important material self-interest may have been in Clinton's November victory, Bush's Wimp Factor vulnerabilities, which were foregrounded once again only weeks after his evanescent glory in Houston and postconvention poll bounce, played a significant role in the final results. In fact, it took only days after the Bush nomination for fellow Republican George Will to declare their candidate "impotently ardent" and his speech "dry, sterile thunder without rain" (borrowing T. S. Eliot's phrase).[90] Of course, Bush had been plagued by attributions of effeminacy throughout the campaign, as was evident even in discussions of fiscal problems. *Newsweek* had used the title "A Wimp of a Recovery" in an article about the feeble economy under Bush.[91] Independent candidate Ross Perot knew exactly what he was suggesting when he told the story about joining Bush on a boat trip during which the president "almost cried" when he couldn't start his motor boat.[92] On another occasion, Perot claimed to have told Bush, "This world is full of lions and tigers and rabbits." Apparently confident of his own manly feline status, Perot declared, "and you're a rabbit."[93] On the PBS program *McNeil/Lehrer News Hour*, the diminutive but combative billionaire attacked Bush's pre–Gulf War support of the Iraqi military regime by saying Bush had "burped, diapered, and pampered" Saddam Hussein for years.[94] While the allusions to being a crybaby, a scared rabbit, and a mother to a dictator were certainly assaults on Bush's masculine credentials, nothing suggested his scrotal vacuity more than the dispute over his Texas residency. Some Lone Star citizens wondered whether owning one-eighth of an acre of an empty lot in Houston made Bush a real Texan. For many people "real Texan" was code for "real man." Columnist Molly Ivins summarized her view of Bush's problem (and echoed the link Americans have long made between the aristocratic and the feminine) thus: "There are certain minimal standards for citizenship: real Texans do not use the word 'summer' as a verb. Real Texans do not wear blue slacks with little green whales all over them. And real Texans never refer to trouble as 'deep doo-doo.' "[95] Bush had his work cut out for him. As the state's governor, Ann Richards, put it, "You have got to prove your manhood down here, whether you're a man or a woman."[96]

Editorial cartoons and TV comedy sketches depicted Bush in drag or otherwise feminized.[97] In fact, every one of Oliphant's images of the president showed him carrying a purse. On the night before the October presidential debates, there appeared on NBC's *Saturday Night Live* a parodic preview of the anticipated debate. At the end of the debate skit, the candidates were asked to make a closing statement. While each man listened to the other's statements, he fantasized about his opponents. In these fantasies the candidates were depicted in terms that represented their most negative popular caricatures. Clinton appeared as a dope-smoking hippy protester, Perot as a wacky Munchkin from *The Wizard of Oz*, and Bush as a dowdy old woman.[98]

The Bush campaign made valiant, if not always compelling, responses to this femiphobic derision. At a photo opportunity in which Bush posed wearing boxing gloves, one labeled "Congress" and the other "Democrat," Republican senator Alan Simpson, bellowed, "George Bush is fully engaged, ready to let 'er rip, a man of confidence and energy, ready to go, and we're excited."[99] In addition to pumping up their man, Republicans tried to reverse the direction of feminine attribution. Bush friend Ray Scott said Clinton was a "sissy," as indicated "by how he kind of swishes his back end."[100]

The boxing motif reemerged in the pre-debate hypermasculine chest thumping by Clinton and Bush. "I've listened to all [his] macho talk," asserted Clinton with a jaunty confidence, "but when it comes time to go man to man, plan to plan, where is he? One of the greatest boxers that ever lived, Joe Louis, said 'You can run but you can't hide.' " Only grazed by this blow, the Bush campaign quickly counterpunched, hitting Clinton in a delicate area. "If Bill Clinton was a real man," a Bush spokesperson insisted, "he would stand up and tell the truth and the whole truth about the draft issue."[101] It was the Democratic candidate, however, who delivered the knockout punch in this pre-debate rhetorical exhibition bout. He joked that the president, along with other Republicans, had been criticizing Ms. Clinton so much, "You'd think [Bush] was running for First Lady, instead of president."[102] As if anyone could forget, Sheila Tate, a Republican public relations executive, reminded the nation that for politicians, debates "are the ultimate test of manhood."[103]

In spite of all the pre-debate posturing, the actual confrontation made little difference in the outcome of the election. Even though Bush performed rather poorly in the debates, he didn't lose much support overall.[104] There was a gender gap in the final exit poll vote tally, but with some interesting variations. By a margin of 5 percent, women voted for Clinton more than men did. On the other hand, Bush did only slightly better among male than female voters.[105] Bush's conservative positions, more typically supported by men, seemed to have been outweighed by a combination of many factors. These include Bush's stubbornly adhesive wimp image, the poor economy that had prompted middle- and low-income males to vote for Clinton (for individuals making less than fifty thousand dollars a year, there was 16 percent income-based gap favoring Clinton), and the presence of Ross Perot in the race (more males than females voted for him by a margin of 4 percent).[106]

Obviously, because it was a three-way race, Clinton got a plurality, not a majority, of votes. But it wasn't just the lack of a mandate that would haunt the first term of his presidency—rather, it would be the image of Hillary, represented in the 1992 campaign by right-wing femiphobes as a power-hungry and castrating vagina dentata who controlled her husband. That image would endure and constitute one of Bill Clinton's primary political vulnerabilities, *his* wimp factor.

4

Vaginas with Teeth and Castrating First Ladies
Fantasies of Feminine Danger from Eve to Hillary Clinton

Women Who Lust Too Much and
Other Terrors in the Male Unconscious

Michael was a thirty-five-year-old Irish-American from a working-class Boston family. A man of numerous talents, he was never able to translate them into work that was either satisfying or adequately remunerative. He survived by moving from one low-paying sales job to another. His reason for consulting me was a lifelong history of erectile impotence and a near total absence of sensation even when he was "functional." He also had difficulty sensing a variety of social cues, especially signals of interest from women. Over the course of our work together, we had come to understand this "obliviousness" as a defensive strategy that helped him avoid intimacy with women. The relationships he did have were fleeting and superficial. In one of our sessions, it became clearer what was so disturbing to him about closeness with females. "The thing is," Michael explained, "I just have a difficult time concentrating when I'm supposed to be making love. I keep thinking about baseball, trivia, things that have to be done that day. I like being with women and they're attractive to me. But you know, it's funny, the sexual fantasies I have while masturbating can't go further than foreplay. If they get to the point of intercourse, I lose my erection."

"Maybe," I wondered, "you're worried about going too far, emotionally and sexually, with a woman."

"You see," Michael replied, "I don't want to go out on a limb with a lover and have it cut off."

Going out on an interpretive limb myself, I said, "It seems like being inside a woman—her heart, her vagina, her world—and letting yourself feel something makes you fear that some part of you might be cut off."

His face reddened as he pondered my comment for a moment and said, "That's strange. For some reason I'm recalling this bizarre but frequent daydream I used to have when I was a teenager. I'd visualize being inside a girl and there would be a scissors there ready to cut my penis off." While this association led, in turn, to several others, he spent most of our remaining time in that hour describing how he avoided being "pussy whipped" in romantic relationships.

In thinking about his castration fantasy, it would be easy to get overly concrete about it. In my view, the fundamental fear in castration anxiety is not so much a physical injury per se but an injury that *feminizes*—a fate that, in some men's eyes, could just as easily result from feeling dependent on ("out on a limb") or controlled by ("pussy whipped") a woman, as it could from vaginal scissors. Although Michael was much more complex than can be rendered in a brief vignette, and there were multiple determinants of his symptoms, his anxieties bear a striking similarity to those articulated by many men throughout the long and varied history of patriarchal societies.[1]

The reader should not construe Michael or any of the examples that follow as somehow typical of all men in all places and at all times, but of particular configurations of masculinity within patriarchy. These have changed over time, but have also exhibited some striking continuities. In spite of the profound differences between men from various historical periods and cultural locations, most social orders based on male dominance seem to have produced men who share similar fears and insecurities. Part of what makes these anxieties so disabling is that, as with Michael, women are desired as well as feared. One way this conflict has been managed is to mentally split females into two mutually exclusive categories of "good" and "bad" women. Good women have been seen as caregiving, desirable but without desire, passive, sub-missive, self-deprecating, fragile, and in need of male protection. Bad women, on the other hand, as they have been portrayed across the centuries, both in word and image, are castrating, engulfing, sexually ravenous, power hungry, and murderous. And, because they are a malevolent and persecutory threat to men, they must be punished or destroyed.

As anyone with a passing familiarity with history knows, misogy-nist fantasies of feminine danger have provided fuel for more than pri-vate neuroses, as the witch-hunt holocaust of early modern Europe can attest. With up to a hundred thousand women murdered (estimates vary) for their putative lusty liaisons with the Devil, some European towns were left completely depopulated of female inhabitants.[2] In 1486, two church-appointed inquisitors, Heinrich Kramer and James Sprenger, laid out the rationale for this epidemic of male hysteria in their treatise on the detection, interrogation, torture, and execution of witches, *Malleus Maleficarum* (The Witches' Hammer):

> What else is woman but a foe to friendship, an inescapable pun-ishment, a necessary evil, a natural temptation, a desirable calam-ity, a domestic danger, a delectable detriment, an evil of nature, painted with fair colors! ... I had rather dwell with a lion and a dragon.[3]

What is so instructive about this passage is that it captures the am-bivalence that makes misogyny a *conflict,* rather than simple hatred—the "calamity" is "desirable"; the "detriment" is "delectable." It might interest those readers comforted by our historical distance from the il-lustrious inquisitors to know that the translator and editor of the 1948 edition of the *Malleus Maleficarum,* Reverend Montague Summers, considered this work to be "among the most important, wisest and weightiest books of the world."[4]

Over the millennia of anxious masculinity, various mythical women have figured prominently in the pantheon of antifemale demonology: Eve, Lilith, Pandora, Diana, Kali, and others. Yet, these characters seem derivative of an even more pervasive and primordial image of feminine monstrosity—the *vagina dentata*, or vagina with teeth. Derivatives of this fantasy have been a recurring motif in the folklore of an astonishing variety of cultures. In the mythology of some North American Indians, there is a story of the Terrible Mother whose vagina is inhabited by a meat-eating fish. To make her into a woman, the hero must overpower the Terrible Mother and knock the teeth out of her vagina.[5] Among the Nandi of Africa, the clitoris was regarded as a dangerous tooth and therefore removed. The severed clitorises, which are tossed into a swamp, are then thought to become leeches.[6] According to Chaco legend, the first women of the Chaco Indians ate with the teeth in their vaginas. To make females safe for men to have sex with, Caroucho, a mythical culture hero, had to break the teeth out.[7] A similar tale from East Indian folklore involves the wife of a Brahmin (a member of India's upper caste) whose vaginal teeth bit off the penises of many lovers. One day the husband returned with a pair of tongs and while pretending to seduce her, removed the teeth. Unfortunately, it left her unable to experience pleasure. After many joyless encounters with men, she tried the Brahmin's horse, but he entered her with such force that she died.[8] This last tale is particularly interesting in that it directly links a woman's destructive impact on men with her capacity for pleasure.

In some myths, the teeth develop endogenously; in others, they result from invading snakes who are attracted to the vaginas of sexually excited women. In the lore of some Polynesian cultures, such as the Tuamotos Islands where snakes are unknown, eels put the bite in the boudoir. Similarly, the folktales of a few Eastern European societies have dragons taking up residence in tempting young maidens.[9]

Variations on the vagina dentata narrative, too numerous to fully recount here, involve men being emasculated in less literal ways—being eaten, poisoned, infected with disease, rendered impotent, and turned into women. These derivations, which are more highly symbolized and metaphorically distant from toothy vaginas, can be found in different fairy tales. For example, one version of Sleeping Beauty, "Briar Rose," features an adolescent girl to whom access is barred by a thorny hedge, upon which numerous suitors have found themselves impaled and dying in agony. For the heroic prince, however, who is able to win the young girl's heart, the hedge turns into flowers. It parts, allowing him to pass uninjured.[10] There is a seemingly infinite variety of fables that involve a male hero who, in the pursuit of some treasure, knowledge, or fair maiden, makes a perilous journey through a dark and dangerous passage often guarded by snarling beasts, crushing rocks, or smiting gates.[11] Once these obstacles are defeated (the teeth extracted), the hero gets his reward and others can pass without fear.

Modern Euro-American culture has been no less replete than those cited above with images and language that covertly or overtly depict women as castrating and/or devouring fanged vaginas. Throughout the late nineteenth century, popular paintings routinely represented women as wild, toothy beasts. In slightly more subtle images, lions, tigers, and other snarling carnivores were often placed next to a well-dressed woman's crotch—inviting the viewer not only to contemplate the supposed animal nature of women but to speculate on what predatory dangers might lurk beneath their sartorial civility.[12]

Contemporary film, especially and most explicitly the horror genre, is another arena in which conscious and unconscious fantasies of feminine monstrosity and male vulnerability find expression. Such movies simultaneously represent the personal artistic vision of the filmmaker and the collective fears, wishes, and concerns of those who attend them. Interestingly, young men constitute the largest single demographic group at theater screenings of horror movies.[13] In many of the classics of this genre, such as *Alien, The Brood, The Exorcist,* and *Sisters,* to name but a few, feminine evil finds representation in the form of deranged wombs, witches, demonic mothers, mutilators of men, and possessed vessels of malevolent spirits.[14] Even films that feature a male monster often attribute his villainy to a previous psychic wound inflicted by a female, usually a mother. For example, the crimes of countless television and movie serial killers have been explained by the story's insightful criminologist as a repetition compulsion, in which the murderer's abusive and/or seductive mother is symbolically killed over and over again through the substitution of the random female victim.[15] At the end of Alfred Hitchcock's *Psycho*, the audience learns that the reason Norman Bates behaved so badly was that he had psychologically incorporated his intrusive mother, whom the psychiatrist describes as having been a "clinging, demanding woman." It was "the mother half of his mind" that compelled him to murder any women who sexually excited him.[16]

Possessive, engulfing, consuming, and annihilating feminine terrors are certainly not confined to the horror genre. In the light comedy *Bull Durham*, a character playfully warns another that men refer to women as "the Bermuda Triangle" because once inside they might never be heard from again[17] (an assumption that seemed to be shared by my patient, Michael). A woman in Ingmar Bergman's *Cries and Whispers* anticipates the arrival of her husband, and while waiting in bed for him, she places broken glass in her vagina.[18]

In all these accounts, it is women's sexuality that appears to be at the core of men's anxieties. Males insecure about their masculinity seem to be caught in a paralyzing conflict: they desire women as sexual objects but fear them as sexual subjects, as creatures of desire. The conjoining of teeth with vaginas suggests that it is women's amorous *appetites* that some men find so threatening. Inquisitors Kramer and Sprenger put it clearly when they said, "All witchcraft comes from carnal lust, which in women is insatiable."[19] In a later passage they describe a witch's curious hobby of collecting penises in a box, and keeping them alive by feeding them corn and oats. While the authors are not explicit about the reason for this strange pastime, it sounds as if the captive organs are being fattened for later consumption.[20]

There are indications, seen in the clinical, literary, and folkloric narratives of many cultures, that some men are so fearful of female sexuality that their own desire becomes a signal of impending danger. Arousal that portends union with a woman becomes an alarm, warning that dissolution of the self is imminent. Under these circumstances, sexual excitement comes to be represented in the anxious male imagination as violence. One compelling example can be found in a "love" scene from a 1929 novel, *The Nation Awakes,* written by a German fascist, Franz Schauwecker:

> In her glowing smile, quite silent, is a bewitching mixture of love, triumph, passion, and promise.... He can contain himself no longer. He draws her close, for she belongs to him and he cannot let her go. She does not offer the slightest resistance. Bending her body almost imperceptibly, she glides over to him.... What else can she do? After all, she belongs to him and her place is with him.
>
> They lie next to each other. She lifts her arms and her dress slips off. Underneath she is naked. Her nakedness assaults him with a sudden glowing shudder, a gust of wind across a placid lake. He says nothing, but with a jolt his breath rushes into his blood, filling it with pearls of pure, quivering bubbles, a gushing froth, just as the blood of men shot in the lungs leaves them lying yellow and silent like corpses, while the blood spurts endlessly, gurgling and seething at every breath—breath which they heave up, groaning, as if by a block and tackle, the air is so heavy and laden.[21]

The blurring of bedroom and battlefield came abruptly to American public consciousness in the 1990s as a result of what the cover headline of *People* magazine referred to as "The Cut Felt 'Round the World."[22] Not until Lorena Bobbitt made her debut in the trashy tabloid venues of American popular culture did stand-up comedians have such a reliable source of nervous laughter. The revelation that she cut off John Wayne Bobbitt's penis with a kitchen knife as he slept, in retaliation for years of marital rape and physical assault, and then tossed it out her car window, produced an anxious, if bemused, identification in men across the country. As Jay Leno said, "Every guy in America is sleeping on his stomach now."[23] But even as men chuckled at the multitude of jokes, T-shirts ("Love Hurts"),[24] and media-sponsored contests (the "Lorena Bobbitt Weenie Toss"—hitting a bull's-eye with a hot dog),[25] they crossed their legs tightly. A pervasive, paralyzing, and often unconscious nightmare had come true. After centuries of vagina dentata fantasies and rhetoric about castrating wives and mothers, a woman actually cut a penis off. As Roy Hazelwood, the FBI's expert on violent sex crimes pointed out, "Genital mutilation is quite common. But it's either a homosexual crime (male against male) or male against female."[26] Such reminders of empirical reality, however, rarely assuage hysteria, especially when driven by such powerful projections. Sidney Siller, founder of the National Organization for Men, was certainly not dissuaded from proclaiming, "It's now open season on men," who are "more exposed to this danger than ever."[27]

The fantasized threat posed by women's desire is managed in various ways by anxious men. One strategy is psychological decapitation— the attempt to deny, suppress, or eradicate women's personhood or subjectivity. Clarence, a fifty-seven-year-old associate in a large corporate law firm, was initially driven to seek psychotherapy after his alcoholic wife of twenty-five years left him. Theirs was a largely sexless marriage, at least after the first few months, when she became pregnant with their son. While Clarence had had a long series of brief affairs, it was her decision to stop drinking that precipitated his wife's departure. During our initial meeting, he complained of immobilizing depression, which he attributed not only to the end of his marriage, but to his inability to sustain any interest in a woman after sleeping with her once or twice. In the course of our first year working together, we returned frequently to this problem. One day, in reflecting upon how rapidly his excitement waned after having met a woman a few weeks earlier, he said, "Maybe, I'm just too perfectionistic. When I wake up next to a woman in the light of day and see the blotches, the freckles, the pores, and especially the body hair, I think, 'ugh!' Maybe a robot would be better." I asked Clarence what troubled him so much about the flesh and blood aspects of a woman. He replied with bracing frankness, "Maybe I just don't like the thought of another person being there. It's like when I'm eating. It makes me queasy to think I'm cutting and chewing on some chicken's leg. Who would want to think about that?" I noted that it seemed to be the thought of touching a *particular* woman's leg that filled him with such disgust, and that perhaps he handles that by doing what he did in his analogy—turning her into dead meat. No wonder he loses interest, I thought to myself. "Yeah, I don't like to be reminded that there's a human there," Clarence responded. I asked if there were any specific humans he didn't want to be reminded of. "Well," he boomed with nervous laughter, "I suppose my parents. I certainly wouldn't want to think about having sex with my mother! But, that's not something that's ever occurred to me."

"Until now," I added.

"Yeah, that's true," he acknowledged. Clarence continued, "Well, uh . . . maybe it's just an evolutionary thing, to want to mate with someone new. I watch all these animal documentaries and think, 'that really fits for humans.' My whole life, as soon as I have sex with a woman, I get kind of depressed and want to get away from her as soon as I can. It must be just some obsolete relic of natural selection." Perhaps, I conjectured, it was more comforting for him to think of his urge to flee any experience of sexual intimacy with women as some kind of biological imperative, rather than consider that there might be something emotional going on inside of him. After a minute of anguished silence, Clarence ended our session by saying, "I guess I don't really want to know that part of me."

Such intense, deeply personal expressions of male anxiety in the face of women's sexual subjectivity—their capacity to be desiring selves, as well as desirable objects—are matched by more public but equally disturbing manifestations in the larger culture. Judge Thomas Bollinger of Baltimore County, Maryland, explained why he gave probation rather than jail time to a man found guilty of raping a drunken woman: the sight of a supine female in an alcohol-induced coma was "the dream of a lot of males, quite honestly."[28] With this comment, the judge may have opened up a new career opportunity for himself—as spokesmodel for the disturbingly popular date-rape drug, Rohypnol. But for that position he will have to compete with Max Factor cosmetics heir Andrew Luster, who was convicted of drugging and raping three women, while videotaping his crimes. On one of the tapes he speaks directly to the camera, and says, "That's exactly what I like in my room: a passed out beautiful girl." Apparently, for this progeny of the makeup dynasty, powerful sedatives can create even greater allure than lip gloss. Since he had the bad luck not to end up in Bollinger's courtroom, Luster was sentenced to 124 years in prison.[29]

While some men have found women who lose their heads to alcohol or drugs to be objects of uncontrollable lust, others have eroticized the *literally* decapitated female body. The oeuvre of comic artist Robert Crumb is known for its curious blend of self-deprecating humor and misogynist fantasy. One story that appeared in *HUP: The Comic for Modern Guys*[30] featured the desperately randy, neurotic, and terminally clueless Flakey Foont and his guru, Mr. Natural, a kind of amoral leprechaun of the id. One day, Mr. Natural arrives at Flakey's apartment with the "gift" of a live but headless woman, called Devil Girl. She has a cover over her "gullet," which must be removed for "feeding." Upon that sits a fake head. After Flakey expresses initial alarm at her decapitation, Mr. Natural assures him of its necessity: "The head was always such a big problem. She had such an irritating set of sensibilities.... So I got ta thinkin' an' figurin'—why not just get rid of th' head? Th' body is what we're mainly interested in, right?" Since her sole function is that of sex toy, *any* sensibility would be disturbing. Thus, as soon as Mr. Natural leaves, Flakey finds even the fake head annoying. He knocks it off and says, "I like it better with just the cap!" While raping her he is abruptly overcome with shame and horror as the image of Devil Girl's enormous decapitated head appears in his mind's eye and intrudes on his orgasm. Her wild, serpentine hair, large glistening teeth, and enraged countenance constitute a Medusa-like return of the repressed for the hapless Flakey. He calls Mr. Natural and implores him to take her back. When the diminutive guru arrives, he reaches down into Devil Girl's neck and, by employing "old African witch doctor stuff," pulls her head out. She is every bit as hideous as Flakey had imagined and, when she regains consciousness, just as furious. Mr. Natural pontificates, "There's very, very powerful, very forceful 'Yin' energy there. It could *kill* you if you're not careful. Y'gotta be cool, detached. It's hard, I know. The attraction is so strong. So irresistible!" (Rarely has patriarchal male ambivalence about female sexuality been expressed so succinctly—at least outside a clinical consulting room.) At this point, Flakey makes a pathetic attempt to apologize to Devil Girl and says, "I'm so sorry . . . something in me that I'm not very proud of—some warped part of my psyche—took over. . . . I can't begin to tell you the remorse I feel. The terrible self-loathing. . . ." This feeble recrimination only excites her fury more. The last frame shows Devil Girl looking for a butcher knife to decapitate the men.

Fantasies of headless women, and the vagina dentata myths discussed earlier, are manifestations of male gender and sexual anxieties that are linked in complex ways. In many cultures and historical periods, symbolic equations have been drawn—covertly and sometimes overtly—between heads and genitals. The vagina dentata is itself a mouth, aberrantly but meaningfully located. According to Jewish Studies scholar Howard Eilberg-Schwartz, the symbolic substitution ("upward displacement") of the vagina for the mouth can be found throughout the Old Testament and Talmud.[31] In some sections the associations are expressed by eroticizing the female voice. "A woman's voice is nakedness," asserts one Talmudic discourse on what qualifies as indecent exposure in females, for it is "sweet" and the face is "comely."[32] Another passage warns, "Do not engage too much in conversation with a woman, for this will lead you to illicit intercourse."[33] Elsewhere we learn it is improper for the man to engage in conversation during sex because this is seen as equivalent to cunnilingus.[34] In another section, God (as male) accuses Israel (as female) of "harlotry" for allowing the name of another god to pass her lips.[35] Thus, if a woman's voice is alluring, it is a dangerous beguilement, one that portends corruption, betrayal, and annihilation. This brings to mind the ancient sirens, the mythological figures with the bodies of birds and the heads of women, who by virtue of their seductive song lured sailors to their rocky doom on invisible reefs, and then ate them. Here is a myth that brings together two dangers of the female's head—her enchanting face and her cannibalistic/castrating mouth.

Surprisingly similar symbolic equations between female heads and genitals have found expression in contemporary Israel as well, especially among the ultra-orthodox. Women in this sect wear either wigs or scarves. While this is done ostensibly for religious purposes, there appear to be other, equally significant motivations, of a more psychosexual nature. Around 1990, in the city of B'nai-Brak, the local "Modesty Brigade," which functioned as the self-anointed guardians of public virtue, lodged a vigorous protest against the owners of an upscale wig store. The complaint concerned the brazen exposure of hair on the be-wigged manikin heads displayed in the shop window. The danger here was the possible sexual disturbance that the sight of female hair might generate in the city's men. The initial demand was for the store owner to use scarves to shield the hirsute hazard. The problem of course was that this would also shield the shopkeeper's wigs from customers. A compromise was finally reached. The wig hair could remain exposed as long as the eyes of the Styrofoam heads were covered, which was achieved by using dark sunglasses. In spite of the artificiality of these disembodied craniums, it seems that the threat posed by the female gaze outweighed the erotic temptation of female hair.[36]

Perhaps the most infamous malevolent female head to ever haunt the patriarchal imagination has been that of Medusa. According to ancient Greek myth,[37] she was a warrior queen and unwed mother, traits which by themselves already rendered her a gender outlaw. She had a hideous face, with giant boar's teeth in her gaping mouth and writhing fanged snakes for hair, and all men who beheld her repulsive visage were turned to stone—immobilized and thus impotent. Though she tried to defend her community from the invading Perseus, he was able to avert his gaze, and with the help of Athena, he cut her head off. Just prior to this battle, Medusa had been raped by Poseidon, and from a hole in her later decapitated torso, she gave birth to two progeny. In a nuanced analysis of this myth, classics scholar Molly Myerwitz Levine concludes, "Voiceless but fertile, the headless Medusa encodes the patriarchal ideal of maternity without sexuality."[38] Removing the head of wild hair, which for the Greeks and many other cultures signified wild female sexuality (i.e., out of male control), can thus be understood as an attempt to "castrate" her, to sever her sexual agency from her function as mother. In fact, Perseus (which means "cutter") used the same weapon Cronus employed to castrate Uranus.[39] Echoing the theme of upward displacement, the late sociologist and all-around radical polymath Phillip Slater described Medusa's fate as a "mythical representation of clitoridectomy."[40]

Ambivalence about maternal sexuality is evident in other aspects of this story. Perseus himself is the result of a kind of virgin birth. His mother Danaë was impregnated by the ever libidinous Zeus, but not through intercourse. Since her father kept Danaë in an underground chamber to preserve her virginity and prevent the birth of a child that an oracle predicted would slay him, Zeus transformed his seed into gold, which dripped through the chamber and onto her lap. And later, as a young man, Perseus himself sought to keep his mother chaste. Danaë's suitor Polydectes said he would marry another if Perseus brought him the head of Medusa.

The fate of Medusa's disembodied head is as interesting as that of her fecund but decapitated body. Perseus appropriates the hideous cephalic monstrosity, which still retains its power to frighten and turn men to stone, and uses it to defeat a multitude of enemies. Later, Athena has the head emblazoned on her shield, which serves to terrify men who may have designs on her virginity. The power of this image of the vagina dentata to ward off men's desire and render them impotent lies, according to Slater, in its capacity to evoke fantasies of the engulfing maternal genitals. In these stories no phallus (such as those that might assault Athena) or phallic derivative (like the enemy swords that might threaten Perseus) can stand up to Medusa's head. She doesn't just represent an image of castration with a head of penile snakes, as Freud reads her severed head,[41] but also a threatening *castrator* whose coiffure of open-jawed dentate serpents and salivating mouth of boar's teeth clearly render her a vaginal danger.[42]

While many traditions within various male-dominant cultures involve the talismanic use of female genitals to ward off or frighten away evil spirits or enemies, the ambivalence about female sexuality is more often expressed in upward displacement—through taboos associated with the exposure of women's heads or hair. Anthropologist Carol Delaney, in her study of Islamic rural villages of Turkey, notes that girls' heads must be covered with scarves by the time they reach puberty, a practice that not only expresses a concern about exposed female heads but also suggests the link in the minds of these villagers between head hair and pubic hair.[43] Loose hair is read as a sign of loose sexuality. And not only must the symbol of female genitality and pubic hair be kept covered or trammeled in braids, but pubic hair itself (and by extension, all female body hair) is taboo and must be removed. While men are also expected to remove their body hair, this cultural stricture is applied to women with much greater severity. This difference is probably a reflection of the culture's disparate views about female and male genitals. Vaginas are so shameful they must never be spoken of. The penis, however, is seen as the precious source of creativity, the fountain of a life force that is perpetuated indefinitely across generations. Semen itself comes from the brain and is the earthly manifestation of divine agency. Interestingly, when the foreskin of a young boy is removed during circumcision, it is spoken of as lifting the "veil of the penis."[44] Thus, even for males, heads and genitals are experienced as symbolic equivalents.

As in the ancient Hebrew texts described earlier, in the patriarchal cultural space of the villagers studied by Delaney, a woman's voice carries the meaning of disruptive sexual power. According to their interpretation of Islam, female speech is "awra [pudenda] and should not be heard."[45] An open (speaking) mouth is an open vagina. A very similar set of concerns can be found in early Christian writings, especially those of the apostle Paul, who declared, "Let a woman learn in all submissiveness. I permit no woman to teach or have authority over men;

she is to keep silent."[46] Along with this pronouncement, he commanded that women be veiled so as not to provide irresistible sexual temptation to the angels.[47]

Paul shares a sensibility that links him to countless other guardians of male dominance across cultures and historical time, and to many ordinary men like the patients I have described. They are all deeply disturbed by women's visibility, agency, intellect, and public voice. A major reason for this, in addition and related to wanting to protect male privilege and ensure paternity, is the felt association between women's autonomy and their sexuality. There is no domain where women's social power generates as much male sexual anxiety as it does in the political arena. And perhaps no contemporary phenomenon more starkly exemplifies this than does the demonization of Hillary Rodham Clinton. From early on she was portrayed as a sexual danger. In a 1992 interview with R. Emmett Tyrrell, editor of *The American Spectator*, ABC's Ted Koppel asked, "What would you do with [Ms. Clinton], put her in a convent for the next four years?"[48]

To Pillory Hillary

In 1993, at the end of a difficult twelve months as First Lady of the United States, Hillary Rodham Clinton declared in astonishment, "The idea that I would check my brain at the White House door just doesn't make any sense to me."[49] But to many conservative men, and even a few women, a decapitated first lady made a lot of sense. That head of hers turned out to be an endless source of difficulty. Perhaps that is why, in the words of the *New York Times*, she "experimented with more hairstyles than Heinz has varieties."[50] As the years unfolded, however, no amount of obsessive cosmetic repackaging could render her self-authorizing intellect acceptable to the femiphobic right.

It should be emphasized at this point that to analyze the epidemic of male political hysteria in response to Ms. Clinton is not to endorse her or her husband's cautious center-right politics. Her Byzantine but conservative failed healthcare plan, for example, was clearly an attempt to preserve corporate control of medical services, and co-opt the early groundswell of support for the more rational and cost-effective single-payer model of healthcare financing. Yet, it is precisely the Clintons' "New Democrat" corporate centrism, support for the death penalty, and gushing boosterism of unfettered global capitalist hegemony that make the manic vituperations, revived Cold War paranoia, and bizarre fantasies of their conservative political enemies so interesting and so important to understand.

Chief among Ms. Clinton's avid foes was right-wing talk jock Rush Limbaugh, who implicated her in an alleged homicide by suggesting, "Vince Foster was murdered in an apartment owned by Hillary Clinton."[51] While the death of the deputy White House counselor had been ruled a suicide, Limbaugh's hysterical claim was welcome grist for the right-wing conspiracy mill. But the sense of the first lady as a vaguely malevolent threat even pervaded the most mainstream of pop culture venues: late-night television. David Letterman's famous Top Ten list featured on one show the "Top ten surprises in the O. J. Simpson video." Number five was listed as "the revelation that the gloves are Hillary's size."[52] This, by the way, was only one of many versions of the same joke that entered circulation, some as editorial cartoons, after the Simpson trial.[53] A link had been made in the shared cultural unconscious between the famously bloody murders in Los Angeles and the terrifying fantasies of feminine menace associated with the first lady.

Other attacks on Hillary got more specific about the kind of peril she presented. For example, the conservative *National Review* referred to her as "that smiling barracuda,"[54] a metaphor that obviously echoes the vagina dentata fantasies described earlier. Along similar lines, comedian Bill Maher referred to Paula Jones's sexual harassment suit against Bill Clinton, and her claim that she could identify certain distinguishing features of the president's genitals: "He had to be careful around the White House because you know how Hillary loves to shred evidence."[55] *Newsweek* featured a cartoon of the first couple in bed together. While Bill is blissfully asleep, Hillary is sitting up, with an ex-

pression of demonic determination on her face, and evidently contemplating some act of wickedness. The thought bubble above her head
reads, "Hillary Rodham Bobbitt."[56] But it was the cartoonists for Mr.
Tyrrell's paper who seemed to dip their pens most deeply in the inkwell
of femiphobic symbolism. The cover drawing for the May 1993 issue of
The American Spectator (p. 132) pictured a terrified young man on an
operating table struggling to get up. His wide-eyed gaze is fixed on the
large saw being held over his torso by a grinning Hillary Clinton in a
surgical gown. Although held down by Ms. Clinton and the President,
the patient seems immobilized, largely by his own panic. The tip of the
saw blade extends beyond the frame of the drawing as if it were threatening the reader as well. The headline that accompanies this image is
"Health Nuts," which suggests that the article inside by Fred Barnes will
talk about those supposedly wacky folks on Hillary Clinton's healthcare
task force. It is actually a rehash of the right-wing denial that there is
any healthcare crisis in the U.S., and a paean to the current system.[57] The
headline has another more ominous implication, however, that ties into
the psychological theme of the drawing. Hillary, and by extension the
Clinton health plan, are about to amputate John Q. Public's erstwhile
healthy nuts, which can be read as signifiers for the existing private
health plans that Mr. Barnes and other wealthy Americans think are
just-fine-thank you and have no trouble affording.

In the classified section of the same issue there appeared advertisements that provided the perfect complement to the front cover.
One promoted a new publication, *Hillary Unleashed*, which claimed
to be "dedicated to uncovering the truth about the *real* power in the
White House ... Hillary! Cookie baking housewife or mud-wrestling
she-devil?"[58] This ad appeared next to a recruitment notice for the
aptly named "Men's Defense Network" ("Defeat Radical Feminism ...
membership $24/yr.").[59] In the personals section, anxious femiphobes
were offered reassuring fantasies by sleazy brokers for "Oriental Ladies,"
a commonplace racist code for passive, obedient Asian women who
know their place.[60] Since the 1990s, *The American Spectator* has become

A castrating first lady

less lurid in its femiphobia, but its greater subtlety of presentation has not been accompanied by any increased sophistication in its paleo-conservative politics.

How to Win Friends and Not Influence People: The Unwritten Rules of First Lady Etiquette

The rhetorical assault on Hillary Clinton has a long and ignoble pre-history. American male political culture has always had a first lady problem. The vexing question has usually been: How can a woman who is sharing the life of the most powerful man in the nation be kept from sharing in any of that power? As described by historian Garry Wills, this has been accomplished, especially in the last forty years, by giving first wives pet projects.[61] These have generally been good works that address noncontroversial social problems entirely isolated from the political and economic contexts that created them. These are projects guaranteed to (1) threaten no vested interest, (2) generate little debate, (3) confer no meaningful decision-making power on the first lady, and (4) have minimal impact. For Jackie Kennedy it was interior decorating. Lady Bird Johnson was devoted to spiffy, immaculate freeways. Volunteerism captured Pat Nixon's imagination. Betty Ford adopted disabled children as her constituency. Mental health was designated a safe cause for Rosalynn Carter, although she did occasionally wander off the first lady reservation. Nancy Reagan was inspired to say no to drugs, while Barbara Bush took a firm stand in favor of literacy. Following in her mother-in-law's footsteps, Laura Bush, a former schoolteacher and librarian, has become a passionate advocate of early reading programs.

Woe is the first lady who deviates from these prescribed modes of innocuous social improvement. Being suspected of advising her Chief Executive husband is perhaps the most common reason a first lady falls from favor. Unlike the feedback provided by a president's unelected *male* advisors, wifely recommendations will evoke unremitting gasps of sanctimonious outrage from the priests of the status quo. While this has not stopped many intrepid first ladies from counseling their husbands, and even passionately lobbying for controversial political causes, it was often at the cost of considerable derision.[62]

Eleanor Roosevelt and Rosalynn Carter are relatively modern examples of first ladies who crossed the line. Franklin Roosevelt was often compelled to issue denials that his bright and politically active wife influenced his thinking.[63] But that didn't keep Eleanor from being widely vilified and portrayed in editorial cartoons as a masculinized dominator of her husband. The fate of Rosalynn Carter is perhaps a more striking example because of the profound effect criticisms of her political assertiveness had on the public image of her husband, President Jimmy Carter. One commentator made much of the fact that she attended many policy advisory meetings with her husband, and concluded that "Carter did not project the image of being a 'real man'" because he "considered the advice of his wife ... when making important decisions." The same author went on to speculate that President Carter was enfeebled by such "despair" that he was forced to "ask women for help."[64] Using similar reasoning, a *Wall Street Journal* writer lamented that while "Jimmy Carter first presented himself to the nation as a masculine personality ... he lost no time revealing his true feminine spirit." The author concludes, "So, in a sense, we've already had a 'woman' president: Jimmy Carter."[65]

But no presidential spouse had ever been viewed as transgressing the norms of first lady comportment more than Hillary Rodham Clinton. Nevertheless, even though she eventually became the object of feverish hatred and paranoid fantasy, she enjoyed considerable public approval in the initial post-election year. In fact, assessments of her were far more positive than those of her husband. Ms. Clinton earned a 62 percent approval rating, compared with the 48 percent who liked the job the president was doing.[66] Even former president Richard Nixon changed his tune to sing her praises, albeit with a touch of intimidation: "I certainly wouldn't take on Hillary, because she is a very intelligent, very strong, very effective First Lady ... She can be a help to her husband, the President, and I think the American people will like that."[67] Surprisingly, given the angry white male backlash to come, at this time there was no gender gap in the first lady's approval ratings.[68] Within two years that would change markedly. By April 1994 there was a 22 percent gender gap among Republicans in support for Ms. Clinton, with men, of course, having the greatest antipathy toward her.[69] There was even a gap among Democrats, albeit much smaller, with men more than women disapproving of the first lady by a margin of 6 percent.[70] By January of 1996 she was less popular than ever, 51 percent of those polled saying they had a negative view of Ms. Clinton.[71] The gender gap overall (not differentiated by party) was 16 percent.[72] Three years later she would experience a surge in her popularity, largely as a result of two factors: a vigorous program of refeminization and the Monica Lewinsky scandal—an event that enabled her to assume the more "feminine" role of wounded woman standing by her man. Both of these developments will be discussed more fully at the end of this chapter, but it may be of interest to note here the perspective of the wife of another male head of state, with regard to Ms. Clinton's struggles for acceptance.

When the First Lady of Poland, Jolanta Kwasniewska, first met Hillary Clinton in Cracow in 1996, the American guest got some unsolicited womanly advice from her hostess: "I told her that from my point of view, I should always be three steps behind my husband." In 1999, Ms. Kwasniewska reflected with some satisfaction on the impact of that counsel: "I think in the next term of President Clinton, Hillary was even more steps behind her husband than I. And that is one of the reasons that she has such good press and high popularity now."

Back in the mid-1990s, however, the question of Hillary's political ambition and influence was the central issue driving the gender gap in her popularity. As early as 1992 this issue was raised in the media. Pollsters were preoccupied with, and thus helped to create, the public perception of Ms. Clinton's putative hunger for power in the White House. They even conducted surveys in which Americans were asked about her qualifications to be president. *Time* magazine began an article, "You might think Hillary Clinton was running for President."[73] In March of 1994 a survey revealed that 53 percent of Americans thought the first lady had too much influence.[74] One month later this increased to 62 percent.[75] By 1996 the anti-Hillary crusade reached across the Atlantic Ocean. British Labor candidate Tony Blair had to reassure voters that his wife would know her proper (nonpolitical) place should he be elected.[76] Bob Dole, in his 1966 presidential campaign, took a leaf from Mr. Blair's notebook. In a speech before a California audience he was careful to let his constituency know just what role his wife Elizabeth would have in any future Dole administration: "When I'm elected she will not be in charge of health. Don't worry about it. Or in charge of anything else."[77]

Hillary as Gender Outlaw:
From Uppity Wife to Phallic Woman

A post-1992-election public opinion analysis showed that Republican efforts to use Hillary Clinton against candidate Bill Clinton failed.[78] She was in fact a net asset to her husband. Nevertheless, the Cro-Magnon boys club at *The American Spectator* magazine, among others, did succeed during the 1992 campaign in sowing the seeds (a seminal metaphor seems appropriate here) for the anti-Hillary hatred and fear that would later take root in the mainstream of American media and culture, far from the loony right fringes represented by that publication. The lead article in the August 1992 issue, "The Lady Macbeth of Little Rock," by Daniel Wattenberg, was a rabid tirade against Ms. Clinton, likening her to every threatening female his anxious imagination could conjure— Eva Peron, Anita Hill (whom his own magazine had been instrumental in slandering, according to recovering Republican David Brock[79]), Thelma and Louise, Winnie Mandela, and of course Lady Macbeth.[80] He recounts the history of her "vicious left wing polemics and activism" at Yale that included "leading campus protests against everything from the Vietnam War to the absence of a Tampax dispenser in the woman's law school john."[81] (The conjunction of these two issues in Wattenberg's mind recalls, and perhaps reflects, a commonly seen demonstration placard of that era: "War is Menstrual Envy.") More interesting than his catalogue of her ideological crimes is Wattenberg's list of her gender sins, her felonies against phallocracy: "consuming ambition, inflexibility of purpose, domination of a pliable husband ... , lack of tender human feelings ... , contempt for traditional female roles." Moreover, the president "is powerless to check his wife's growing influence."[82]

Above all, Wattenberg seems to regard the greatest transgression against the destiny of her anatomy to be Ms. Clinton's insistence on a distinct identity. "There is a pattern of details about their relationship that suggests it is not as fully fused as an old-fashioned marriage," he sniffs.[83] It is noted that the Clintons are members of different churches, give to different charities, and manage their financial assets separately.

They not only take some of their vacations separately, but one of Hillary's favorite destinations is that Sodom of political and gender perversity, San Francisco.[84] Believing that he has uncovered a major scandal, Wattenberg reveals that her 1991 tax return used her maiden name, Rodham. He concludes this jeremiad against female independence by derisively presenting a quote by a family friend of the Clinton's, actress Mary Steenburgen, as if he had come upon eyewitness testimony to the first couple's unapologetic depravity: "Steenburgen puts it this way," Wattenberg exults, "'They're two whole people. One hasn't given away huge parts of themselves to the other.'"[85] No doubt he would prefer to see a return to the English common law, adopted by the early American colonists, that declared a woman, upon marriage, to be a legal nonperson—disallowed from owning or selling property, making wills, negotiating contracts, or suing or being sued, and whose obedience to men could be ensured by beatings if necessary.[86]

Obviously, Wattenberg was not alone in his defense of archaic notions of marital rectitude. The antifeminist backlash that later crystallized around the persona of Hillary Clinton had become pervasive enough among the self-anointed political kingmakers of the media, especially in talk radio, that the Clintons themselves felt compelled to play down the egalitarian nature of their relationship. A friend from their days in law school revealed, "She and the President have a private arrangement that is based on power sharing—she is his equal, and he acknowledges it. But they realized that the American people weren't ready for that, and so they are trying to do it without telling people. And that is what is creating this sense that they are hiding something."[87] The Clintons' understandable, if cowardly, attempts to dissimulate the truth of their relationship turned out to be largely in vain. Not only did Ms. Clinton's attackers remain undaunted, but their propaganda crusade against the first lady achieved such a frenzied momentum that a 1994 survey of over one hundred talk radio programs found that Hillary Rodham Clinton was more vilified than Saddam Hussein.[88] She was even burned in effigy by tobacco farmers.[89] At about the same time, the Affinity Marketing Group of Fairfax, Virginia, was promoting its nearly

30,000-name "Hillary Haters List." It must have been viewed as an effective direct-mail solicitation tool by two of its bigger purchasers, the Republican National Committee and the American Life League.[90]

In spite of her many efforts to retraditionalize her image as a woman
(which will be examined more fully later), nearly all the rhetorical assaults against Ms. Clinton directly or indirectly concerned her failure
to be a properly subordinate female. Republican strategist Roger Ailes
declared, "Hillary Clinton in an apron was like Michael Dukakis in a
tank."[91] With apron and tank as the symbolic poles of a gender continuum, Ailes implies here that Ms. Clinton is as fraudulently female as
Dukakis was fraudulently male, that they were both gender imposters.
Accusations and images concerning the first lady's counterfeit femininity, which will be detailed later in this chapter, ranged from relatively
subtle editorializing about her unwifely power, ambition, and assertiveness to depictions of her chomping on cigars and swaggering about
in androgynous power suits or men's clothes, and retouched photos of
her having a literal penis. All of these representations are versions of a
(predominantly) male fantasy that psychoanalytic scholars refer to as
the "phallic woman." Too often this archetype is confused with that of
the castrating woman. Since both of them can be found in the iconic
vocabulary of anti-Hillary demonology, clarifying the distinction may
allow a more nuanced understanding about the nature of the conflicts
anxious males are unconsciously enacting in the political arena. At this
point, it might be useful to review and deepen the discussion begun in
the Introduction on the notion of the phallus.

Interpreters of popular culture, whether in academic or commercial publications, will often talk about an image or object as being a
"phallic symbol." While this may frequently be a persuasive decoding
of aspects of a cultural representation, such as might be found in a film,
photograph, or novel, certain nagging questions may come to mind.
What have we understood when we designate something a phallic symbol? What does a phallus symbolize? These are really two ways of asking the same question. The second one may be more startling because
it is often assumed that a penis is simply a penis, that once you have de-

termined that something represents a penis you've reached the bedrock of meaning, and there is nothing further to be understood. But there are problems with this assumption. Listening to everyday speech can reveal some of the *many* things that, at this cultural moment, penises might mean: "My boss is a real prick" (aggression and hostility), "We've been fucked over" (the capacity to exploit, betray, and destroy), "He stuck it to them" (the power to dominate, humiliate, and punish), "Your ass is mine" (the prerogative to satisfy vengeance through real or symbolic rape), and "Fuck you" (defiant rage).[92] Since these sound like rather negative meanings, it may seem strange that they would circulate in a society where political and economic power is held by penis owners. But the zero-sum nature of power in most patriarchal societies means, in the minds of many people, that it is better to be a "fucker" than "fucked over," better to be the one capable of intrusive control and sadistic aggression than to be "on the receiving end" (to use an appropriately anal metaphor). Yet, there are some unambiguously positive meanings associated with having phallic status that rely on more testicular metaphors, such as "that takes a lot of balls" (courage) and "the author is a seminal thinker" (productive and creative).

So, when cartoonists, reporters, or political commentators have sought to convey what they see as Hillary Rodham Clinton's excessive ambition, cruelty, aggression, fearlessness, hunger for power and control, autonomy unseemly for a proper wife, and inappropriate financial independence, they will portray her in *phallic* terms, since that is the culture-wide symbolic shorthand for these "masculine" qualities. (Needless to say, every one of these attributions would be regarded as flattery, were they directed at a man.) For example, when *Spy* magazine wanted an image to accompany its "follow-the-money" article on Ms. Clinton's "power brokering" and "dubious investments" that "performed extremely well,"[93] they created a front cover illustration (p. 140) that could condense all those meanings. It featured a skillfully retouched photograph of the first lady displaying a radiant, smiling face, which had been grafted onto the body of a younger woman. She is wearing a sexy black sheer dress, which is billowing provocatively in

Hillary as *literally* phallic

the wind, in a manner that is obviously intended to recall the famous image of Marilyn Monroe standing over the heating grate. Unlike the 1950s bombshell, this woman is carrying a different payload. Bulging beneath her exposed male jockey shorts are the unmistakable outlines of a penis. The headline is "Hillary's Big Secret," subtitled "Where that shady $100,000 came from and what it bought."

Spy both establishes and exploits a symbolic equation in the mind of the reader between penis and cash. In other words, with images as well as text they reinforce and depend on the link already in the cultural unconscious between phallic power and purchasing power. (The pornography industry has a similar way of representing liquidity. Their term for the penile ejaculation scene that used to be required in nearly all heterosexual adult films is "the money shot."[94]) Ms. Clinton's display of other qualities the culture views as masculine, such as political assertiveness and personal independence, prompted these writers, like others, to lift up the hem of her financial records, find out what she's got, and reveal the fiscal/phallic truth that had until then been hidden from public view—but which they knew all along had to be there.

Slick Times, a conservative magazine of political satire that had been devoted exclusively to demolishing the Clintons, was in wide circulation during the 1990s, and drew on similar associations in the cultural unconscious. The caption on top of one cartoon read "Inside the newly remodeled White House Master Bathroom." Below are two men's urinals, one labeled "Bill," and the other labeled "Hillary."[95] In another, Hillary's phallic status is established a bit more symbolically by having her refuse to comply with her husband's request for the television remote control, telling him to "put a sock in it, chump."[96] In a different issue, the "Share a Joke" page, which features reader contributions, continues the theme with even less subtlety:

Q: What do Hillary Clinton and J. Edgar Hoover have in common? A: They're both female impersonators.

Q: Why did the Rodhams name their child Hillary? A: There was a mistake on the birth certificate. It should have read H.I. Larry Rodham. (They always regretted not having a girl.)

Q: Why do the Clintons have only one child? A: Because Hillary had a vasectomy.[97]

In an anthology from *Slick Times,* there are others that are equally witty:

Q: Why doesn't Hillary Clinton wear mini-skirts? A: So her balls don't show.

While Clinton was in the middle of a very heated discussion with the Joint Chiefs of Staff, Hillary walked in and sat right down. The Joint Chiefs stopped their conversation, and just glared at her. Hillary smiled, and in that "tone" of hers asked, "What's the matter boys, do I threaten your masculinity?" To which the Joint Chiefs responded, "No, do we threaten yours?"

Q: What happened when Bill got a shot of testosterone? A: He turned into Hillary.[98]

This is a small but representative sampling of numerous cartoons, jokes, and articles in this (unofficial) Republican magazine that symbolize Hillary's putative power and influence in explicitly phallic terms. Many of them were recycled on talk radio programs. Throughout the mid-1990s, representations of her disturbing political competence continued to permeate even the editorial cartoons of mainstream publications. There she was most often in male drag, or at least significantly defeminized by, for example, having her breasts removed.[99] The artists who designed the June 1994 cover of *The American Spectator* seemed to be channeling their witch-hunter progenitors, Sprenger and Kramer. The headline is "Air Clinton: David Brock on the Travelgate Cover-Up." It features the image of Hillary Clinton dressed as a witch. Her giant head faces the reader with a mannish countenance and an expression of triumphant evil. Between her legs is a passenger jet, which she is riding broom-like above the clouds, and stroking with both hands in a masturbatory manner.[100]

What may strike the reader about all these depictions of the first lady's penis is that they not only express worry about and contempt for her phallic potency, but also evince, notably in some of the jokes and sexy poses in the altered photos, a certain pleasure. It is as if these and other men are unconsciously torn between the fear that a woman might have a penis, and the wish that she did. This brings to mind the classical Freudian reading of the phallic woman, an archetype that shows up in the dreams of patients as much as it does in the various domains of popular culture.[101] According to this view, a woman with a penis is a re-assuring image that counters the infantile unconscious male fantasy that females lack a penis because they have been castrated. In the boy's imagination, the thought is: "If she lost hers, then I could lose mine." As adults, men will sometimes unconsciously "add" a penis symboli-cally by requiring their female lovers to wear certain fetish items, like stiletto heels, leather corsets, and garter belts, or they may become erot-ically overinvested in certain body parts, such as feet. For many of these men, sexual arousal is impossible without the fetish object, perhaps be-cause its absence elicits castration anxiety. Interestingly, a number of re-touched fetish photos of Hillary Clinton found wide circulation in the 1990s. In one that appeared on the cover of *Spy* magazine in 1993, Hillary's head is grafted onto the body of a sexy dominatrix attired in a studded black leather bikini, and holding a long black riding crop across her thigh. The headline reads: "What Hillary Problem? Power Playing in the Clinton White House." This rendering of the first lady's phallic qualities was a bit more subtle than the *Spy* cover described earlier that gave her an actual penis. But both embody the ambivalence I have sug-gested—each of the images depicts her as sexy and appealing, in spite of the critical content of the articles.

Another fetish picture made its appearance across the country in 1995 as a postcard put out by The American Postcard Company. This one featured the heads of Hillary and Bill Clinton placed on the buff, black-leather-clad bodies of, respectively, a female dominatrix and a compliant male "slave." Hillary is holding a metal leash that is latched to a leather collar around Bill's neck, and is leading him in the direction she wants to go, while he wears an expression that conveys both sexual arousal and willing submission. On the one hand, although done play-fully, the scene contains the familiar criticism of a controlling first lady and a weak, submissive president. On the other hand, the image por-trays a certain pleasure—it not only represents a fetishized version of a phallic Hillary, but reveals the erotic excitement felt by a man under the power of a phallic woman.

There are other ways to think about the conflictual pleasure some men might take in the notion of a phallic woman. One of the obvious implications of possessing a penis is that it suggests the possibility of penetration. Even though being subject to penetration is regarded as a feminizing and thus a dreaded experience by femiphobic men, that dread, as explained in chapter 1, is quite possibly the transformed residue of an infantile pleasure that was once taken in being penetrated by the mother's erect nipple, her warm and life-giving milk, and (psychologically) her attunement to and modulation of the child's internal states. Whether we understand these phallic interpretations of Hillary Clinton as a bulwark against castration anxiety, as a conflictual expression of a disavowed fantasy of being psychically and erotically permeable to an all-powerful, omniscient, and nurturing mother, or as some combination of factors, we are still left trying to make sense of a mind-boggling phenomenon—that scores of right-wing femiphobic men across the country and dozens of publications had spent years in the 1990s using jokes, editorial cartoons, and magazine covers to put an actual or symbolic penis on the first lady, and evidently took great pleasure in the process. Whatever our explanation, these men seem to have been doing far more than warding off a terror. By all appearances, they were also expressing a powerful sexual fantasy.

Regardless of the complex motivations for the various attacks on Hillary Clinton's perceived gender deviations, they took a toll not just on her own popularity but on that of her husband's administration as well. Her response was to launch a series of refeminization programs.

From Lady Macbeth to Betty Crocker: Hillary Clinton's Extreme Makeover

Rush Limbaugh, the designated angry white male hit man for the Republican war on the Clintons, has always been free from some of the constraints that tempered the maliciousness of his right-wing office-holding colleagues who, in spite of their slash and burn politics, still had to be soft-focus baby kissers and unctuous glad-handers for campaign commercials. Limbaugh has not had to worry about reelection, only about keeping his ratings up. So, when it came to the sexual politics be-hind the attack on the first lady, he could afford to be quite direct and pander to the primitive femiphobia of his mostly male listeners. Lim-baugh told the following joke on his radio program in 1993: He gets into an elevator in which Hillary Clinton is the only other passenger. In an impulsive fit of lust, she rips off all her clothes, throws herself on the floor, and pleads, "Rush, make a woman out of me." His response is to tear off all his clothes, throw them at her, and say, "Fold those."[102] Ob-viously, what Limbaugh is telling us is that what really makes a woman is not sexual aggression—no, that kind of erotic agency would be much too phallic for his anxious sensibilities. The true sign of femininity, he is saying here, is *submission*. And this is precisely the deficit in Ms. Clin-ton's image that has marked her like a scarlet letter since her early days as a political wife in Arkansas. The terrible irony of Limbaugh's humil-iating joke is that Hillary Clinton herself eventually came to accept its premise, or at least struggled to make it look as if she did.

"My first responsibility, I think," the first lady explained to an in-terviewer in 1995, "is to do whatever my husband would want me to do that he thinks would be helpful to him. It may be something of great moment, but more likely it's just to kick back, have a conversation or even play a game of cards and just listen to him ruminate. I mean, what-ever it takes to kind of be there for him, I think is the most important thing I have to do."[103] While this Stepford-Wife manifesto may seem like a radical departure from the highly competent legal scholar/policy wonk identity of her early career, the truth is that ever since Bill Clinton was governor of Arkansas, Hillary Clinton had always been plagued by a conflict between being her ambitious, intelligent, self-authorizing self, and enacting the deferential wife role demanded by political expediency. This has led to the cyclic nature of her efforts at refeminization. Her first gesture of compromise followed her husband's defeat for the guberna-torial reelection, after having served only one term. Widely seen as an "uppity woman" by the voters of Arkansas, Hillary decided to finally take her husband's last name and remove her glasses.[104] The latter gesture was presumably intended to make her look less intellectual and more fem.

There were, however, periodic, irrepressible eruptions of feminist authenticity. In a 1992 televised damage-control interview following public allegations of her husband's infidelity, she told a national audience that she was "not sitting here, some little woman standing by my man like Tammy Wynette."[105] Several months later, in another gaff that belied her wifely docility, Ms. Clinton reminded the public that her role was not to simply "stay home and bake cookies and make tea."[106] Both of these remarks produced the predictable outrage from Republican defenders of Neanderthal family values, anger that was kept alive for years on right-wing talk radio.

The combination of the first lady's independence, her all-too-prominent brain, and the relentless crusade against her, produced, as we have seen, a tidal wave of negative male public opinion toward her, and threatened to wash away the reelection hopes of President Clinton. It was makeover time again. Advisors were brought in to make Hillary "softer" and more conventionally "feminine." This move was a centerpiece of the effort to strengthen Bill Clinton's candidacy, which the consultants themselves referred to as "The Manhattan Project."[107] This time around, however, the nuclear energy being utilized was that of the nuclear *family*. It didn't take long before she did, in fact, stay home and bake cookies, and even distributed her recipe, competing (in a ladylike manner, of course) with the one published by Barbara Bush. Next came a tour of the White House's Blue Room after it was extensively remodeled. The caption accompanying an Associated Press photograph of this event seemed to grasp, if only unconsciously, the symbolism of the occasion, namely that it was celebration of parallel makeovers: "Hillary Rodham Clinton, wearing a royal blue suit with seven gold buttons, admired a new rug in the refurbished Blue Room at the White House during a tour for the press yesterday. Her suit was a shade or two brighter than the sapphire hue of the satin draperies and silk upholstery."[108] Ironically, the first lady had succeeded so well at her program to retraditionalize herself that during an official visit to famously patriarchal India, a reporter for *The Calcutta Telegraph* criticized her for being "solely decorative."[109]

The *New York Times*, in their coverage of Ms. Clinton's role in the 1996 campaign, observed that "For every pointed political appeal she made, she offered half a dozen expressions of her concerns as a mother for America's future"—an apparent bid to out-fem childless Elizabeth Dole.[110] In addition, the paper noted the conspicuous absence of "my plans" in her speeches, and the frequent repetition of the phrase "my husband."[111] Also in evidence was an exclusive focus on noncontroversial "maternal" social issues, such as the value of education and the perils of drug abuse. And, consistent with her new role as first-lady-who-finally-knows-her-place, Ms. Clinton's speech before the Democratic National Convention in Chicago was scheduled for "family night."[112]

Around the same period, Hillary got sympathy from an unlikely quarter, right-wing hatchet man David Brock. In a book on the first lady, *The Seduction of Hillary Rodham*, published eight years before his aforementioned political repentance, he engaged in his own oddly chivalrous effort to refeminize her.[113] He saw her as good, but her goodness was predicated on having been the helpless victim of "the greatest seducer who ever lived"—her husband. This fate, according to Brock, was even worse than the tragic and unwitting ideological deflowering she suffered at the hands of the various liberal Lotharios of her innocent youth—commie cads like labor organizer Saul Alinsky and leftist lawyer Robert Treuhaft. Such a sympathetic, if condescending, assessment of Hillary Clinton might seem shocking, having come from a former writer for *The American Spectator*, and the man famous for referring to Anita Hill as "a little bit nutty and a little bit slutty."[114] It seems unlikely that Brock had undergone any kind of feminist conversion at that point, if he ever has. But there is a consistency in his radically disparate views of these two women. Both portraits are positioned on the same continuum—female sexual agency—but at opposite ends. There is really nothing surprising here. For many centuries conservative males have managed their anxieties about the fantasized dangers of female sexual and political power by splitting women into nutty sluts and seduced but virtuous victims. The greatest mystery is what motivated him to write the book in the first place. Perhaps this was the moment of his first, inchoate pang of conscience. Or, maybe he identified with her, and projected his own sense of being seduced by the conservative Casanovas in his midst. Brock's recent confessional was, after all, titled *Blinded by the Right*. While we may never know his true motives, his book on Hillary did ironically presage the event that would be more successful at refeminizing her and increasing her popularity than any deliberate makeovers had been up to that point—the Monica Lewinsky scandal. Not only was the first lady publicly humiliated and rendered a sympathetic victim, but she stood by her man. Ms. Clinton's popularity went up markedly,[115] paving the way for her successful run for the New York Senate seat, leaving an incredulous Maureen Dowd to ask: How is it possible that, politically "she grows stronger only when she seems weaker?"[116]

In spite of Hillary Clinton's renewed popularity, she has not lost her honored place in the GOP pantheon of political demons. As Al Mitchler, a Republican wizard of direct-mail propaganda, crowed after Ms. Clinton's Senate victory, "Without a doubt, she is going to be the best fundraiser the Republican Party has had in a generation. We're going to have six years of hyperbole over her and people are making it up right now. I'm making it up right now. By God, this is a gift."[117] In a letter mailed out by the New York Republican Party to the well-heeled faithful, potential donors were reminded that Ms. Clinton is "abrasive and annoying, brash and bitter, calculating and scheming, distant and deceitful, polarizing and power-hungry."[118] Needless to say, these descriptors, which could have been lifted from Sprenger and Kramer's *Malleus Maleficarum*, have rarely if ever been applied to a *male* politician. Another fund-raising solicitation asked the rhetorical question, "How dangerous is she?"[119] Indeed, that is the question always on the minds of femiphobes, from the bedroom to the halls of government.

While Hillary Clinton was clearly a beneficiary of the Lewinsky scandal and the associated impeachment hearings, she was not the only one. By virtue of his status as incorrigible ladies' man, it seemed as if the phallus was finally taking up residence with its rightful owner, President

Bill Clinton, and this led to a surprising increase in his popularity. As we will see in the next chapter, in spite of all the legal costs, the intrusive investigations by Grand Inquisitor Kenneth Starr, the televised shaming, his groveling public apologies, and sinner-looking-for-redemption lip biting, the scandal would turn out to be just the remasculinizing tonic the president needed.

5

Permutations of the Presidential Phallus
Representations of Bill Clinton, from Emasculated Househusband to Envied Stud Muffin

The phallus, that coveted signifier of masculine invulnerability and self-sufficiency, is a fantasy, not an organ. Yet, the symbolic subtext of nearly every debate between and concerning male (and even some female) politicians is about who is the true possessor of this imagined trait. Most political campaigns and advocacy groups, therefore, are at some level devoted to ensuring that their candidate is the chosen object of this projection, and that their opponent is deprived of it. In 1994, the right-wing anti-Clinton satirical magazine *Slick Times* printed this joke: "Q: What does [*sic*] a pair of panty hose and Clinton's suit coat have in common? A: They both contain a pussy."[1] Only four years later, in his August 6, 1998, broadcast, ultraconservative AM radio talk jock Michael Savage said of former President Bill Clinton, "I think about this walking erection of a president and I get furious!" By means of what political alchemy was Clinton transmuted from pussy to walking erection in only four years? That is the question this chapter aims to answer.

Savage's statement seems to be revealing his envy as much as his contempt. And, what I suspect he found even more galling than the president's moral turpitude was the fact that Mr. Clinton's job approval rating actually went *up* at the height of the Lewinsky scandal.[2] In other words, what Savage seemed to detest the most was that in the popular imagination, the president's penis became the phallus. Of course the phallus, unlike the penis, is only psychically attached, and temporarily

Al Gore was seen as unfit to receive the presidential phallus

at that. Depending on the capricious fluctuations of public opinion, the phallus is subject to sudden and embarrassing departures. This chapter will trace the wanderings of Bill Clinton's peripatetic phallus, especially as it moved from him to his wife, and at the moment of his putative disgrace, back to him. Unfortunately for Clinton's failed heir apparent, Al Gore, the phallus bypassed the vice president altogether. Maureen Dowd, noting Gore's strained efforts to render himself appealing to women, said, "The guy practically lactates."[3] Even the vice president himself said he was, "the woman behind the man," when describing the supportive role he had played in relationship to Clinton.[4] During the last presidential campaign, comedian Bill Maher, in his monologue on ABC's *Politically Incorrect,* was ruthlessly succinct in his description of Mr. Gore's image problem: "Essentially, he's Clinton without the dick."

In many respects, Bill Clinton's actual achievements, positive or negative, are far less interesting than the role he played in the shared conscious and unconscious fantasies of the American public. The elaborate conspiracy theories and histrionic denunciations by assorted right-wing Clinton haters are particularly notable. One of the most striking aspects of these crackpot conjurings is how irrational they were from the perspective of conservative political self-interest. Bill Clinton was more effective at implementing Republican policy goals than the Republicans themselves. It was due to *his* efforts that GATT, NAFTA, Welfare "reform," and the defeat of the movement for single-payer health insurance (by offering up his and Hillary's own labyrinthine and doomed-from-the-start managed-care-lite plan) were realized— not those of Newt Gingrich, Trent Lott, or Dick Armey. Two of Clinton's proudest achievements, ending welfare as he knew it and balancing the budget, were, by the time he left office, the only promises in the Republican Contract with America to be fulfilled. He even presented bouquets of accommodation to right-wing culture warriors, by, for example, signing the anti-gay Defense of Marriage Act and forcing the resignation of Surgeon General Joycelyn Elders when she suggested that information about masturbation should be part of any sex education curriculum. In spite of this kind of public record, President Clinton felt compelled to point out that he wasn't "a closet liberal."[5] "If you peel away Nixon's paranoia, basically I'd say they're not so far apart," claimed political scientist Walter Dean Burnham in 1996 about Mr. Clinton.[6] Of course, this assessment was not shared by ultraconservative North Carolina Republican senator Jesse Helms, who warned, "Mr. Clinton had better watch out if he comes down here. He had better have a bodyguard."[7]

Regardless of how diligently Clinton, the New Democrat corporate cheerleader, attempted to hew to the right edge of the middle of the road, or how carefully he pitched his focus-group-derived positions, right-wing fundamentalist Grand Inquisitors and free-market crusaders were not dissuaded from designating him, respectively, the Antichrist and a crypto-Marxist class warrior. The specific hysterical accusations, frequently aired on right-wing talk radio, were as amusing as they were astonishing—murder, fraud, treason, drug running, and multiple inchoate conspiracies on a global scale involving UN troops, black helicopters, and computer-chip tracking devices implanted in the buttocks of governmental critics. But more notable in some ways have been the symbolic means employed by Bill Clinton's political enemies to convey their hatred.

She's Got It; He Doesn't:
Bill Clinton, the Estrogen Years

An examination of the linguistic and visual imagery through which Clinton has been portrayed shows that after the 1992 election, the president's critics relied largely on feminine attributions to attack him. In most instances, this was in relation to his more phallically construed wife, Hillary. As described in the previous chapter, he was variously represented as infantilized, dominated, and castrated by her. The cover of the *Big Clinton Joke Book* (shown on p. 154, and published by the same people who put out *Slick Times*) featured a cross-dressed reversal of the painting *American Gothic*, with Bill in farm-wife drag and Hillary wearing the overalls in the family and holding a large pitchfork.[8] In case the joke was too subtle for its readers, the writers were kind enough to repeat it numerous times: "Q: What does Hillary do after she shaves her pussy in the morning? A: She puts a suit on him and sends him to work."[9] A mock replica of the president's daily schedule repeats one item on an hourly basis: "check with Hillary."[10]

Bill Clinton is pictured at a podium at "The National Battered Men's Conference," his eye blackened from a recent encounter with the first lady. He says to the audience, "I'm pleased and honored to be here today, and I know Hillary would be, too, but she couldn't come. Heh heh."[11] While the latter image appeared as a cartoon, it was part of an entire genre of rumors, urban myths, and unsubstantiated news items that had the shared theme of Hillary physically abusing her defenseless husband, usually involving Ms. Clinton hurling various objects— briefing books, lamps, and furniture—at him.[12]

These narratives and images of a feminized Bill Clinton were not confined to the pages of conservative publications, like those cited here.

When Hillary possessed the phallus

They could also be found in much of mainstream popular culture. The premiere of Dana Carvey's short-lived comedy show featured a portrayal of an empathic and nurturing "estrogen-enhanced" President Clinton offering up his lactating nipples.[13] In an April 1, 1993, National Public Radio broadcast, The Capital Steps, a pallid, risk-averse, middle-of-the-road group of political satirists, sang a little ditty that located the presidential phallus for the larger culture: "When Bill's cabinet starts behaving like a bunch of jocks, tell those macho laughingstocks I'll neuter 'em just like Socks [their cat]. To find out where the power went, you should never be hesitant. You could ask the President, or you could just ask her husband."

The fantasy of Hillary Clinton's feminizing influence on Bill Clinton even spilled over onto the president's Republican White House aide, David Gergen. When Rush Limbaugh referred to him as "David Rodham Gergen," the implication seemed to be that he, like the president, had become a mere instrument of the first lady's power.[14] Other men positioned around Mr. Clinton were said to be similarly imperiled. David Brock, the now-repentant right-wing hatchet man discussed in the last chapter, alleged that Hillary Clinton, when the first couple lived in the Arkansas governor's mansion, had ordered state troopers to "fetch feminine napkins."[15]

In 1993, a White House proposal set the stage for a new genre of Clinton representations. In July of that year, a Pentagon-commissioned study implemented by the Rand Corporation concluded that a ban on open homosexuals serving in the military was neither necessary nor advisable.[16] They recommended an end to discrimination based on sexual orientation. This study was not released, however, until more than a month after President Clinton announced his own incoherent but controversial "don't ask, don't tell" approach to ending institutionalized antihomosexual bigotry in the military.[17] Though far less bold than the Pentagon's own recommendations, the president's plan catalyzed a firestorm of homophobic hysteria. War hero and Iran Contra fixer Oliver North, who had in his military career faced the Viet Cong as well as a nuclear-armed Soviet Union, found the move to permit homosexuals in the armed forces to be "one of the most dangerous things to happen in my lifetime."[18] Virginia Republican senator Warren E. Barry referred to the president's proposal as the "fags in the foxhole" plan, and said that it lent a new meaning to the old battlefield cry "watch your rear flank."[19] To dramatize this supposed peril, Senators John Warner and Sam Nunn toured Navy ships and staged photographs that appeared on the front pages of newspapers from New York to San Francisco. These images featured sailors looking worried and vulnerable while lying prone, rear flanks exposed, on their narrow submarine bunks.[20] In response to the plethora of comments issued by various anxious male pundits about the dangers that would lurk in military shower rooms should Mr. Clinton's plans ever be realized, openly gay midshipman Joseph Steffan noted dryly, "Heterosexual men have an annoying habit of overestimating their own attractiveness."[21] As might be expected, there was a 21 percent gender gap in opinion polls concerning any plan to end the gay ban in the military, with the majority of men and a minority of women opposing it.[22]

A cultural climate emerged from this controversy that became a kind of hothouse for homophobic anxieties. The aforementioned Michael Savage went on a rant about "gay and lesbian Nazis" who were "trying to steal our freedom."[23] There were numerous highly publicized gay bashings and murders, all committed by men in the military.[24] And within three years after "don't ask, don't tell" was adopted, the number of service members discharged for homosexuality actually increased dramatically.[25] Partially as a result of these developments, along with the pervasive depiction of Hillary as the phallic partner in the first marriage, a wide range of homoerotically tinged representations of Bill Clinton showed up in editorial cartoons, satirical publications, and the metaphors of newspaper writers. Most of these portrayed him as a masochistic bottom, but a few pictured him as a menacing phallic penetrator. In these images his phallic status hinged not so much on his imagined sexuality but, as among the ancient Greeks, on his role as top or bottom.

Some depictions lacked any subtlety, such as the cover of *Slick Times* on which, courtesy of altered photos, Bill Clinton and Ross Perot were shown naked and snuggling in bed together.[26] On February 1, 1995, one discussion question that got listeners to right-wing talk station KSFO-AM in San Francisco especially excited was "Is President Clinton controlled by a coven of Communist lesbian members of the Trilateral commission?"[27] A more symbolized but unmistakable representation of Clinton as a political bottom was found in an editorial cartoon that had multiple iterations (drawn by different artists) and showed up in numerous publications. On the surface, it referred to the Republican rout of the 1994 midterm Congressional elections. The GOP is represented by an elephant with massive phallic tusks, which in every version of the cartoon are seen penetrating the president from behind.[28]

What followed shortly thereafter was a series of editorial cartoon images and articles prompted by Clinton's efforts to seek a bipartisan collegiality with and endear himself to the newly victorious House Speaker, Newt Gingrich. In most of these, Clinton is portrayed as the masochistic bottom. For example, Jeffrey Klein, editor of *Mother Jones* magazine, in an article that was actually quite sympathetic to President Clinton, saw this new courtship coming to a dire end, largely because "Gingrich is hell-bent on domination." Klein goes on to compare the likely outcome of this budding relationship with the outcome of the Speaker's first marriage, and notes that Gingrich "campaigned for Congress on the issue of family values, while cheating on his wife. After the election, he ditched her, then appeared at her hospital bedside after she had a cancer operation to present his terms for divorce." Then Klein draws the predicted parallels more sharply: "Gingrich's likely terms to Clinton: Gingrich keeps the House and gets the White House as well; Clinton leaves town humiliated. . . ." The imagined scenario is based, we are told, on who is currently sticking it to whom in this relationship: "Gingrich's favorite chess move is the fork, a simultaneous attack on two of the opponent's pieces. *He has forked the Clinton administration* by forcing the President to choose between the Democrat's traditional pro-underdog stances and the surging conservative, anti-government populism [emphasis added]." Klein goes on to argue that Clinton is being set up to lose either way—by moving rightward and alienating his base, or by not responding to the growing angry white male hatred of government. I would not necessarily take issue with Klein's argument, nor would I disagree with his assessment of Gingrich as a Machiavellian player in politics as well as personal life. But the issue here is not the manifest content of the article. Rather, what is being illustrated is how hard it is, in spite of one's conscious politics, not to be embedded in the unconscious register of political discourse. In this example, that embeddedness seems to have been a powerful determinant of the author's choice of metaphors. Thus, we have a supporter of Clinton painting him as an abandoned, humiliated wife who is being "forked" by a powerful man "hell-bent on domination."[29]

One month after Klein's article appeared, another liberal, Jules Feiffer, published a cartoon that repeated the same theme. Titled "Newt

the Brute," it features a Gingrich who here is hell-bent for leather. Attired in a sort of medieval s/m outfit—featuring a mask, studded leather
accessories, boots with spurs, a spiked belt, and, in his hand, a cat-o'-
nine-tails—he faces Bill Clinton, who is naked and chained to a dun-
geon wall. With a sadistic grin, Gingrich taunts his prisoner, saying,
"I'm going to assault you, degrade you, humiliate you, make you whine,
whimper, and follow my command." Clinton, with an expression of
eager anticipation, replies, "And then will you like me?"[30]

In the same time period, 1994 to 1995, the president's missing phallus was represented in other ways. In one series of cartoons, he is
feminized by being rendered pregnant. Several of them show Clinton
struggling to bring a Surgeon General nomination to term.[31] In another,
more telling example, he is shown impregnated by Hillary, in this case
by her healthcare reform plan.[32]

A cartoon in the *San Francisco Examiner* locates the phallus in the
first lady, and thus reiterates the theme of the latter image. It shows Ms.
Clinton glad-handing male members of Congress, while in her other
hand she holds a briefcase labeled "Health Care." The congressman
shaking her hand says to her, "Thanks, Hillary, and give our best to the
little man."[33] In spite of all these feminine attributions, Bill Clinton was
already formulating a strategy for recapturing the phallus—not only
from Hillary but from the Republicans as well.

The Phallus Returns

After the 1994 midterm election, a disaster for Democrats, it was clear
that the Republican "Revolution," led by Newt Gingrich, had acquired
a taste for liberal blood and would (as Jeffrey Klein predicted) continue
its long march to the White House, if not stopped. Bill Clinton seemed
to read this as an indication that his best chances lay with coopting the
right's agenda, rather than challenging it, especially as he approached
his 1996 reelection bid. To do this he had to shore up his support among
men, which in part required remasculinizing his image. This involved
a range of approaches. There were the major rightward shifts in policy

discussed earlier, in which Clinton sought to steal the punitive patriar-chal thunder from the Republicans, and which were favored by more men than women. In a master stoke of political theater, the president ignored much-publicized advice from aides to leave San Francisco off his list of California speaking engagements, and decided to face the crowds of enraged gay and lesbian protesters who were angry about his opposition to gay marriage, and who he was told were waiting to con-front him. When he did show up, he gave a speech that focused on his support for gay civil rights (other than marriage). This enabled him to have it both ways. He could appear to be standing up to "militant" ho-mosexuals, and thus please conservative and homophobic voters, while at the same time making it clear to his liberal/centrist constituents that, compared to Dole, he was without a doubt the lesser evil on such social issues.[34]

There were also fatuous photo opportunities. One example of the latter was a widely printed picture that was apparently designed to erase the memory of Clinton pushing through a ban on assault rifles, an act Michael Savage described as "the de-balling of America."[35] The photo depicted President Bubba, shotgun and dead ducks in tow, and fully ac-cessorized in camouflage, strutting down a muddy Arkansas road at the end of a manly hunt[36] (an image that prefigured the nearly identical per-formance a decade later by John Kerry, as described in the Preface). Then there was the other equally fatuous pseudo-event in which Clin-ton threatened to punch conservative columnist William Safire in the nose for calling his wife a "congenital liar" after she denied any wrong-doing in the various Republican-manufactured scandals.[37] However silly, by threatening violence against another man who insulted his wife, Clinton was seizing a vital opportunity. This was his chance to show that he was *not* Michael Dukakis—the unphallic Democrat who fa-mously balked at expressing a desire for manly vengeance in response to a hypothetical threat against his wife, and thereby ended his politi-cal career.

Although the Democrats had the women's vote locked up, the Clin-ton campaign took no chances. Demonstrating their commitment to equal-opportunity pandering, they mailed out gender-coded voter guides, both of which were received at my home. The flyer sent to me was labeled *The Law and Order Guide,* and claimed, "President Clinton hasn't just *talked* tough on crime. He's *fought* the gun lobby and made our neighborhood safer." (The italicized "fought" was presumably intended to reframe gun control as a form of macho tough-on-crime pugilism.) My wife, on the other hand, received a flyer entitled *The Pro-Choice Guide,* and was exhorted to "protect YOUR RIGHT to make YOUR most personal choice" by voting for the president, as well as other Democrats. The point here is not that fault should be found with Clinton's stand on these issues—it remains a bizarre fact of contemporary civic life that keeping guns out of the hands of felons, terrorists, or paranoid schizophrenics, and allowing women to make their own reproductive choices continue to be controversial concerns. Rather, these gendered voter guides illustrate how conscious the Clinton campaign was of the fine line it had to walk between remasculinizing its candidate and holding on to its female supporters.

To a certain extent Clinton's manly makeover program was working. Just before the 1996 election, a *Saturday Night Live* skit featured a conversation between Bob Dole and former president George Bush (played by Dana Carvey). Bush says to Dole, referring to Bill Clinton, "Come Tuesday, he's gonna make you his woman, and you'll enjoy it. I did." Nevertheless, in spite of some shifting perceptions, and Clinton's efforts to present his candidacy as the testosterone ticket, the male side of the gender gap still favored opponent Bob Dole. Although he emerged as the victor in the 1996 election, none of Mr. Clinton's efforts to recapture the phallus yielded any enduring success. Of course, Mr. Dole's grip on the monolith of manhood would also turn out to be unsustainable, especially after he assumed his fallback position as Viagra spokesmodel.

Once a young female intern named Monica Lewinsky appeared on the political stage, a deus ex machina for Clinton masculinity, the entire country became fixated on the president's anatomy and its fantasized derivatives. Ironically, it took the worst scandal of his political career to restore his phallic credentials. Widely castigated by some for having illicit sex, yet widely admired and even envied by others for doing so, President Clinton was, on balance, significantly more popular as a result of what was largely seen as a virile transgression. According to a 1998 Gallup poll conducted after news of the scandal broke, Clinton was viewed as the most admired man by the greatest plurality of respondents—far ahead of Pope John Paul II and Michael Jordan, who were respectively, a distant second and third on the list.[38] Moreover, the president was admired significantly more *after* than before the world knew of the Lewinsky affair. As described in the last chapter, even Hillary benefited from the seemingly terrible events her husband's philandering set in motion. As a victim who nevertheless stood by her man, the same Gallup survey found, not only was the first lady the woman most admired by Americans, but her rating was twice that of the previous year. As Bill Maher might have said, she was now the Clinton without the dick.

Given this unexpectedly positive fallout, the Monica Lewinsky affair could be described as the most successful disgrace a politician had ever suffered. Many pundits referred to the affair as "zippergate," an appellation that in one word condenses both the political near disaster and the phallic restoration that Ken Starr's investigation facilitated for Bill Clinton. A guest on MSNBC effectively captured the post-Monica *Zeitgeist* when he joked that the new Viagra slogan should be "take the pill and be like Bill."[39] Another journalist described the president as "sporting an EverReady erection like an ancient fertility statue."[40] Specialized Bicycle, in a poster used to market a new seat designed to take pressure off the perineum, and thus "help alleviate impotency," put the head of Bill Clinton on the lean, aerobicized body of a cyclist. In the poster, which was distributed to bicycle shops nationally, the president is facing the viewer and giving a firm thumbs up sign, indicating that with this new seat he will remain a stand-up guy.[41] Other advertisers seized the opportunity to link their product with the newly acquired phallic aura of the Clinton presidency. A Tommy Hilfiger ad featured a lubricious twenty-something woman, barefoot and poured into black leather pants, coiled like a voluptuous serpent on the president's desk, and beckoning the viewer. Far from seeing this transparent allusion to the Lewinsky scandal as somehow disrespecting the authority of the president, Donny Deutsch, an advertising executive and former Clinton campaign aide said, "The Hilfiger ad glamorizes the scandal, brings it to true fantasy as opposed to the tawdry reality. A beautiful woman in the most powerful universe in the world—it's right out of a romance novel. A young maiden in a castle—it adds to the Clinton potency."[42]

Even those who disapproved of the president's conduct ended up affirming the phallic status it afforded him. Michael Savage bemoaned Clinton's "satyriasis" and "priapism."[43] George Will castigated the impulsive Chief Executive for "behaving like his incorrigibly glandular self."[44] As mentioned in the Introduction, conservative columnist A. M. Rosenthal expressed outrage that Americans did not "gag" at the fact that the media focused more on "oral sex" than it did on "Iraqi biological weapons." He was especially disgusted that "most Americans seem to be relishing it all, drawing vast entertainment from a Presidency involved as much in matters of genitalia as of state," and "that journalists can write about the President's penis, and most voters accept with calm, even admiration, the possibility that he employs it in the Oval Office with female members of his staff."[45] Mr. Rosenthal must have been particularly perturbed by Ed Bradley of 60 Minutes, who seemed to be aiming for more than the usual infotainment prurience when he asked Clinton sexual harassment accuser Kathleen Willy if the president was "aroused" when he allegedly placed her hand on his crotch. "Inquiring minds want to know" was no longer a motto limited to The National Enquirer, but apparently had been adopted by CBS.[46] It was as if the priggish, inquisitorial voyeurism of Ken Starr gave mainstream journalists like Bradley license to go for the salacious details—rationalized, as with Starr, in terms of public service.

Bill Clinton's new phallic image even became an international phenomenon. In China, a book titled Clinton: A President of Strong Drives became a hot seller.[47] Sergei Markov, a political analyst for a Russian television program, observed, "People here watch and think, well, there may be something wrong with it but on the other hand, he is a real muzhik [real man]. They think this is the guy we need to rule the country."[48]

Meanwhile, back in the U.S., mainstream as well as right-wing publications that only a few years earlier had been making jokes about Clinton *being* castrated were now printing cartoons that conveyed a sense that he *needed* to be castrated. In *Newsweek,* for example, a cartoon depicted the president and the first dog, Buddy, sitting side by side in a veterinary clinic. Hillary says to the nurse, "We're here to have him neutered." To which the nurse replies, "Which one?"[49] Several weeks later, a cartoon by a different artist, from a different part of the country—but with the identical theme—was also printed by *Newsweek.* In this one, Clinton is holding Buddy by the leash, and listening attentively to a veterinary surgeon who says, "And which one of you is here for the operation?"[50] In a *Slick Times* feature that adopted the style of television stand up shtick, the fictitious host, "Jay Letterman," said, "The Oklahoma Senate passed a bill that would make the state the first to allow judges to order the surgical castration of sex offenders. President Clinton called it a landmark decision and announced that from now on, all fundraising in Oklahoma would be handled by Al Gore."[51] This was just one among a number of similar jokes in the same issue. This magazine's shifting representation of Clinton from pathetic pussy whipped househusband to phallic predator was manifested in other ways. A few years earlier *Slick Times* had published the image described above of a cross-dressed first couple in a take-off of *American Gothic* (which they called *American Pathetic*). By 1998 they were marketing a poster (p. 164) featuring a Photoshopped image of Clinton as an inebriated libertine surrounded by champagne-swilling bimbos in party hats.[52]

It was not only men who took note of Clinton's ascendant phallus. In a droll column published in July of 1998, Maureen Dowd details some of the fulsome female adulation evoked by the scandal-plagued but lusty Chief Executive. Celebrity culture maven Tina Brown wrote about the president in a manner reminiscent of the steamy musings of a Harlequin novel: "His glamour is undersung ... a man in a dinner jacket

The phallus returns to Bill Clinton

with more heat than any star in the room (or, for that matter, at the mul-
tiplex) ... his height, his sleekness, his newly cropped, iron-filled hair,
and the intensity of his blue eyes.... He is vividly in the present tense
and dares you to join him there."[53] In a similar vein, and even more over
the top in her breathless praise of the president's new phallic stature,
Mirabella writer Nina Burleigh described her own stirrings while playing a game of hearts with Clinton on an Air Force One jaunt to Jasper,
Arkansas:

> The President's foot lightly, and presumably accidentally,
> brushed mine once under the table. His hand touched my wrist
> while he was dealing the cards. When I got up and shook his hand
> at the end of the game, his eyes wandered over my bike-wrecked,
> naked legs. And slowly it dawned on me as I walked away: He found
> me attractive.... There was a time when the hormones of indignant
> feminism raged in my veins. An open gaze like that, at least from a

man of lesser stature would have annoyed me. But that evening . . . I felt incandescent. It was riveting to know that the President had appreciated my legs, scarred as they were. If he had asked me to continue the game of hearts back in his room at the Jasper Holiday Inn, I would have been happy to go there and see what happened.

Comparing Clinton to Zeus in William Butler Yeats's "Leda and the Swan," Burleigh's prose becomes even more engorged: "Yeats honored the magnetic sexual pull a powerful male can have on a weaker female. The beating wings of the giant swan enwrap the helplessly infatuated woman, whose 'terrified vague fingers' cannot 'push the feathered glory from her loosening thighs.' "[54] After recounting a number of similarly wanton acclamations authored by various women, Dowd wryly concludes, "We should stop blaming Ally McBeal for killing feminism. We should even stop blaming Bill Clinton. It was clearly a mass suicide."[55]

What got easily lost by both revilers and idealizers of the president's new phallic eminence was the ironic contrast between fantasy and the actual sex between Lewinsky and Clinton. Thanks to the widely publicized testimony of many figures in the case, and especially Lewinsky's autobiography and many television appearances, we know that their erotic encounters were for the most part little more than very adolescent episodes of foreplay. Largely due to *his* inhibitions, their rendezvous were fleeting, guilty, and measured. In her testimony, Lewinsky described Clinton's vigilant though doomed attempts at self-regulation, as if they had ensconced themselves in the church basement after Sunday school. The former intern quotes the president as saying, "I'm trying to not do this and I'm trying to be good." She goes on to note, "It seemed a little strange to me. . . . There was sort of foreplay to the foreplay."[56] As we all know, much to her dismay, he only let himself orgasm once. The resulting dress stain became, as feminist critic Jane Gallop put it, a sort of scarlet letter.[57] This was much more the case for Clinton than Lewinsky because it signified not just an illicit liaison but an unpresidential loss of control. In a way, he was really only phallic in his *refusal* to orgasm—in maintaining his self-possession, in keeping his interior (and thus the scandal) from leaking out. Indeed, ejaculation is the moment when the bodily phallus becomes merely a penis—a soft, leaking opening to the outside, and thus no longer the rigid, sealed-off citadel of power. This brings to mind the work of classics scholar John Winkler, who, in his study of ancient Greek masculinity, described the equation, broadly held at the time, between managing one's desires and managing the state. A failure of the former was regarded as a poor prognosis for the latter.[58] This may shed some light on the concern, frequently expressed on call-in talk shows at the time, over reports of the president being fellated while speaking on the phone with some government official about the situation in Bosnia. The crucial question concerned Clinton's ability to manage his desire while managing the state. What callers seemed to be wondering was: What was in play at that moment—the impulse-driven, secreting, and out-of-control penis, or the masterful, self-contained phallus whose owner could discuss state secrets?

What also got lost in the scandal discourse was much discussion of Monica Lewinsky's desire, *her* sexual agency. In spite of the clear power imbalance, she was aggressive and, however naively, she went after what she wanted. Most discussions of their oral sex were fixated on an image of her on bended knee, in a supposed posture of submission. Very few journalists or nonacademic critics gave much consideration to her oral pleasure. That would have been taboo because it would have positioned the penis as an *object*, not just an agent of desire. The possibility that oral sex could be an expression of sexual mutuality might threaten the phallic status of the erect penis. It was in part this eliding of Lewinsky's oral erotic agency, her active rather than merely passive role, that sustained the phallic aura around Clinton.

One question that might arise in considering President Clinton's transformation from "pussy" to "walking erection" is whether he has retained possession of the phallus, especially in the era of George W. Bush, whose regime, as we will see in chapters 7 and 8, has become perhaps the most phallic in U.S. history. There are few clues that might lead to an answer to that question. In February of 2001, Marshal Wittman, a former member of the Christian Coalition and current associate of the right-wing Hudson Institute, made a statement that ended up on the front page of the *Washington Post*'s "Style" section: "The heart will be the favorite organ of the Bush administration. That's to distinguish it from the favorite organ of the Clinton administration."[59] Christopher Hitchens, in his commentary on Wittman's pronouncement, noted "the comparison between these two throbbing items ... and the strong subliminal connection between them."[60] Wittman is clearly affirming a lingering view of Clinton as phallic. It is less clear what to make of his link between the two pulsating organs. While this is evidently not its intended meaning, we could read it as foreshadowing the fact that the "heart" of Bush's "compassionate conservatism" would actually be manifested as a kind of phallic heartlessness, but without any of the messy genital acting out of the Clinton era.

6

Voting Like a Man
The Psychodynamics of the
Gender Gap in Political Attitudes

Republican Class War and Blue-Collar Manhood

White privilege isn't what it used to be—especially if you're a working-class male. Median annual wages for blue-collar men went down by 11.5 percent between 1979 and 1995, according to the Labor Department.[1] Since then, as a result of global trade agreements and the consequent export of manufacturing plants, industrial jobs have been steadily hemorrhaging from the United States. From the time Bush assumed the presidency in 2000, the nation has lost nearly five million jobs—the bulk of which have been in manufacturing.[2] Seventy-five percent of the positions that *are* available as of this writing are low-wage service sector jobs.[3]

The president's tax cuts not only provide the greatest relief to the wealthy, but working-class families are going to suffer consequences from which the economic elite are immune, such as declining revenues for public schools. The Bush administration has put forth a proposal to overhaul the guidelines that determine mandated overtime pay for American workers, which if enacted would deprive up to eight million wage earners of that benefit.[4] The elective war in Iraq is maiming and killing mostly young male (and some female) blue-collar bodies. Republican agricultural policies privilege large corporate agribusiness over the interests of smaller family farms, leading to a record level of bankruptcies for the latter.[5]

As the ex-lobbyists for industrial polluters and food industry giants, who now head federal regulatory agencies, undo the regulations that once constrained their former employers, the quality of air and water, and the safety of the food supply, have steadily declined. This is a development that disproportionately affects working-class families, who are less able to move to cleaner environments (where the cost of housing can be prohibitive), or afford water filters or organic foods.

According to a *New York Times* series on workplace injuries, 100 workers a year die as a consequence of intentional wrongdoing on the part of employers, such as removing safety devices or denying protective equipment to employees. Reporters also found that the Occupational Safety and Health Administration (OSHA) has declined to prosecute 93 percent of cases in which their own investigations found that employers had engaged in practices they knew would lead to worker injury or death. The *Times* also revealed that in a number of cases, OSHA employees were actually penalized for going ahead with prosecutions.[6]

This decline in the economic and physical well-being of blue-collar workers has been largely, though not exclusively, the result of explicit Republican governing philosophy and practice. Since none of these facts is garnered from classified sources, one would expect that the majority of white working-class men, acting in their own obvious material self-interest, would be firmly opposed to GOP candidates. The reality of current public opinion, however, sits in stark contrast to such an expectation. A survey conducted in December of 2003 by the Pew Research Center for the People and the Press found that non-college-educated white men preferred George W. Bush to a Democrat in the 2004 election by 60 percent to 25 percent.[7] An ABC/*Washington Post* poll revealed that white men in general were inclined to vote for Bush over an unnamed Democrat by 62 percent to 29 percent, an astonishing 30 percent margin, while white women preferred a Democrat by a small margin.[8] The Pew survey found that men without college degrees actually supported Bush more than did men who had graduated from college.[9] Of course, these numbers could change in either direction as we approach November of 2004. But the question will remain: How could a majority or even a plurality of working-class men ever have endorsed a politician who has played such a central role in their loss of well-being and security?

The gender gap in political attitudes and voting behavior began after Ronald Reagan, the founding father of the Republican Revolution, ascended to power in 1980—precisely the period that marked the most precipitous decline in the economic status of working-class men. This makes the political history of the last two and a half decades seem even more startlingly counterintuitive: as men's wages went down, their conservatism went up. The more the Republican agents of the economic elite made the life of white male workers difficult, the more these men flocked to the GOP. Those inclined to interpret this paradox as simply an expression of political naiveté and ignorance, secondary to the center-right bias of the corporate media, might be discomfited to know the results of a study conducted by the Roper Center for Public Opinion Research on the Bush tax cut. Among the poorest blue-collar men (with incomes of thirty thousand dollars or less) who *agreed* with the statement that "this tax plan benefits mainly the rich," 53 percent nevertheless favored it.[10] In contrast, only 35 percent of those in the seventy-five thousand dollar income bracket favored the tax cut, in spite of believing that the wealthy were the main beneficiaries.[11] How can we make sense of what looks like an astonishing display of economic irrationality, if not masochism?

The sociologist Arlie Hochschild, in an insightful article that addresses precisely this issue, argues that what the Republicans in general and the Bush administration in particular have so skillfully finessed is the methodical engineering of displaced rage. She notes that the anger of working-class men has been effectively "directed downward— at 'welfare cheats,' women, gays, blacks, and immigrants," outward "at alien enemies," and definitely away from "job exporters and rich tax dodgers."[12] Hochschild also describes the Republicans' facile exploitation of the fear and vulnerability generated not only by economic insecurity but by the uncertainties and pervasive sense of threat that characterizes the post-9/11 world. As she describes the situation, "George

W. Bush is deregulating American global capitalism with one hand while regulating the feelings it produces with the other. Or, to put it another way, he is doing nothing to change the causes of fear, and everything to channel the feeling and expression of it."[13]

Although I would not take issue with Hochschild's trenchant formulation, there is one question that could be addressed more fully: Why men? Why are males particularly susceptible to this manipulation? While men in general tend to vote Republican, I started this chapter looking at the conservatism of *working-class* men precisely because it seemed the most counterintuitive. In other words, it defies the conventional wisdom that economic self-interest is the primary driving force in shaping political allegiances. It does seem that the right-wing tendencies of blue-collar men militate against a simple economic motive for the gender gap, and highlight the role of *masculinity* in the political disparities between men and women.

That said, class and gender can be slippery categories, and at times exchangeable with one another. For example, to be a subordinate, to have others "on top," is often construed by members of a patriarchal culture as assuming a feminine position. So, even though notions of blue-collar manhood are saturated with fantasies of primitive muscularity, this is in tension with the "feminizing" experience of being at the bottom in an economic hierarchy, or at the lowest rung in a workplace command structure. In addition, regardless of the significant presence of women in the labor market, masculinity is often defined in terms of a man's capacity to be a provider—a position that is far more likely to be precarious for working-class men, given their lower wages and their vulnerability to underemployment and job loss. (While the focus here is on some of the ways that class positions get *gendered*, it should be noted that gender can also be a *class* position, the major manifestation being patriarchy itself—the distribution of power, resources, and privilege based on maleness.)

There is another way that class can morph into gender. The reader may recall from chapters 2 and 3 the tradition in American politics of equating certain expressions of luxury and upper-class comfort with effeminacy. While this was a problem for the Republicans during the reign of George Herbert Walker Bush, the faux-populism of the Bush II regime and their allies seems to have convinced many men that it is the *left* that drips with the effete accoutrements of feminizing wealth. Conservative talk shows are filled with denunciations of "latte liberals" and the "Volvo-driving, *New-York-Times*-reading liberal elite." This rhetoric, combined with the regular-guy persona of George W. Bush—his inarticulateness and anti-intellectual presentation—has successfully disguised the president's own patrician roots. One of Bush's more shrewd performances, widely denounced at the time, was his joke during a speech at Yale, his alma mater, that his success proves you can get a C–average and still become president. But, as important as these considerations of class may be, it should not be forgotten that the gender gap involves men of all economic strata, making the role of masculinity the most important factor in understanding the growing political chasm that now divides men and women.

In Bed with the Opposition

Within days after the 2000 election, newspapers across the United States printed color-coded maps in red and blue to denote, respectively, the states that went Republican and those that voted Democratic. This visual aid also highlighted the stark political divisions in the country, especially the radically disparate values that constitute the psychological borders between America's various geographical regions. If reporters had wanted to give a more detailed picture of the fault lines that separate citizens from one another, they could have created a different color-coded portrait of the nation, one divided between *pink* and blue. For the first time since the election of Ronald Reagan in 1980, women and men, as distinct groups, elected different candidates—most women voted for Gore, while the vast majority of men selected Bush.[14] Of course, this sort of division would not have lent itself well to a national map because the political fissures would in many cases would have run right down the center of middle-class bedrooms. This is even truer now than it was then. In a recent survey conducted by Democratic pollster Celinda Lake, married voters were asked if their partners had chosen the same candidates that they did. Half the women said "no," in contrast to only a quarter of the men. Lake's understanding of the discrepancy is that the women were reluctant to disabuse their husbands of their fantasy of political agreement. "We call it the 'Sure, honey' factor," Lake explains.[15] It appears that the more educated a woman is, the more likely she is to disagree with her husband politically, and thus favor Democratic candidates. According to a *USA Today*/CNN/Gallup poll conducted between January and November of 2003, the gender gap among those with a high-school diploma or less was 10 percent. For college graduates it jumped to twenty percentage points, while the gap became a gulf for voters who had taken postgraduate courses, leaping to 28 percent.[16]

There is another kind of marriage gap that should not be lost in this focus on the gulf between husbands and wives—the gap between married and single women. In the campaign leading up to the last election, married women favored Bush over Gore by fourteen percentage points, and married mothers voted Republican by a margin of thirty-three points.[17] By the time of the election, exit polls showed that Gore had managed to reduce the marriage gap to only one percentage point.[18] This seems at least partially attributable to his efforts to foreground his warm family life, his happy and still passionate marriage (as the famous convention kiss was intended to demonstrate), and most importantly his marital fidelity (by strenuously presenting himself as the un-Clinton). While the phenomenon of conservatism among women will be explored briefly in the next chapter, there are a number of explanations that can be offered at this point for the gap, however variable, between married and single female voters—a gap that promises to be a major factor in the upcoming election. Married women, in contrast to those who are single, are likely to be more religiously and culturally conservative, more financially secure and thus less in need of government-based social services, and, if they became mothers early in life, less likely to obtain a higher education, which, as we have seen, is an important variable in determining political affiliation.[19]

"Why Can't a Liberal Be More Like a Man?"

That's how columnist Christopher Matthews framed the puzzle of the gender gap.[20] Republican senator Trent Lott offered up a kind of neuroastrology to answer the question: "Republicans and Democrats think with different sides of their brains, just like men and women.... We think with our left brain.... I like to think we are the party of Mars."[21] One thing is clear: the gender gap has been driven by men's growing conservatism, not by women's liberalism.[22] This was noted as far back as 1996 by Everett C. Ladd of the Roper Center, who said, "In truth, women are not really more Democratic than they were fifteen years ago. It's that men have become more Republican."[23] Since women's support is more equally divided among the two parties, the net benefit goes to Republicans. Since men are the ones who have changed, it is the *male* side of the political divide that most urgently calls for an explanation. In other words, if we can understand the dynamics behind male conservatism, we will be in a much better position to make sense of the dramatic lurch to the right that has marked the last two and a half decades—because to a certain extent, they are the same phenomenon.

Just prior to the 2000 election, the *Los Angeles Times* interviewed a young man who summarized his impression of the two main candidates: "Bush is a guy's guy. He's from Texas, so he's more of a he-man, leatherneck type.... Gore, he's sensitive. He's supposed to be for the environment. He's always talking about kids and families."[24] While not offering the most nuanced analysis, this man effectively illustrates two key components of political thinking that inform the gender gap for men: an assessment of the masculinity of a candidate, and a perception, however unconscious, that certain issues or political stances are gendered. In this example, the two are linked—the supposedly unmanly candidate is naturally taken up with "feminine" issues like the environment and concern for children. In some ways these two components are hard to disentangle. A male politician with a hypermasculine image, who (temporarily) possesses the phallus, can sometimes masculinize an issue that might otherwise have a feminine cast, at least enough to have his view prevail. Lyndon Johnson, a manly hawk on the Vietnam War, had enough phallic "street cred" when it came to battling Southern racists and supporting the issue of racial equality, a cause which even today is of much greater concern to women than men.[25] The 2000 election primary campaigns within both parties showed how a solid masculine image can trump the gender of specific policy stands when it comes to winning over men. Former basketball star Bill Bradley, a Democrat, and veteran and former POW John McCain, a Republican, were both more liberal than their respective front-running opponents, Al Gore and George W. Bush. Yet, among men, each ran ten or more points ahead of their main rivals.[26] Unfortunately for Bradley and McCain, their advantage with male voters was ultimately insufficient to compensate for their larger disadvantage among women.

On the other hand, a male leader who seems to have lost the phallus can imbue a feminine quality to an issue typically gendered male. Bill Clinton, during the "estrogen years" described in chapter 5, transformed military intervention into what right wing femiphobes widely viewed as a global expansion of the nanny state. As I will describe more fully shortly, some of these combat operations even garnered more support from women than they did from men. Much of the book up to this point has focused on the mercurial phallic status of male *politicians*, on their anxious obsession with presenting a macho persona to their equally anxious male constituents. Now attention will shift to understanding how certain *issues*—those on which there is a significant gender gap—have acquired their masculine or feminine aura.

Each of the two major parties has been acutely aware of this gender gap, and both have sought to shape their rhetoric in such a way that they could make forays into the gendered turf of the other party, without simultaneously alienating their base—which, as we have seen, is women for the Democrats, and men for the Republicans. For example, many center-right Democrats, such as Bill Clinton and former California governor Gray Davis, tried to minimize the flight of men to the GOP by proclaiming their unqualified enthusiasm for certain erstwhile conservative positions. For Clinton this meant being a champion of Welfare "reform" and a deregulated global capitalism in the form of NAFTA. Davis, for his part, became an enthusiastic booster of the prison-industrial complex and capital punishment.

Republicans, on the other hand, have relied more on rhetorical camouflage and less on actual policy accommodations, in their efforts to make themselves more palatable to women. In 1997, GOP pollster Frank Luntz fired off a memo to Congressional Republicans titled "Language of the 21st Century." He told his comrades, "[We need not] change our substance or create a separate women's agenda" because "listening to women and adapting a new language and a more friendly style will itself be rewarded."[27] Elsewhere in the memo, he waxes more brazenly Machiavellian and instructs his fellow Republicans, "Women consistently respond to the phrase 'for the children' regardless of the context."[28] Linguist Deborah Tannen did an exacting content analysis of a number of George W. Bush's speeches, orations which we can safely assume were constructed with great care by his speechwriters and by advisors like Luntz. Tannen found that talks on everything from education to tax cuts and farm policy were filled with "women-friendly words" repeated many times. She notes that in one speech "children" showed up thirty-five times, and that there was "a dizzying array of other emotion-laden words: seven 'loves,' nine 'hopes,' three 'dreams,' and three 'hearts.' "[29] Tannen noticed this pattern in all the speeches she analyzed. The most famous of Bush's woman-friendly phrases from the last campaign was, of course, "compassionate conservatism," which, under the current reign of swaggering paleo-Republicans, is even more oxymoronic than it might otherwise be. As it turns out, this slogan was actually coined many years earlier by right-wing über-talk-jock Michael Savage, whose own typical rhetoric sounds about as compassionate as the burst of machine gun fire and the boom of exploding ordinance that constitute the "musical" opening to his program.

It remains to be seen whether these efforts by the Democrats and Republicans will have much effect on their respective gender gaps in the long run. Meanwhile, there remain profound differences between men and women on a wide range of issues. My own research, which was described in the Introduction, found that men are more likely than women to take the typical conservative position on military intervention (with some interesting exceptions to be discussed later), environmental protection, the caretaking functions of the state (such as Welfare), and homosexuality. Other studies have shown men to be more pro-capitalist, less egalitarian, more racist, and more punitive than women.[30] Interestingly, in spite of all these differences, men and women have tended not to disagree as much on so-called "women's issues," such as abortion rights and the Equal Rights Amendment.[31]

Canadian sociologist Michael Adams, who has done a landmark study of social values, found that men and women differ significantly on a dimension he refers to as "global consciousness."[32] This refers to the sense that one is first a citizen of the world and only secondarily a citizen of a particular nation. This means, in other words, that one feels an empathic connection to and identification with people from other countries and cultures. Women, perhaps not surprisingly, score much higher on this factor. Along similar lines, other researchers have found that, by a stunning margin of 30 percent, women are more interested than men in studying anthropology.[33] It seems reasonable to surmise that this difference in "global consciousness" would likely translate into a range of political issues that would differentiate women from men. This might include support for international agreements (such as those related to human rights, the environment, and arms trafficking), an interest in multilateralist as opposed to unilateralist approaches to problems of global security, an investment in improving the standard of living and well-being of all the world's citizens, and an unwillingness to sacrifice civilians of other nations in order to achieve a strategic military goal. Obviously, these are attitudes that are anathema to the current militantly virile Republican administration. While there are currently no studies (to my knowledge) that could confirm such a speculation, it seems quite possible that Bush's stance on these global issues may have much to do with women's lower level of support for him, as contrasted with men's considerable enthusiasm for the president. One area where the male/female difference in "global consciousness" seems to contribute to the gender gap is in attitudes toward war.

When War Making Gets Gendered

The notion that men are more likely than women to be military hawks may seem like such self-evident common sense that an analysis of the gender gap on war might appear to be a tedious belaboring of the obvious. The most familiar conventional wisdom on the reason for male pugnacity, whether expressed with fists or laser-guided missiles, derives from the simplistic formulations of pop biochemistry. The culprit, in this view, is the "male" hormone. Since testosterone is to aggression and dominance as gasoline is to flame, the argument goes, why look for a more complex explanation? There are a number of problems with this sort of biological reductionism. First, the "gender" of testosterone is more ambiguous than is generally appreciated. Men and women each have estrogen as well as testosterone circulating throughout their bodies—affecting multiple organ systems, not just sex organs—and, under certain conditions, one hormone can be converted into the other.[34]

Second, the relationship between testosterone and social behavior, such as aggression and dominance, is anything but straightforward, and in many circumstances surprisingly counterintuitive. For example, researchers have been unable to find any significant or reliable effect of surgical or chemical castration on the aggressive behavior of male sex offenders.[35] In one study of sixteen incorrigibly violent men who were castrated to diminish their aggressive tendencies, nine later died as a direct consequence of violent conflicts with others.[36] In research that sought to explore the link between testosterone and scores on tests measuring hostility, no consistent correlation could be found.[37] Moreover, under conditions of stress, such as combat, testosterone levels actually plummet.[38] One study of American soldiers during the Vietnam

War found that men on the verge of entering a battle exhibited a marked decrease in this hormone.[39]

Dominance behavior, as well, does not reliably correlate with testosterone. What seems to be more important in this regard is the social and ecological context, a conclusion supported by studies of non-human primates, as well as those conducted on people. For example, male baboons that live in open plains—where food is scarce, predators are plentiful, and there are few places to hide—will determine troop movements, fight attackers, protect females, and, when dominant, have priority in choice of food or sexual partners. On the other hand, male baboons who reside in forest environments exhibit no dominance hierarchies, seem more "cowardly" than females, and follow the dictates of the females when it comes to where and when the troop will move.[40]

Sociologist Theodore Kemper has written one of the more comprehensive reviews of the human studies on the relationship between dominance behavior and testosterone, and developed a dialectical model to explain that relationship.[41] He refers to a "social-bio-social" chain of causality, by which he means that changes in testosterone levels are often preceded by certain social experiences. But once hormone levels are changed, they in turn affect the likelihood that particular behaviors will be expressed. Those behaviors will then lead to experiences that can further alter hormone levels, and so on. Other than stress, as mentioned earlier, the experiences that seem to initiate (and result from) shifts in testosterone have to do with achieving some socially valued position or status. For example, when men are victorious in a tennis match, their testosterone levels will rise,[42] which can act as a catalyst in increasing the likelihood of further victories, producing in turn higher levels of the hormone. This is what physiologists call a "positive feedback loop." We could substitute job promotion, election victory, or any other socially valued attainment, and Kemper believes that women are subject to the same process.[43] Of course, if events cascade in the other direction, then both status and hormone levels will tend to decline. Kemper argues that this dynamic can also occur *vicariously,* such as when a sports team, political candidate, or military force with which one identifies either van-

quishes an opponent and achieves a special eminence, or suffers a humiliating defeat.[44] So, if male support for military intervention cannot
be explained solely in terms of testosterone toxicity, how are we to make
sense of it? One answer does seem to lie in the nature of men's identifications in times of threatened or actual war.

In my own research on the gender gap, which I conducted using 294
subjects (140 males and 154 females) after the first Iraq war and before
the second one, men were much more likely to endorse statements that
linked military victory with one's own self-esteem. For example, significantly more men than women strongly agreed with the statements
"When I saw our powerful American forces on TV 'kick Iraqi butt' during the Persian Gulf War, I too felt powerful," and "Seeing our President
stand up to America's enemies, in some ways makes me feel like I stand
taller." This might help explain the results reported by another researcher who studied the gender gap in attitudes toward the Persian
Gulf War. She found that not only did far more men support the war,
but their support was only minimally affected by the changing goals of
the military operation. Conversely, women's favorable view of the war
changed considerably as the stated ends shifted.[45] Along similar lines,
one psychologist who studied the differences between male hawks and
doves found that hawks were more influenced by the *symbolic* value of
military power than by the actual military utility of any particular use
of force.[46] And consistent with my own research, the hawks in this study
were more concerned than the doves with not being feminine.[47]

While to my knowledge no similar research has been done on attitudes toward the current conflict in Iraq, men's support for that
military intervention has not waned as the Bush administration's
rationalizations for the war changed from finding weapons of mass destruction (WMDs), to hunting down the Al Qaeda members supposedly being harbored by Saddam Hussein, to building democracy in Iraq.
As of this writing, no WMDs have been found. But what *has* been found
is a document authored by Hussein after his fall from power and prior
to his capture that directs his followers not to trust any of the Islamic jihadis or foreign Arab fighters—a discovery consistent with the testi-

mony of Al Qaeda leaders in U.S. custody who said Osama bin Laden rejected any suggestion by subordinates of forming an alliance with Hussein.[48] As far as building democracy is concerned, the U.S. is currently trying to fend off demands by Iraqi Islamic leaders for direct elections. Yet, in spite of the collapse of all the main rationalizations for the military intervention, in the face of these very public developments, there has been no discernible decrease in men's support for the war or Bush. Of course, unforeseen developments could cause this support to change or even evaporate. Nevertheless, at this time, it seems likely that men's opinion regarding the conflict in Iraq is related to the vicarious boost in their own self-esteem resulting from a powerful identification with the American victors.

And, we should not overlook the obvious—defeating an enemy is, more than anything else, an expression of *domination*, which, as I have argued throughout this book, is the bottom-line criterion for masculinity in nearly all patriarchal cultures. The link between domination and manhood has also been confirmed by empirical studies. Several researchers have found that men exhibit a greater "social dominance orientation" than women, which leads them to hold a variety of anti-egalitarian positions. In particular, males, in contrast to females, are not only more likely to be pro-war but are also more comfortable with racial and class inequities.[49] It does seem likely that dominance, whether vicarious or direct, may be a primary motivation for men to support war, and at times may underlie more lofty and principled rationalizations. "Operation Kiss My Ass" does sound far less exalted than "Operation Iraqi Freedom" but would probably poll well, at least among men. Surprisingly, there are certain justifications for military action that would lead women to be significantly more hawkish than men.

When War Is for Wimps

"The U.S. military has become a slave service for the wealth distribution schemes of internationalists and gangs of weeping do-gooder mystics," said the anonymous author of an article that appeared in a right-wing dissident newspaper, *The Resister,* which was run by disgruntled Army Special Forces soldiers based in Fort Bragg, North Carolina, in 1995.[50] The writer went on to point out that "one need simply note the circling of media carrion eaters to predict in which third world toilet these altruists will flush hundreds of millions of U.S. dollars and the lives of U.S. servicemen. Peacekeeping is a monumental fraud."[51] The secret group that produced this publication was equally frank in announcing the political tendencies they sought to crush, which consisted of "statism, liberalism, tribalism, socialism, collectivism, internationalism, democracy, altruism . . . and the New World Order."[52] They were not alone in their opposition to using the American military for humanitarian purposes. Republican senator Phil Gramm insisted, "You can't run foreign policy like social work."[53] The political context for these concerns was the decision on the part of the Clinton administration to threaten the use of the military to reinstate the elected populist president of Haiti, Jean-Bertrand Aristide, who had been exiled in the U.S. after a military coup overthrew him and then subjected the country to a horror show of human rights abuses. Without addressing the merits of this threatened but later aborted intervention by American armed forces, it is instructive to look at the gender subtext of the discourse surrounding these events. Intervention was almost uniformly opposed by the right, primarily because of the human rights rationale. Republican senator Dan Coats decried Clinton's plans as "gunboat liberalism."[54] Fellow GOP senator John McCain got more to the point, denouncing the impending invasion as the "emasculation" of American armed forces.[55] These sentiments were reflected in the complex nature of the gender gap on this planned military intervention.

A Gallup survey conducted in September of 1994, unlike so many other polls, effectively captured some of the important nuances of the gender gap on the planned Haiti invasion. It also revealed the degree to which the framing of an issue can determine whether the use of military force will be construed as a masculine or feminine endeavor. Researchers went beyond asking subjects whether they approved of such

an intervention; they measured men's and women's responses to different *rationales* for sending U.S. troops. When the reason for invading was
based on an appeal to a relative abstraction ("to restore a democratic
government"), men favored it over women by a very substantial margin of 14 percent. When it was presented with a justification anchored
in the need to preserve America's esteem and respect among nations
("to maintain U.S. credibility in the world by carrying out Clinton's
pledge to remove the current military government"), men were persuaded over women by a 10 percent margin. If the rationale presented
for the use of force was to keep out immigrants ("to reduce the flow of
Haitian refugees to the U.S."), more men than women endorsed the plan
by a margin of 4 percent. When the motive for military intervention was
framed as an altruistic effort to help suffering Haitians ("to stop the
abuse of human rights by the current government"), women supported
it slightly more than men.[56]

At the risk of overstating its importance, we have in this one survey
more information about the variegated psychology of gender regarding
war than in a hundred other polls that give no consideration to their respondents' reasoning for holding the positions they do. In the *first* version of the question, where the motive is restoring democracy, we find
confirmation of the study cited in the Introduction that showed that
men are more likely than women to support war for reasons of abstract
principle. One explanation for this would derive from the work of psychologist Lawrence Kohlberg, who studied the development of moral
reasoning. Kohlberg's analysis would suggest that men's responsiveness
to abstract principle demonstrates an appreciation for the importance
of universal principles of justice—a sign of a highly developed moral
sensibility. One problem with that interpretation is that it would not
jive with men's relatively diminished responsiveness, in this survey, to
human rights protection as an acceptable reason to deploy the American military. Another consideration is that while abstract principle
might inspire one to take up arms, it can be emotionally content-free,
a kind of intellectual cover for the more primitive satisfaction and mas-

culinizing effect of subjugating another that was described earlier. And that leads us to what the responses to Gallup's second version of the survey question might tell us.

The greater male concern for "U.S. credibility," the *second* rationale for war, bespeaks a particular kind of identification with the American nation state not shared (to the same degree) by women, one that is personified as an individual warrior whose honor (read "phallic manhood") is on the line in any potential conflict. This interpretation is consistent with the findings of my own research on the nature of men's psychological investment in the outcome of a war. In other words, a military intervention in which one's country might assert manly dominance over another is an opportunity to achieve (or fail to achieve) a vicarious sense of personal worthiness and efficacy, which in phallic terms is experienced as potency.

Lyndon Johnson captured this sensibility well when, after bombing North Vietnam, he announced to a reporter, "I didn't just screw Ho Chi Minh. I cut his pecker off."[57] As we all know, this chest-thumping phallic hubris did not last, and was ultimately replaced by the "Vietnam Syndrome," a vicarious but enduring sense of shame and humiliation, suffered primarily by men, as a result of the eventual military defeat. But even before America lost the war, there was a sense of what was at stake, which was reflected in the way opponents of U.S. involvement were derided. While Richard Nixon was vigorously prosecuting the war and arguing that "pulling out" would risk national humiliation, a member of his own party, Senator Charles Goodell, took a stand against America's military presence in Vietnam. Vice President Spiro Agnew attacked Goodell by calling him "the Christine Jorgenson of the Republican Party."[58] Obviously, by comparing the GOP dissident to the world's first male-to-female transsexual, Agnew, following LBJ, was revealing his administration's phallic conception of the U.S. war in Southeast Asia—a view that many American men came to share.

The *third* rationale for invading Haiti, keeping refugees out of the U.S., which men more than women found compelling, is worth considering, even if the margin of difference was a moderate 4 percent. A number of other studies have found that males are far more concerned about immigration, especially of undocumented aliens, than women are. In one of these surveys, men by a margin of 13 percent favored deporting illegal aliens who have remained for many years.[59] In 1994 California voters approved a measure, Proposition 187, that required doctors and teachers to refuse services to undocumented immigrants, and then turn them in to the police. A Field Research exit poll found that, by a margin of 6 percent, men more than women voted for the initiative. But this gap masks an even greater gulf of 22 percent among men themselves, in contrast to a gap among women of 12 percent[60]—yet one more study that indicates the male nature of the overall shift to the right. These findings—combined with the greater propensity of men to be racist, ethnocentric, and fearful of being penetrated—suggest that men have a much deeper psychological investment in national boundaries than women do.

The *fourth* justification for invading Haiti, stopping human rights abuses, shows that there are circumstances under which women would be more eager to go to war than men. In this case, it seems driven by women's greater "global consciousness," to use Adams's term. Conversely, as we have seen, *this* motive for war making tends to be regarded by right-wing males as suspiciously feminine. The gendered debate over the invasion of Haiti was similar to the one that later characterized the argument over sending troops to the Balkans to stop the wholesale slaughter of civilians—war crimes that were perpetrated in large measure, though not exclusively, by the Serbs under the direction of Slobodan Milošević. While the left was split between interventionist and noninterventionist sentiments, the right was almost uniformly opposed. Conservative talk show host Spencer Hughes spoke for many of his compatriots when he averred, "Liberals are in favor of using the military for politically correct causes, like stopping ethnic cleansing, but not when it came to stopping communism in Viet Nam."[61] Here, condensed in one sentence, we have the two gendered rationales for war making, set against one another—human rights versus political abstraction. In one, the goal is stopping mass murder; in the other, the aim is to defeat a system. The attitude of the right has not modified appreciably since the 1990s. Even though the inability of the Bush administration to find weapons of mass destruction in Iraq has led them to abruptly shift their rationalization for the invasion, and become reborn crusaders for human rights, very little beyond the line of the day has changed. In January of 2003, Bush speechwriter David Frum, in an allusion to the past use of the military for humanitarian purposes, said, "Republicans returned to office in 2000 fed up with the random do-goodery of the Clinton years."[62] The questions of why and against whom we go to war—and by extension, the proper role of the military—are linked to another major issue on which we find a significant gender gap: the caretaking functions of the government.

Self-Made Men against the Welfare State: Denying Dependency and Punishing the Poor

"Wolves" and "alligators" were only some of the appellations Republican members of Congress gave to female recipients of Welfare during debates over funding for Aid to Families with Dependent Children (AFDC) in the 1990s. As an explanation for the grisly murder of a pregnant mother and her two children, and the abduction of the baby she was carrying, GOP House Speaker Newt Gingrich said the killings were "the final culmination of a drug-addicted underclass with no sense of humanity, no sense of the rules of life in which human beings respected each other," and went on to blame "the welfare state."[63] The fact that none of the parties involved was either a recipient of Welfare or addicted to drugs seems not to have influenced his rant against the undeserving poor. Some may recall that Gingrich's own Dickensian version of Welfare reform was to take children away from mothers and house them in state-run orphanages—a solution that fellow conservative Douglas J. Besharov, a scholar at the right-wing American Enterprise Institute, estimated would carry an annual cost of about seventy-two thousand dollars for two children, in contrast to the fifteen thousand that a two-child welfare family got at the time.[64] The scorn, willful ignorance, and punitive vindictiveness that characterized these examples of anti-Welfare hyperbole were echoes of the widespread misunderstandings and myths that were shared by many Americans around the time that Clinton's Welfare reform measures were being debated. Prevailing opinion among both the public and the punditry during that period, which has only become consolidated since, was that the typical recipient was an African-American teenage girl who had never worked and never wanted to, and who decided that multiple pregnancies while on Welfare would be a shrewd career move and an easy path to highly paid indolence. One survey found that almost half the Americans polled thought that Welfare or foreign aid (the latter being viewed as Welfare for the undeserving poor of *other* nations) was the largest item in the federal budget.[65] Needless to say, the facts were not only contrary to these myths, but known (at least by policy makers) at the time.

According to sociologist Ruth Sidel: (1) Black recipients may have been overrepresented in Welfare programs, because their percentage in the Welfare population is greater than their percentage in the general population, but whites constituted a larger proportion of those getting benefits, (2) the overwhelming majority of those who receive Welfare are children whose average age is about seven years, (3) more than 80 percent of teenage pregnancies are unintended, (4) between 1975 and 1994, the average AFDC benefit went down by more than a third, and in no state did Welfare and food stamps combined bring recipient families even up to the official poverty level, (5) more than 70 percent of adult beneficiaries of Welfare had recent work histories, and half of them went off Welfare to return to work, and (6) families receiving AFDC had an average of only two children.[66] In fact, one study conducted in the same period found the birthrate for women on Welfare to be lower than that of the general population.[67] Moreover, back when the Welfare debate was at its hottest, it was well known that the main middle-class entitlements, Social Security and Medicare, cost four times more than all the low-income programs combined.[68]

The most glaring oversight in the crusade against Welfare was the other "AFDC" programs, namely those we could lump under "Aid for

Dependent Corporations." A short list of these business entitlements would include tobacco subsidies, government donation of the public airwaves to a handful of media empires, royalty-free mines on public lands, federal giveaways to big agriculture and logging companies, land grants to the railroads, free grazing on public lands, industry bailouts, sweetheart deals to defense industries, business-specific tax loopholes and off-shore escape opportunities, and the incalculable benefits of ubiquitous corporate deregulation. According to a 1994 book by conservative commentator David Frum, just one of these items— subsidies to large corporate farms—dwarfed the annual federal contribution to the cost of AFDC.[69]

If the myths about Welfare are unsupported by the social and fiscal realities, how can we account for the vitriolic discourse surrounding AFDC and its recipients? What has made it such a compelling rallying cry for conservative males in particular? As noted throughout the book, Welfare dependency is something that men are more likely than women to find disturbing. One clue to the basis for this sensibility can be found in the history of American views about dependency. Since the nineteenth century, dependency in the United States has been increasingly regarded as a feminine condition—natural and good in the case of married mothers and wives, and suspect, if not bad, in the case of unwed or abandoned poor mothers reliant on charity or government relief.[70] Eventually, the Internal Revenue Service established the dependency of married women as normative by designating them dependents.

Men, on the other hand, were not understood as dependent, regardless of how much they might actually rely upon or be controlled by others. The exception to this was the male slave, who was regarded as dependent in the way any colonial subject might be. But this perspective was not a static one. In the eighteenth-century view, the involuntary process of being conquered rendered one dependent. One hundred years later, the conventional wisdom was that the "natural" dependency of supposedly childlike slaves or colonized natives predisposed them to and justified subjection.[71]

A similar view of inherent inferiority was later extended to the poor in the early twentieth century. Even though Progressive Era reformers—principally upper-middle-class feminist women—ironically sought to erase the stigma attached to poverty by substituting the word *dependent* for *pauper* in the social conversation about government relief, the pejorative associations to Welfare dependency did not disappear, and only became more deeply fixed by the end of World War II.[72]

In terms of its impact on men, the discourse of Welfare dependency has served an especially powerful, if unconscious, function. It has rendered nearly invisible other social manifestations of dependency, such as the middle-class entitlements and corporate subsidies and bailouts mentioned earlier, which, unlike Welfare, involve no means testing or humiliating moral supervision. But the real elephant in the social living room, occluded by the rhetoric of Welfare dependency, has been the experience of wage labor.[73]

As discussed in earlier chapters, since the industrial revolution, the workplace, with its supervision, its often arbitrary exercise of authority, and its dominance/submission hierarchies, has become—first in factories and later in office cubicles—the primary locus of male dependency. Needless to say, compliance with these conditions is enforced with an unstated imperative—submit or join the ranks of the homeless, or worse, the despised Welfare dependent. This is becoming increasingly the case as the power of unions steadily erodes.

Male dependency in private life can also be eclipsed by diverting attention to Welfare mothers. In single-earner nuclear families where husbands or fathers are the ones employed, men can easily deny their profound dependency on female partners who provide childcare and housework, as well as love and recognition. Even in many dual-income marriages, men are still dependent on women to care for them in these ways.[74] Welfare, as the culture's designated site of pathologized feminine dependency, became a receptacle for the reviled and disavowed experiences of male dependency—a kind of psychological toxic waste dump. This leads me to wonder: What will right-wing male femiphobes do if they actually succeed in ridding the world of this terribly useful "enemy"? How will they maintain the delusion of being "self-made" men?

And speaking of making oneself, we cannot leave the topic of men's aversion to Welfare without calling attention to one of the central features of the Welfare dependency narrative—the bizarre assertion that mothers who receive AFDC are not already working. This denial of the life-sustaining nature of maternal labor presents an obvious example of one of the more common defenses against womb envy described in chapter 1, *devaluation*. What better way to deny one's envy than to proclaim the worthlessness of what the envied object has to offer? Thus, Welfare mothers cannot be viewed as parents who work extraordinarily hard, under conditions of dispiriting material deprivation, to provide and care for their vulnerable and dependent children. They must instead be seen as lazy bon-bon-eating and crack-smoking slackers who pass their days watching Jerry Springer reruns, while their feral children play among the broken glass and discarded needles of inner-city mean streets. The best solution is to conscript such women into the Wal-Mart minimum-wage army of service workers, and put their incorrigible brood in strict, paternal, Gingrichean orphanages where they can finally learn discipline. Who needs mothers anyway?

There is another problem conservative males have with AFDC, one that is masked by the outrage over dependency on government aid: Welfare allows poor women a degree of independence from men. It keeps women from having to choose between starvation and staying with an abusive, philandering, alcoholic, or otherwise inadequate male partner. When Jeb Bush was running for governor of Florida, he got a lot of mileage out of demonizing AFDC recipients who somehow failed to appreciate "the virtue of work."[75] The future governor insisted Welfare mothers "should be able to get their life together and find a husband."[76] Archconservative and antifeminist culture warrior George Gilder lays out this position more fully in an essay in which he argues that "the chief cause of black poverty is welfare state feminism." He elaborates:

"Monogamous marriage is based on patriarchal sex roles, with men the dominant provider. . . . The welfare state attacks the problem of the absence of husbands by rendering husbands entirely superfluous. 'Welfare reform' continues the policy, giving welfare mothers new training and child-care benefits and further obviating marriage by pursuing unmarried fathers with deadbeat dad campaigns."[77]

As it turns out, the same government that has become a subversive feminist instrument threatening to undermine men's rightful domination of women is also construed by many conservative males as the primary impediment to man's biblically ordained dominion over the natural environment.

Cutting the Umbilicus to Mother Earth: The Political Consequences of Making Nature Feminine

"Die Liberal Pinko Tree-Fucking Wimps!" The placard carried by the contemptuous ultraconservative heckler who protested one of San Francisco's antiwar demonstrations in 2003 was as condensed a political manifesto as it was a vulgar one. The man's highly abbreviated message linked seemingly disparate enemies. Someone opposed to the war was assumed to be a communist, an environmentalist pervert driven to incest with mother earth, and an effeminate man. This anonymous rightwing ranter is not the only one subject to loose political associations and what appear to be ideological non sequiturs. In a Congressional debate over a water pollution bill, California Republican representative Randy Cunningham equated politicians who wanted to apply environmental regulations to land managed by the armed forces with those who "want to put homos in the military," and then attempted to silence Patricia Schroeder, Democrat of Colorado, by yelling "Sit down, you socialist!"[78]

Right-wing men seem to experience their opposition to environmental protection through the metaphor of war. When Republican representative Tom DeLay (whose occupation prior to politics was exterminating insects) heard that the Nobel Prize for Chemistry was given to scientists who established a causal association between atmospheric ozone depletion and the proliferation of chlorofluorocarbons, he dismissed the honor as the "Nobel Appeasement Prize."[79]

As I found in my own research on the gender gap, and as earlier chapters have probably made evident, disidentification with the natural world and the valorization of war are two factors that are highly correlated with one another, and with male femiphobia. There are some instances when this link is made surprisingly explicit. George R. Brown, a military psychiatrist, conducted a study looking at the way some non-surgical transsexuals try to use enlistment in the military as an attempt to overcome a feminine identity they find disturbing. In a description of one group of potential recruits, Brown notes, "Of the three civilian patients evaluated, one had received written and verbal recommendations from his internist to 'join the Army, go to boot camp, and learn how to run over trees with a tank' as treatment for his transsexualism."[80]

For some, the manly battle against a feminized environment is a holy war. Those who attended the Earth Summit II in Johannesburg in 2002 were presented with a draft of the U.N. Earth Charter, a document that emphasized the interdependence of people across the globe. William Jasper, a writer for *The New American*, a publication of The John Birch Society, wrote that this statement was "actually a diabolical blueprint for global government," and warned fellow Christians that if "the Earth Summiteers have their way, Johnny and Suzie will not be able to pledge allegiance to 'one nation, under God,' but they will be able to pledge to 'One World, under Gaia'—that is, Mother Earth."[81] The battle lines being drawn here are notably gendered—patriarchal dominance, personified by the Heavenly Father and the Christianized America he favors, versus a natural environment construed as a usurping woman who doesn't know her place. Fundamentalist holy warrior Pat Robertson has also made his sentiments known in these matters. To illustrate his claim that environmentalists are promoters of "alternative lifestyles" (i.e., homosexuality), he noted that these eco-perverts were trying to get government grants to study the "sexual proclivities" of spotted owls. Behind his odd homophobic attribution to environmental scientists, there seems to lurk in Robertson's mind a troubling suspicion that owls may not be exemplars of Christian family values.[82]

Perhaps as a consequence of imagining the planet in feminine terms, conservative men seem to have the same ambivalence toward the natural environment as they do toward women—they are ineluctably drawn to it, but largely to assert phallic dominance. Republican representative from Alaska Don Young seemed to take a very concrete approach to showing who had the phallus when it came to the environment. In a hearing to consider strengthening the Marine Mammal Protection Act, an enraged Young pulled a walrus penis bone out of his pocket and waved it menacingly at an Interior Department official.[83] This is the same congressman who refers to the pristine Arctic National Wildlife Refuge (ANWR) as the "Arctic Oil Reserve."[84] Young's ardor to extract oil from this extraordinary wilderness area is certainly shared by the Bush administration. What is most interesting about the uncontainable Republican lust to drill in ANWR is its *economic* irrationality. Were this exploitation to proceed, it would yield no more benefit in fuel availability than would a three-mile-per-gallon increase in gasoline mileage.[85] Since the Bush White House has adamantly opposed any significant increase in fuel efficiency standards for American cars, as well as other conservation measures, we are left with only noneconomic motives. And chief among these, I would argue, is a need to establish dominance over nature through the phallic penetration of the oil drill—the more "virginal" the landscape, the more imperative the assertion and the more manly the achievement. While this may sound like an interpretive leap to some, the reader would do well to recall from earlier chapters that this language—the metaphors of rape and gendered subordination—was used *explicitly* by male scientists, colonial adventurers, pioneers, developers, and presidential administrations of prior centuries as a way of talking about the proper and divinely ordained relationship real men must have with the natural world. But hidden beneath this phallic bluster is another, less obvious motive for conservative men's femiphobic stance toward the environment.

My own research on the gender gap did show that men were less inclined than women to support government measures to protect the environment from corporate predation. But it revealed a more specific difference, namely women's greater tendency to *identify with* and *feel connected to* the natural environment. For example, significantly more female than male subjects agreed with the statement, "When I pass through a wilderness area that has been clear-cut, I feel like an important part of my world has been taken from me." A year after formulating that item for my research questionnaire, I serendipitously came across an astonishing expression of the same psychological stance I was trying to capture in the survey item. It was manifested in the bodily metaphors employed by a female book reviewer, Patricia Holt, in her appraisal of a disturbing collection of photographs, published by the Sierra Club, that documents the horrific destruction wrought by the practice of clear-cutting forests. She describes "lush forests shaved down to the skin," and the "welts and keloids of logging roads." In other passages she notes the ways the landscape had been "checkerboarded with open wounds," and mountaintops "scalped down to the rock underneath." "After a while," Holt reveals, "the effect of the book is like looking at scars on one's own body."[86]

I certainly would not argue that Holt represents some sort of archetypal woman, that women are essentially closer to nature, or that the attitude she evinces can only be present in a mind saturated with estrogen. Such an essentialist account could neither explain the minority of men in my study who agreed with the above survey item, nor the minority of women who disagreed with it. Nevertheless, the fact that far more women did endorse it cannot be ignored. So, if we are not going to look to mystical or reductively biological explanations, how can we make sense of this gender difference?

One answer may be found in remembering that the environment has not just been the object of men's feminine projections for centuries but, more specifically, of *maternal* ones. If we apply the theory and research discussed in chapter 1 regarding the developmental conflicts that young boys must negotiate in male-dominant cultures, a likely answer emerges: Right-wing males not only construe the earth as a mother but as one from which they must disidentify in order to retain their precarious sense of masculinity—just as they struggled to do with their own mothers. Of course females are embedded in the same patriarchal discourse that depicts the earth as global mother. But unlike men, they do not typically have a sense that their gender identity depends on feeling a psychological distance from mothers, whether actual or symbolic ones, and they therefore are free to experience themselves as linked to the larger "maternal" body of the planet.

Regardless of how we explain it, this gender gap on the environment has been noted by political consultants across the spectrum, and has played a central role in campaign strategy. As far back as 1990, a study by the Roper Organization found that twice as many women as men were committed to taking individual actions to protect the environment.[87] Not only has the difference between men and women's attitudes persisted, but the issue has moved front and center in the minds of political advisors. In 1995, House Speaker Newt Gingrich failed in his efforts to dismantle a number of environmental regulations. In light of the GOP presidential defeat that followed a year later, Republican pollster Kellyanne Fitzpatrick, in 1997, advised him, along with other Republicans, to modulate their antienvironmental fervor. "If I want any of them to pay attention to the environment," she said in an interview, "I start out with two words: 'gender gap.'"[88] By 1999, the pro-environmental "Soccer Mom" was commanding even more attention. Republican consultant Alex Castellanos claimed that the "feminization of politics" arose in response to concerns about "quality of life issues, from health care to the environment," in contrast to "Joe Six-Pack," who "is not concerned about green space."[89]

Needless to say, all this attention to the gender gap on green matters reflects a concern only with how to *package* environmental policy, not how to change it. But all the greenwashing and Orwellian Newspeak (such as calling deregulatory initiatives "Healthy Forests" and "Clear Skies") that GOP spinners can engineer cannot camouflage Bush's record on the environment. A short list of the Bush administration's achievements would have to include: decimation of the Clean

Water Act, especially by allowing the debris that is created when coal-mining companies destroy Appalachian mountaintops to be dumped into creeks and streams; undoing the Clean Air Act by permitting old power plants and refineries to operate without updating their pollution filtration technology; the invitation to logging companies to denude American forests of old-growth trees in exchange for clearing brush; and a refusal to even acknowledge the reality of global warming, let alone develop a plan to reverse it.[90] Of course, this list does not include those measures they have sought to enact but have not yet been able to implement, such as raising the acceptable levels of arsenic and mercury in the environment, and reintroducing fume-belching snowmobiles into Yellowstone Park. It is no wonder the Bush administration is so eager to go to Mars, and perhaps leave Earth behind. Even more than the regulation-averse "red states," the red planet can offer the perfect Republican landscape—one with no troublesome vegetation or pesky protected species to impede development and keep minimalls and free-ways from metastasizing across its surface.

Last, on the issue of the environment, it may be of interest to note one particularly ironic consequence of femiphobia-driven antienvi-ronmental policies. The deregulation of pollutant emissions is leading to the disregulation of male hormones. As it turns out, many of the chemicals becoming increasingly pervasive in the environment mimic the effects of estrogen. Male animals among a variety of species have been anatomically feminized by these contaminants, including fish (who have been born with ovaries and eggs instead of sperm ducts), al-ligators, birds, river otters,[91] and frogs.[92] Scientists have also linked low sperm counts in human males to pesticides.[93] Manly indifference to the natural world may turn out to have not-very-manly consequences. While conservative men may be clueless when it comes to *real* threats to their manhood, they are, as we have seen, ceaselessly vigilant when it comes to fantasized dangers.

Where Fear Lies for the Straight Guy:
The Political Psychology of Male Homophobia

Antihomosexual hatred—whether expressed as discrimination, harassment, or violence—is the last socially acceptable form of bigotry in
the United States. It is a prejudice manifested in nearly every quarter of
American culture, from the back-alley gay bashings and murders in U.S.
cities and towns to the formal pronouncements, judicial rulings, and
legislative proposals of our nation's most esteemed authorities. This is
not only a bigotry that is sanctified in law, but one that the organized
homophobes of the right want to inscribe in the Constitution in the
form of an amendment that denies homosexuals the rights and privileges associated with legal marriage.[94] The Republican-controlled Montana state legislature passed a law in 1995 that placed consensual gay sex
between adults in the same category as murder, rape, aggravated assault,
and incest. According to GOP senator Al Bishop, mutual homoerotic
love is "even worse than a violent sexual act."[95] After serving their prison
time, those convicted under the law would have to register with the police as sex offenders for the rest of their lives. So far, no one has been
prosecuted under the law, but it remains on the books. Montana politicians are not the only governmental authorities who regard homicide
as far more benign that homosexuality. The Florida Court of Appeals
upheld a trial court ruling that awarded custody of a twelve-year-old
girl to her convicted murderer father because the mother was a lesbian.[96]

Judicial discrimination against homosexuals has been manifested
in other ways, as well. In January of 2004, a ruling by the Kansas Court
of Appeals affirmed a lower court decision to sentence a young man to
more than seventeen years in prison for having sex when he was eighteen with a boy of fourteen. Had the underage child been a girl, he
would have been sentenced to a maximum of one year and three months
in jail. The statute that applies to heterosexuals is rather romantically
designated the "Romeo and Juliet" law.[97] While the U.S. Supreme Court
did overturn the Texas sodomy law that criminalized consensual adult
gay sex, the greatest impact of the Court's decision seems to have been

a furious antigay backlash reflected in public opinion polls as well as various legislative initiatives across the country.[98] A similar response can be expected in the wake of the Massachusetts High Court ruling in February of 2004 that only full and equal marriage rights for homosexual couples would be considered constitutional. Whereas at one time an African-American was regarded as three-fifths of a person, we are now in an era in which a similar official status obtains for homosexual citizens. When leaders of national and local governments so openly challenge the humanity of anyone who is not heterosexual, can we be at all surprised that those who harass and assault gay men and lesbians do so with such a sense of guiltless impunity?

High-school students have paid attention to their elders, and seem to have learned their lessons well. In a 1998 survey, 48 percent acknowledged being prejudiced against homosexuals—twice the number who admitted such bigotry a year earlier.[99] Even more startling, this poll was conducted among the nation's most high-achieving sixteen-to-eighteen-year-olds, those listed in that year's *Who's Who Among American High School Students*.[100] Since not everyone would be comfortable admitting such a prejudice (although some males may be more uncomfortable *denying* it), we can probably assume that this study, like any research based on self-reports, does not reflect the true prevalence of antigay bias. The data for those who have gone on to higher education are no more reassuring. A study by forensic psychologist Karin Franklin of college students in the liberal San Francisco Bay area found that, in spite of an intellectual endorsement of civil rights for gays, 70 percent of her subjects said their male friends had engaged in verbal harassment of individuals believed to be homosexual. Twenty-four percent directly admitted to doing name-calling themselves. When Franklin just looked at men, the number went up to 50 percent. Among the same population of college students, one in ten actually admitted to threatening or physically attacking someone he thought was homosexual.[101]

According to FBI statistics, from 1996 to 1997 there was a nearly 10 percent increase in antigay hate crimes, even though the same period

saw a 2 percent decline in other felonies.[102] A study that looked specifically at murders found that the level of violence in the killings of homosexuals is much greater than that seen in other homicides, and that
such slayings are less likely to lead to arrests.[103] Data collected by the California Department of Justice for 1997 showed that the incidence of hate
crimes against perceived gay men was five times that of similar crimes
perpetrated against women thought to be lesbians.[104] Given anecdotal
reports from around the country, there is no reason to doubt that these
statistics reflect the situation in other states. So, if we consider together
all the research on antihomosexual attitudes and violence, one particularly notable pattern emerges that begs for an explanation: homophobia appears to be largely a male set of thoughts, emotions, and behaviors
directed with the greatest ferocity against other males. But to assert
this obvious point is not to give short shrift to the multiplicity of
homophobias. As cultural critic and psychoanalyst Elisabeth Young-
Bruehl has argued, antihomosexual bigotry is really a composite of
hatreds.[105] In other words, men or women can be prejudiced against
men or women who seem either masculine or feminine. In Young-
Bruehl's scheme, there are eight different variations. The most common
and most virulent forms, in my view, are those versions manifested by
men, especially when directed against other men. This is what I will endeavor to explain shortly. There is also a multiplicity of motivations that
drive homophobia, but the principal ones are, broadly conceived, religious and psychological. Obviously, within any particular individual,
both motives can operate to varying degrees, and in ways that may
be impossible to disentangle. Nevertheless, the research on the psychological dynamics of homophobia, which will be addressed next, is quite
illuminating—not only in understanding the private behavior of individual homophobes, but also in making sense of how antigay bigotry
has become a political movement. I shall leave it to theologians to de-
construct the religious rationales for antihomosexual prejudice.

In examining the wealth of psychological studies on homophobia,
one is stuck by the enormity of variables associated with this form of
prejudice; it is clear that antigay attitudes cannot be reduced to a single

explanation. There are, however some that seem particularly salient. Researchers have repeatedly found, as argued earlier, that males are significantly more homophobic than females, and more prejudiced against gay men than lesbians,[106] a finding that has been replicated in a study of exclusively African-American subjects.[107] Homophobia has also been correlated with authoritarianism,[108] cognitive rigidity,[109] opposition to gender equality,[110] traditional gender-role orientation,[111] racism,[112] a variety of personal and interpersonal difficulties,[113] and an intolerance of ambiguity.[114] One study established empirically what many of us might assume intuitively, namely that homophobic men have a notable lack of intimacy in their friendships with other men.[115] As described in chapter 2, ever since the decline of male romantic friendship at the end of the nineteenth century and the concurrent appearance of the category of homosexual, intimacy between men has been regarded with some suspicion and uneasiness. Perhaps it was a similar concern that prompted Republican senator Trent Lott during a press conference to offer an odd qualifier to his description of the closeness between himself and the late senator Strom Thurmond. Strangely, Lott felt the need to point out that the relationship he had with the deceased segregationist was "platonic."[116]

Another researcher studying the correlates of antihomosexual prejudice in men found that homophobic attitudes, especially toward gay men, tended to co-occur with misogyny.[117] He also discovered that these men were much more likely to have an exclusive, rather than inclusive, masculine identity,[118] along the lines I described in chapter 1. In other words, their ideal self was one purged of most qualities deemed feminine. Both of these findings are consistent with my own research on the gender gap, which found that men who scored high on measures of homophobia were much more likely to detest femininity in men and exhibit greater rigidity and conflict in their attempts to adhere to male gender norms. In appears, then, that femiphobia is a major factor in male antigay prejudice. And if, as I have argued in the first chapter, men's fear of being feminine is driven in large measure by a disavowed and unconscious identification with women, we might expect male homophobes to exhibit a particular kind of paranoia. In other words, they might be unduly concerned about being feminized in their contact with gay men, and project onto them a predatory sexual aim that would render the straight homophobe an effeminate bottom (i.e., a submissive and anally receptive partner). As it turns out, this sort of paranoia is indeed a central feature of homophobia.

In Franklin's interviews with men who acknowledged assaulting males they perceived as gay, one of the most common reasons cited by her subjects was "self-defense" against "advances" by the victims. When asked how the attackers knew they were being threatened, they said it was the putative gay men's "eye contact and body language." Franklin was also able to elicit the femiphobic basis for this paranoia. She set up a group discussion after administering the formal written part of her research (the various tests and questionnaires). Franklin then asked her subjects if it was really necessary to hit a man in response to perceived flirting. She paraphrases their collective answer to her question: "If they're going to come on to me, I have to hit them. Otherwise, I'm a chump or a sissy, or I'm like a woman."[119]

A related motive for homophobic paranoia is disavowed homoerotic desire itself. That is, after all, the most widespread and intuitive understanding of the term homophobia—the fear of one's own unacknowledged and unconsciously despised homosexuality. In this formulation, the male homophobe projects his own self-hatred onto the perceived gay man, and in assaulting his victim, he is attacking a reviled part of himself. This theory, held not only by psychoanalysts but increasingly by many members of the lay public, received in 1996 an astonishing empirical confirmation. Henry E. Adams and his colleagues, in a novel but simple experimental design, divided exclusively heterosexual men into homophobic and non-homophobic groups, based on their scores on a measure of homophobia. The subjects were then exposed to a variety of explicit sexual imagery in the form of heterosexual, lesbian, and gay-male videos, while their arousal was assessed using a device that measured changes in penile circumference. Both groups of men showed signs of increased sexual excitement in response to the straight and lesbian films, but only the homophobic subjects were aroused by the gay male images.[120]

Sigmund Freud was the first person to theorize a link between repressed homoerotic feelings and paranoia. This was based on his analysis of the autobiography of a nineteenth-century German jurist, Daniel Paul Schreber, who provided his readers with a vivid account of a psychotic break in which he suffered a number of delusions. Chief among Schreber's paranoid fantasies was that his psychiatrist was the architect of a plot to ravage him sexually and transform him into a woman. On the basis of this case and his own clinical work, Freud hypothesized that paranoia might function as a defense against homosexual desire.[121] In an extensive review of the empirical literature regarding contemporary efforts to test Freud's hypothesis, the authors concluded, "The majority of the better-controlled experimental tests of the theory have supported its validity."[122] This rather bland and measured phrasing disguises what is a really a remarkable conclusion—that a century-old speculation, widely regarded as a fanciful conjecture based solely on anecdotal evidence, now appears to have been an original insight with some explanatory value. We should not, of course, read into this that paranoid schizophrenia or paranoid thinking in general is *caused* by repressed homosexuality. Rather, the reasonable conclusion, consistent with most of the research on homophobia, is that in many cases men's paranoid fear and hatred of gay males can be a way of managing and keeping unconscious their homoerotic desire and feared feminine aspects. In other words, a threat from one's internal world is mentally transformed into a peril from the external world, where it can be experienced as "not me," and then attacked. This brings us directly to the psychological importance of the identity category of "homosexual" to the straight male homophobe.

It may be recalled from chapter 2 that at the close of the nineteenth century the view of homosexuality changed. Instead of being considered a set of *behaviors* people engaged in, it came to be seen as a characteristic that identified a certain kind of *person*. In both perspectives there was social disapproval. In the old view, it was one's practices that might bring moral disapprobation, of the sort that excessive gambling and drinking might evoke. In the new understanding, however, it was one's character or personhood that would be seen as disordered, which pointed to a need for scientific study and medical intervention. Terms like "invert" and "third sex" were used to label this kind of person, at least until "homosexual" entered wide usage. While the term has been officially shorn of its pathological connotations, at least in medical and psychiatric discourse, we have retained the view of homosexuality as a category of identity.

Young-Bruehl, in her study of prejudice mentioned earlier, argues that this category is vital to the psychic equilibrium of homophobes. Perceived differences between straight and gay must be maintained if the homosexual is to function as the despised "not me." The category of homosexual is as fundamental a boundary for the homophobe as is his own skin. Dissolving it threatens a terrifying experience of similarity. This is why, as Young-Bruehl points out, homophobes can take great delight in being photographed with drag queens at the Mardi Gras in New Orleans, but are livid when gay men or lesbians publicly express affection and tenderness like ordinary heterosexual couples.[123] Gregory Herek, a social psychologist who has probably contributed more to the social science literature on homophobia than any other researcher, points out that some homophobes are more likely to feel hostile to homosexuals who *defy* stereotypes, such as conventionally masculine gay men or traditionally feminine lesbians.[124]

These insights may help us understand the widespread aversion to gay marriage, even among Americans who might otherwise oppose discrimination based on sexual orientation. Just the name of the most famous piece of anti-gay-marriage legislation, the "Defense of Marriage Act," tells us much. While Bill Clinton's signature on this law was probably a simple case of cowardly realpolitik designed to appease the prevailing prejudices of the electorate, the right-wing architects of this bill, and others like it that have passed through state legislatures across the country, clearly feel that marriages need to be defended from some danger. This movement to outlaw gay marriage is perhaps the most stark example of homophobic paranoia that has ever been enacted in public life. It is certainly not as amusing as fundamentalist Reverend Jerry Falwell's assertion that Tinky Winky, a purse-carrying character on the children's television show *Teletubbies,* was guilty of "role-modeling the gay lifestyle" and was "damaging to the moral lives of children."[125] But is it any less absurd to believe that one's marriage will somehow be damaged or imperiled because homosexuals can also marry?

On countless talk shows one can witness conservative pundits, who on many issues are able to make reasoned arguments for their positions, being at a total loss to ground this paranoid fantasy in even a semblance of logic. The best they can do is cite biblical passages, which of course requires no reasoning capacity beyond discerning the perceived word of God. Other than the absolutist adherence to holy books, the main reason homophobes oppose gay marriage is that it makes "them" more like "us." Were nonheterosexuals free to marry, it would diminish the projective value of the category of "homosexual"; homophobes would be deprived of their much-needed despised other. To recognize their common humanity with gay men and lesbians would involve the psychic trauma of reclaiming desires and identifications homophobes have worked so hard to evacuate into others.

Male Conservatism: The Big Picture

As we have seen, men are much more likely than women to hold rightwing views on a number of major political issues. I have chosen to look closely at the gender gap in only four of these areas—warfare, the caretaking functions of government, environmental protection, and homophobia—largely because these were the primary issues covered in my own research, and in so doing I was able to establish some interesting correlations. Since references to this research are scattered throughout this chapter and in the Introduction, it might be clarifying at this point to summarize my findings. Not surprisingly, the men who scored in the conservative direction on one of these four issues were also conservative on the other three. And, as mentioned throughout the book, on all the issues, men were significantly more likely than women to embrace the right-wing position. Perhaps the most notable findings, and those that to my knowledge have not been assessed by other researchers, were the positive correlations between male conservatism and measures that assessed fear of men's femininity and gender role conflict.[126]

The male subjects in my study were much more likely than the females to be made uneasy by the prospect of a man doing something stereotypically feminine. Those men who held the most conservative positions were also the ones to evince the greatest concern about not being like a woman. My study only established a correlation, not a causal relationship, between fear of men's femininity (femiphobia) and political conservatism. Nevertheless, because gender identity and gender role socialization developmentally precede the formation of abstract concepts such as political ideology, it seems likely that if one of these variables were causal it would be femiphobia.

At first thought, it would seem most objective and fair-minded to regard the conservative political views more typical of men as merely one point on a continuum of equally reasonable ideas, no more or less healthy, valid, or problematic than liberal or progressive beliefs. However, the correlation between adherence to right-wing ideology and male gender role conflict makes it difficult to view men's conservatism with such relativistic equanimity. To score high on the measure of gender role conflict administered to my subjects means that one tends to have chronic anxieties about personal achievement, competence, failure, and career and financial success. Such a man is also more likely to be preoccupied with attaining dominance over others. In addition, he is likely to experience a severe constriction in his ability to express any positive emotions toward other males. In other studies, high scores on the measure of gender role conflict used in my research have been positively correlated with sexual coercion, hostility toward women, impaired intimacy, negative attitudes toward help seeking, low self-esteem, marital dissatisfaction, depression, anxiety, authoritarian personality style, general psychological distress, and some of the most extreme manifestations of paranoia, psychotic thinking, and obsessive-compulsive behavior.[127] This may seem like a harsh assessment, but a recent study of the psychological correlates of political conservatism paints an equally discouraging view.

In May of 2003 four psychologists published an encyclopedic assessment, called a "meta-analysis," of nearly all the research conducted over the last fifty years on the psychological traits that tend to characterize politically conservative individuals more than liberals.[128] From their perspective, right-wing ideology, like all political world views, can be understood as a function of what they call "motivated social cognition." By this they mean that political attitudes and perceptions of the social world result in part from unconscious psychological needs and concerns. They point out, and I concur, that just because someone's politics are motivated by unconscious wishes, emotions, or ways of thinking, we should not conclude that their beliefs are necessarily false or irrational, or that such individuals are somehow less principled. Clearly, everyone's political attitudes are determined by many factors, some conscious and some unconscious. But under certain circumstances, a tendency to believe what we *need* to believe can distort our perception of social reality, and at times even obscure our own self-interest. In extreme situations, motivated social cognition can lead us to scapegoat others, and even consent to their murder—as numerous historical episodes of genocide can attest.

The study undertaken by these four researchers is enormously comprehensive and nuanced, and I could not do justice to it with a brief summary here. But some of their conclusions are worth noting. Individuals who embrace right-wing ideology tend to be more dogmatic, intolerant of ambiguity, threatened by social change and instability, and accepting of relationships of domination between social groups.[129] Conservatives have also been found to demonstrate decreased cognitive complexity, a higher need for order and structure, and greater authoritarianism.[130] The authors of the study argue that people tend to adopt a politically conservative world-view, in part, because to see things that way helps them reduce fear and uncertainty, decrease ambiguity, and account for and justify inequality between people.

One way to think about femiphobia is as an unconscious factor motivating the political cognition of conservative males in particular. More specifically, femiphobia drives men to support issues and candidates that seem to provide a bulwark against the threat of gender instability. This helps them ward off their deeply conflictual identification with the feminine, and shore up conditions of inequality, which is a central pillar of both conservatism and patriarchy.

But this discussion raises another question that may have lingered in the reader's mind all along: What about right-wing women? How do we explain the psychology of *their* political passions, especially when it involves, as it usually does, an endorsement of male domination? It is really beyond the scope of this book to provide a thorough analysis of the psychodynamics of female conservatism, but the phenomenon seems so contradictory it cannot be ignored entirely, and will be taken up briefly in the next chapter. Suffice it to say, in my own research, there was a puzzling minority of women who not only embraced the politics more typical of men, but were also homophobic, and shared with the majority of male subjects a fear of men's femininity. As with men, the explanation for this cannot be reduced to a single factor. While not driven by the kind of gender anxieties that beset men (in my research politically conservative female subjects did not score high on gender role conflict), these women would still be motivated by the same needs and concerns identified by the meta-analytic study described earlier. But for the purposes of this discussion, perhaps the most important thing that can be said about female conservatism is that it is the statistical exception to the rule. Not only is the right wing, in government and among the electorate, composed mostly of males, but it is these men, sadly, who seem to be driving the rhetoric and outcome of elections. In the next chapter, we will see how the terrorist attacks of 9/11 and the ensuing war in Iraq have exacerbated these tendencies and helped to usher in a new era of untrammeled phallic arrogance and unilateralism—assaulting civil liberties and governmental transparency at home, and generating new enemies abroad.

7

Gender in a Time of Holy War
Fundamentalist Femiphobia
and Post-9/11 Masculinity

"Soul" Brothers and Their Discontents

Christian-right crusaders Jerry Falwell and Pat Robertson agree with Osama bin Laden on one key theological point: America had it coming. "The pagans, and the abortionists, and the feminists, and the gays and lesbians ... and the ACLU ... helped make this happen," explained Mr. Falwell. Moreover, he warned shortly after the 9/11 terrorist attacks, "What we saw on Tuesday, as terrible as it is, could be minuscule if, in fact, God continues to lift the curtain and allow the enemies of America to give us probably what we deserve."[1]

Christian and Islamic fundamentalists, who are dramatically increasing their numbers and their influence across the globe, share more than a general distaste for the moral pollutants emanating from liberal Western culture and a dream of the apocalyptic violence that could cleanse the world of them. They are particularly aligned in their concern to discipline the feminine, whether it is women in social life or female identifications in the inner lives of men. Every variety of fundamentalism—ethnic, political, or religious—has as a key element an inability to tolerate ambiguity, and this has, in many places, wrought catastrophic devastation on bodies, cultures, and psyches. And the ambiguity these crusaders for certainty seem the least able to tolerate is that of gender. Thus, fundamentalists everywhere share a creed that includes the restoration of a fantasized golden age of unfettered patriarchal domination, harsh punishments for those who stray from their prescribed gender roles, a fascistic priggery mixed with terror regarding women's sexuality, and an absolute—and often murderous—intolerance of homosexuals. Of course, there are significant differences among various fundamentalisms, and none can be reduced to only its gendered aspects. Nevertheless, it is not without significance that the zealous adherents of every form of tyrannical monomania tend to make policing the borders of masculinity and femininity central to their mission. These movements are, in other words, driven to a great extent by what this book calls anxious masculinity. The aim of this chapter is to shed light on the links between the external holy wars of fundamentalists and the internal wars of femiphobic men. It will also look at how the terrorist attacks in New York and Washington, and later the war in Iraq, catalyzed new configurations of masculinity in American culture and politics.

Misogyny in the Name of God

In the various media profiles of the 9/11 hijackers that appeared in the months following the terrorist attacks, many commentators struggled to make sense of these apostles of mass murder—perplexed not only by their nihilist vision of Islam, but also by the apparent paradoxes within their characters. For example, a number of reporters remarked on what they viewed as a contradiction between the antisexual fundamentalism of the jihadis, and their apparent enjoyment of lap dancing at the bon voyage strip-club bash prior to the suicide missions. Such behavior, however, should have come as no surprise, since numerous American fundamentalist preachers, such as Jim Baker and Jimmy Swaggert, have demonstrated similar predilections. More importantly, what these journalists overlooked was that participation in a form of prostitution is quite consistent with that familiar theme of fundamentalist psychosexuality, the Madonna/whore split, whereby a dichotomy is constructed between good (veiled and private) and bad (unveiled and public) women. As described in chapter 4, this split not only helps to keep women in their proper domestic place, but shores up the psychic quarantine of motherhood from sexuality.

Of course, the gothic horrors of fundamentalist misogyny are legion and go well beyond amusing peccadillos. In Pakistan the local governmental response to the trauma of a twenty-six-year-old female rape victim was to sentence her to death by stoning. Her crime consisted of violating a law against adultery, under which the issue of consent is irrelevant and an accusation of rape is regarded as a confession of forbidden sexual behavior. The man accused was set free, since the testimony of women in such courts is inadmissible.[2] According to human rights groups, 80 percent of all women in Pakistani jails are there for violating laws against extramarital sex.[3] It may be surprising for some to learn that the *hudood,* the legal code putatively based on the Koran, under which these women have been prosecuted, is not some ancient, time-honored tribal code. Rather, it was enacted only twenty-three years ago,[4] a fact that supports the assertion made by some scholars that fundamentalisms are not all centuries-old cultural and political systems, but (like Nazi Germany, which was also based on a fantasized past) are more like mutant forms of modernism, complete with their own Web sites and networks for purchasing and deploying exterminationist weaponry.

In Saudi Arabia, another U.S. ally against evildoers, religious police—otherwise known as the Commission for the Promotion of Virtue and Prevention of Vice—allowed fifteen young girls to be incinerated in a school fire in Mecca. Authorities stopped the men who tried to attempt a rescue because the girls were not wearing head scarves and *abayas,* traditional robes. As the would-be rescuers were "male strangers," argued officials, it would have been "sinful to approach" such inadequately attired females.[5] Apparently, a charred corpse is more virtuous than an uncovered female head.

Of course, the status of American women is in no way comparable to that of women who live under the iron fist of fundamentalist male domination in parts of Africa, the Middle East, and elsewhere. To make such an equation is to indulge in the sort of mindless relativism that some of the more naive postmodern leftists have embraced. At least women in the U.S. enjoy a significant measure of legal equality with men, including the right to receive an education, to vote or run for political office, to sign and enforce contracts, to take employment, to choose a spouse, and, for the moment anyway, to exercise reproductive choice. But these rights remain intact because Christian fundamentalists only *influence* the government, and have yet to actually constitute it.

America's Aspiring Ayatollahs

The selection of John Ashcroft for Attorney General—a man whose obdurate brand of Christianity would make Cotton Mather look like a depraved libertine—was a significant payback by George W. Bush to the Christian right, which provided generous donations of money and labor during the 2000 campaign. Mr. Ashcroft set the tone for his reign when early on he instructed aides to cover the naked breasts of Justice Department statuary.[6]

In 1996, then senator Ashcroft incorporated into the Welfare reform bill a "charitable choice" provision that allowed religious organizations, with minimal government oversight, to compete for federal funds to provide a variety of social services. Four years later, this desire among religious conservatives, in and out of power, to render the separation between church and state a more porous boundary found expression in the White House Office of Faith-Based and Community Initiatives. In addition to taking over government functions and receiving taxpayer dollars, participating religious institutions are free to engage in discriminatory hiring practices based on sexual orientation.

Even higher education has been subject to the surveillance and intervention of our fundamentalist Attorney General. In Texas, a biology professor posted an announcement on his Web site that students who wish to receive a letter of recommendation to science graduate programs had to honestly accept the scientific consensus on the origins of humanity, evolutionary theory. After having this heresy brought to their attention by a group of Christian lawyers, the Ashcroft Justice Department decided to launch an investigation.[7] Other prominent Republicans would doubtless applaud such federal actions, especially House majority leader Tom DeLay, who, following the school shootings at Columbine, said the carnage had happened "because our school systems teach our children that they are nothing but glorified apes who have evolutionized out of some primordial mud."[8]

Impeding the theocratic aims of the Christian right, along with those of their point man in the Bush administration, Attorney General Ashcroft, are certain legal constraints, as well as tensions with Bush administration social policy moderates such as Colin Powell. Ashcroft, nevertheless, continues to battle against an international women's rights treaty, the Convention on Elimination of All Forms of Discrimination Against Women (CEDAW), already ratified by 169 countries, which could help to prevent the kinds of institutionalized atrocities previously mentioned.[9] While the treaty contains no enforcement mechanism, CEDAW has already been cited as the basis for a variety of legislative efforts to protect women from domestic violence, to grant women inheritance rights equal to those enjoyed by men, and to establish laws against sexual harassment, in a number of countries that have ratified it. Nevertheless, Paul Bonicelle, a Bush appointee and a dean at Patrick Henry College—where courses in creationism are featured in the curriculum—regards the possibility of American ratification of CEDAW as "unthinkable" and "not something social conservatives can accept."[10] According to Janice Crouse, another Bush appointee, who is also a senior fellow at the Beverly La Haye Institute, a right-wing think tank, the treaty is part of a "frivolous and morally corrupt agenda designed to legalize prostitution, promote homosexuality, and abolish Mother's Day."[11] Needless to say, CEDAW mentions nothing about the latter two issues, and it calls on signatories to "suppress all forms of traffic in women and exploitation of prostitution of women."[12]

Strategic Spiritual Alliances

In spite of real differences, the parallels between Christian and Islamic fundamentalism are striking. This is not just my view; there are many among these otherwise divergent religious guardians of gender and sexual purity who view one another as essential allies. In early 2002, a large consortium of American Christian right organizations formally aligned itself with over fifty Islamic governments, including those of Iran, Libya, and Sudan, to prevent the adoption of measures at United Nations conferences that would expand civil rights for women and homosexuals. "We have realized that without countries like Sudan, abortion would have been recognized as a universal human right in a U.N. document," declared Austin Ruse, a conservative Catholic member of the American branch of the coalition.[13] Appreciation of this new partnership, and of the special affinity that binds it, was expressed on the Islamic side by Mokhtar Lamani, a Moroccan diplomat speaking for the fifty-three-nation Organization of Islamic Conferences: "The main issue that brings us together is defending the family values, the natural family. The Republican administration is so clear in defending the family values."[14] He went on to explain how offensive he found a proposed declaration at the June 2001 U.N. General Assembly on AIDS because it included, among other things, references to the need to protect "men who have sex with men" from becoming infected with the virus. Mr. Lamani seems to concur with his Christian fundamentalist comrades who insist that AIDS is God's punishment for homosexuality, and that no attempt should be made to save hell bound sodomites from their just and divinely ordained fate. Summing up the official Bush administration position on this new Islamic-Christian alliance, a government spokes person said, "We have tried to point out there are some areas of agreement between [us] and a lot of Islamic countries on these social issues."[15] Another zone of commonality was marked out at the 2002 World Summit on Sustainable Development, where the U.S., along with the Vatican and a group of Islamic countries, took a position opposing any agreement that included language portraying forced marriage, honor killings (murders of women whose sexual behavior has "dishonored" their families), and female genital mutilation as human rights violations.[16] Of course, there is a significant realpolitik motive behind the American government's conduct in these global forums; the administration wanted to cultivate support among Muslim nations for the global war on terrorism, and get them to at least look the other way when it invaded Iraq. Nevertheless, the fact that the U.S. does *not* resemble Saudi Arabia, Iran, or some other fundamentalist theocracy in its gender relations is a source of great consternation to many increasingly well organized Christian conservatives, and thus, not something those with feminist sensibilities can take for granted.

It is quite astonishing, however, the extent to which the prayers of the Christian right have been answered—not by any celestial being, but by the powerful mortal in the White House. A partial list of domestic and foreign policy positions adopted by the Bush administration makes clear the degree to which it functions as the political arm of Christian fundamentalism:

• *On Israel*: The White House has shown unconditional support for Prime Minister Sharon, whose strategy to handle conflict in the region consists of collective punishment of Palestinians, the expansion of West Bank settlements, and what appears to be the ultimate goal, the expulsion of the Palestinians. Not only have these policies increased terrorist attacks, but by doing so, and by increasing Israeli Jewish hegemony in the area, they seem to bring the Holy Land closer to fulfilling the Christian Right's reading of Biblical prophecy, their wishful fantasy of apocalypse, and their conviction that Jews who fail to convert when Jesus returns will perish in the horrors of the ensuing tribulation.

American fundamentalist Christians have not relied solely on their agents in the White House to realize their vision. Some groups have played a direct role in creating the preconditions for their "End Time" scenario by, for example, establishing privately funded social services to make it easier for Eastern European Jews to emigrate to Israel. On the surface, the explicit and ardent support the Christian right has expressed for the Sharon government in general, and for Jewish settlement in Palestinian areas in particular, may seem to contradict the affinity, described earlier, they have shown for some theocratic Arabs. These two stances are not mutually exclusive, however. The fundamentalist Christian concern with Israel is a spiritual one—doing what is necessary to fulfill prophecy. Their kinship with Islamic fundamentalists regimes has more to do with shared moral imperatives in this life—principally those related to gender and sexuality.

• *On the environment:* Many Christian fundamentalists are indifferent to the effects of Republican-initiated environmental deregulation, because they see in the ruination of the planet—whether by melting ice caps or dying coral reefs—yet one more harbinger of the much welcomed End Time when Christ will return.

• *On women's reproductive health:* The Bush administration has sought the restriction and, where possible, the prohibition of reproductive choice, whether in the form of abortion or contraception. It has pursued this fundamentalist goal not just in the U.S., but globally.

• *On human rights treaties:* As previously mentioned, the Republicans have addressed a key concern of femiphobic fundamentalists everywhere by opposing any international agreement that might promote gender equality or mitigate male domination.

• *On domestic civil rights legislation:* The GOP has been in perfect sync with the Christian right in its unflagging efforts to prevent American citizens from obtaining any legal protections against discrimination based on sexual orientation.

• *On education:* Republicans have acted in lockstep with their Christian fundamentalist constituents by supporting school vouchers, prayer in school, the elimination of sex education, the inclusion of Creationist fairy tales in science curricula, and the censorship of "unpatriotic" and "antireligious" textbooks.

Women Warriors for Patriarchy

Fundamentalist agendas, even those that seek to establish or extend male domination, are not the exclusive provinces of men. There are many conservative women who argue unapologetically and campaign *aggressively* in favor of female subordination. As mentioned in chapter 6, there is a significant minority of women who share the political views of right-wing men, although for different psychological, cultural, and political reasons. While these women do not constitute a homogenous group, they often share the antifeminist gender ideology of their male counterparts. In the U.S., one subgroup of neotraditional women has become especially visible in public life over the last decade. They constitute a growing brigade of carefully coiffed, stiletto-heeled conservative female pundits who identify with the phallic slash-and-burn style, as well as the politics, of their right-wing male counterparts.

In a monologue on his new program, *Real Time with Bill Maher*, Maher referred to Rush Limbaugh's prescription drug problem, and then noted, "This has been the toughest week for conservatives since Ann Coulter admitted she had a penis."[17] The audience got the joke because they intuitively understood that she is the paradigmatic right-wing phallic woman—combative, arrogant, impermeable to reason or attack, and reliant on femiphobic epithets like "girly-boy" and "panty-waist" to respond to her male critics.[18] Even the butch *National Review* tossed her out when she wrote of Islamic states, "We should invade their countries, kill their leaders and convert them to Christianity."[19]

With no discernible sense of irony, independent, wealthy, and highly educated upper-class women like Coulter, who relish leadership roles in business and politics, cynically praise the lives of domestic docility and deference led by their lower-middle-class Christian-right sisters. While they take a condescending I've-got-mine-thank-you attitude toward mothers who might need government services, and deride females who complain about sexual harassment, these conservative women save their greatest contempt for feminists, who are dismissed as an undifferentiated group of whiny victimology mongers. Insulated by class privilege, this subgroup of right-wing women is able to remain unmoved by the continuing global feminization of poverty, the extensive international slave trade in women, the remaining pay gap between the sexes, and the double shift of wage labor and unpaid housework most wives without domestic servants tend to perform. And then they accuse *feminists* of elitism. In addition, their historical amnesia apparently renders them unable to recall the debt they owe prior generations of women's rights activists, or the fact that there was a time when even money could not buy equality with men. These polished Republican spokeswomen have become so commonplace in the allegedly liberal media that most TV political talk shows would seem incomplete without at least one dominatrix of right-wing rectitude, like the relentless culture warrior Coulter, extending her pink lacquered talon to point out the liberal traitors in our midst.

Female crusaders for gender conservatism, of all classes and religions, can be found across the globe, from the United States to the Middle East. The late Beverly La Haye, founder of Concerned Women for America (and the person for whom the aforementioned right-wing think tank was named), was a politically outspoken and active woman who nevertheless insisted, "The woman who is truly spirit-filled will want to be totally submissive to her husband.... Submission is God's design for women."[20] The right-wing Christian men's organization Promise Keepers has held massive revival meetings across the country, which fill stadiums with tens of thousands of weepy reborn patriarchs who pledge to take back the familial throne. They are ardently supported in their efforts by a number of women's auxiliary groups. One of these, the Promise Reapers, sees itself as "born from the side of Promise Keepers, as Eve from Adam's side."[21] Another, the Heritage Keepers, instructs wives how to "let go of the reins" of marital authority. Their motto is "Submission is a place of honor."[22]

Echoing similar sentiments at religious schools in Pakistan and in Muslim towns and villages across the globe, many girls and women are devout practitioners of fundamentalist Islam, and firmly believe in social systems that deny women their most basic human rights. Some would fight to the death to support such systems. Wahida Kamily, a twenty-three-year-old, high-school educated Afghan woman explained, "We obey our husbands, and our husbands have more rights than us— that is our culture. If a wife doesn't listen to her husband, it's right for him to beat her."[23] Shafia Salaam, a sixteen-year-old Afghan girl living in Pakistan, was even more adamant. When discussing efforts of the American-led alliance to unseat the Taliban, she insisted, "I believe in

Jihad. I will do whatever I can do. If I am provided the opportunity to get weapons, I will use them."[24]

The paradoxical point here is that women who happily, even fervidly, accommodate the demands of cultures and communities predicated on the political and sexual subjugation of women, and the privileging of all things male, do not necessarily do so from a position of passivity or as a result of coercion. To focus—as this book does in places—on the ways some men seek to control and punish women (as well as other men, at times) does not require seeing women only as helpless victims, even when they appear to gladly obey the patriarchal imperatives of their local culture.

No form of oppression can be understood without acknowledging that members of a subordinate group (in this case, women) sometimes identify with the interests of their rulers, or play an active role in perpetuating the limits the culture imposes on their freedom. This does not mean that those who appear happy to be subjugated fulfill their roles without conflict—internal or external, conscious or unconscious. It is *internal* conflict that fundamentalists are especially anxious to erase because it is ultimately the greatest impediment to compliance. Within a woman, conflict may involve the mental struggle between a longing to be seen (and to see herself) as a "good wife," and a sometimes inchoate urge for greater self-determination. A man too, in spite of being in some respects a beneficiary of women's subordination, may be unconsciously torn by inner conflict. On the one hand, he may desire, identify with, and depend on women, and on the other hand, may fear, envy, and feel a need to control them. This erasure of conflict is usually achieved through projection—an unconscious process in which one's inner suffering is perceived as coming from an external source, which is then regarded as a threatening enemy. Each absolutist theology has its own name for this enemy—infidel, heretic, witch, unbeliever, crusader, and, of course, old reliable himself, Satan. "It is not my own desire to transgress the social order, to sin, to be unshackled from the venerable traditions of our fathers, or to enter the forbidden territory of the other

gender," the true believer, in essence, proclaims. "Rather, it is that demonic force out there that is trying to do it to me, to contaminate me
with its corrupting badness." This is what makes campaigns for moral
or religious purity a pastime of paranoids.

Clean and Dirty in the Fundamentalist Unconscious

With these dynamics in mind, it is not hard to see how every fundamentalism is driven, at base, by a defense of purity. And, for men in
such a world, the feminine is often the impurity that evokes the greatest anxiety. Conscious and unconscious links are made between women
(especially their bodies) and filth. While particularly marked in the history of the Christian West, as other parts of this book have noted, the
same associations have been made in the minds of men around the
world, from New Guinea Highland tribes to Afghan villages. Anthropologist Mary Douglas once defined dirt as "matter out of place."[25] In
fundamentalist public space, as well as in the inner world of male identity, womanliness is dirt that must be contained or expelled. One Pashto
aphorism describes with chilling concision the proper location of
Afghan females: "A woman belongs in the house—or in the grave."[26]

This sensibility was expressed with startling clarity by an earnest
young man who participated in the post-lecture schmooze session that
followed a talk by conservative author Christina Hoff Sommers, at
Dowling College in Long Island, New York. Fired up by the speaker's
bitter lamentation against the liberal/feminist "war against boys," he
came up with his own remedy for this peril: "All we would have to do is
take all the boy babies away when they're born to live on desert islands
and be raised by themselves, away from the influence of feminists and
women, and then they would be protected. And when they are grown
we can bring them back. And they'll be pure."[27] This young man's femiphobic statement is redolent of two major themes common to the
psychology of male fundamentalists around the world: (1) seeing the
feminine as a kind of contaminating impurity, and (2) finding a solu-

tion in exclusive male nurturance and rearing. The latter, here, is a kind of right-wing couvade fantasy, proffered as an antidote the pollution of having been born of woman. Were the speaker Pakistani, he would be an ideal candidate for one of that nation's many madrassas—the rigidly gender-segregated Islamic boys' schools that produced so many zealous soldiers for Al Qaeda.

When women defy the boundaries of gendered space, all manner of male hysteria can be unleashed. After Julie Pennington-Russell was appointed to head Calvary Baptist Church in Waco, Texas, making her the first female senior pastor of a Southern Baptist church in the history of Texas, another local pastor, W. N. Otwell, threw a public hissy fit. Demonstrating in front of Pennington-Russell's church with thirty members of his own congregation, God Said Ministries, Otwell announced that the selection of a female pastor was a "crime against God, the home, the children and society as a whole." His jeremiad continued: "We hold Calvary Baptist responsible, along with feminists, as the main cause of child abuse, abortion, domestic violence, divorce, teen pregnancies, drug and alcohol abuse, pornography, teen crime, gang violence, racial tensions and the ever-increasing coming out of the closet of the sodomites and lesbians." The female pastor responded dryly, "I was surprised he left out global warming."[28]

Fascist Femiphobia

The drive to expel a woman from an erstwhile male-dominated institution can lead, as in the case of Pastor Otwell, to amusing histrionic enactments. However, when men need to abjure the feminine from their mental *interior,* to evacuate any vestiges of female identification, the consequences can be far more disturbing. In times of war, enemies, especially if they are of another race, can readily become the projective repository of the disavowed feminine pollution. To exterminate a feminized adversary is then an act of purification. Fascist regimes such as Nazi Germany and Milošević's Yugoslavia, both of which produced propaganda that feminized their enemies, presented mass murder as the solution to a sanitation problem, as acts of "hygiene" or "cleansing." Fittingly, the Germans chose showers as the sites where unmanly Jews, homosexuals, and Gypsies could be washed off the Aryan body politic. In the case of the Serbs, the ethnic enemy was forced into the feminine, degraded position, and Serbian masculinity affirmed through the systematic rape of both male and female prisoners.

Contemporary neo-Nazi and Christian fascist movements can be understood as another form of fundamentalism, which exhibit the same preoccupations with purity, feminized and feminizing external demonic enemies, and imperiled masculinity as do more conventional fundamentalists. Peter Langan, the leader of one hypermasculine "patriot" group, the Aryan Republican Army, was eventually captured after a bloody shootout with the FBI. Nurses tending to his bullet wounds discovered that his body was not only marked by the predictable scars of a fascist tough guy, but was also completely shaved. Residual pink polish was still visible on his toenails. Langan acknowledged to his physicians that for months he had been taking black-market estrogen.[29] Having failed to forge a solid male gender identity in the crucible of organized right-wing thuggery, he had decided to embrace, albeit in the closet, a far more compelling, lifelong, and surprisingly conscious feminine sense of self. His father, a World War II combat veteran and Viet Nam–era CIA agent, produced a son who could, alas, only adopt militarism as a kind of masculine drag. After his arrest, Peter Langan recalled, "As a child, I wished I was a girl and not a boy. I identified with my sisters, my mother, and the amahs [nannies] more than with my brothers and my dad."[30]

In contrast, the self-styled soldiers of the Army of God, a fundamentalist Christian antiabortion terrorist organization, could only acknowledge the centrality of the feminine in their inner worlds through their battles against it. While responsible for numerous bombings and anthrax threats directed at family planning clinics across the U.S., the Army of God garnered the most attention when one of its members, a Presbyterian minister, Paul Hill, was arrested and later convicted and executed for the murders of Dr. John Bayard Britton and his escort,

James Barnett, outside a Pensacola, Florida, abortion clinic. In a revealing HBO documentary on the organization and the larger movement
of which it is a part, there is a surprisingly unguarded dialogue between
two members, Bob Lokey and Neal Horsley, that takes place in Horsley's home. Both men are ex-cons who became born-again Christians
in prison. Lokey did twenty years for murder, while Horsley was locked
up for drug dealing. At the time of the filming, Horsley maintained a
Web site, The Nuremberg Files, that functioned as a kind of antiabortion hit list, publishing the names and addresses of physicians and clinic
staff, some of whom have been subsequently attacked or killed. Toward
the end of the film, the camera follows Lokey on a trip to Horsley's
home.

After Lokey arrives for the visit, Horsley regales his friend with a
story that demonstrates the ease with which any experience in life can
function as a Rorschach test, revealing to the observer what one conceals
from oneself as well as others. He describes a pair of wild ducks that have
taken up residence in his pond. The male, Horsley notes, seems to follow the female everywhere she goes, as if he is being pulled along by an
invisible string (umbilicus?). He concludes that the male duck has been
"vaginally defeated." While this bizarre deduction might strike some as
a non sequitur, Lokey knows a meaningful cautionary tale when he
hears one. He replies, "Hey, I've been vaginally defeated all my life....
Finally, God said ... 'Son, you've got to leave this thing alone.' I was so
attracted to women that at one time I thought they were gods. And He
made me cut women loose then and there. I quit smoking, quit drinking, quit meat. I circumcised myself." Lokey, it turns out, is a pretty literal guy; the *cut* he made had to be concrete, as well as metaphoric.[31]

We learn in the film that, under divine inspiration, Lokey lopped
off his own foreskin without anesthetic while in prison. Although this
may seem to be a strange, if not psychotic, gesture, Lokey was simply
doing to himself what is done to preadolescent males in many patriarchal cultures as a means of symbolically conferring maleness, repudiating the feminine, and propelling them out of the all-too-appealing
orbit of mothers. Numerous cross-cultural studies of prepubertal male

initiation rites have found that circumcision (as well as other severe or painful rituals) occurs mostly where males are socially dominant, and fathers are psychologically or physically absent during the infancy of young boys. There results in these cultures a great anxiety about the psychological centrality of mothers, and thus cross-gender identity in boys. "Freeing" the penis from the foreskin seems to be a way of highlighting the anatomical distinction between the sexes, and the associated pain and bleeding appear to function as symbolic purgatives of the feminine/maternal aspects of self.[32]

It seems that prison was not only the site of Lokey's conversion to fundamentalist Christianity, but also the place where he became a born-again femiphobe. Perhaps it is only in their crusade in defense of unborn fetuses, with which they seem to unconsciously identify, that men such as these can manifest the other, denied, side of their masculinity—a longing for the womb, and the fantasy of maternal symbiotic merger.

Feminizing the Enemy

By focusing on the fringe lunacy of groups like the Army of God, it is easy to lose sight of the fact that fundamentalist manhood is only a somewhat more inflexible, anxiety-driven form of *mainstream* masculinity. One expression of this continuity is the femiphobic cultural discourse surrounding the post-9/11 American war on terrorism, especially the numerous ways the terrorist enemies have been rendered more despicable by portraying them as somehow feminized—examples of which were given in the Introduction. The point here is not to draw any sort of moral equivalence between this femiphobic rhetoric and the actions of terrorists, nor even to pathologize the understandable rage and hatred so many Americans felt for the mass murders committed by Al Qaeda. Rather, the aim is to call attention to, and encourage further thought about, the narratives through which that hatred gets represented, the projections that are delivered along with our retaliatory bombs, and what this all might reveal about mainstream American masculinity.

Domestic critics of Bush's "homeland security" policy, whom members of the Republican administration *did* regard as the moral equivalent of the terrorist enemy, were the object of similar femiphobic derision. Even the erstwhile conservative allies of the president, such as *New York Times* columnist William Safire, were attacked when they dared to call into question the secret military tribunals designed to try and execute terrorism suspects. Those who argued in favor of retaining some semblance of ordinary due process for arrested suspects were dismissed by unnamed Bush administration sources as "professional hysterics" reminiscent of "antebellum Southern belles suffering the vapors."[33] This followed in a rhetorical tradition that dates back to the 1988 Republican campaign against Michael Dukakis, in which the Democratic candidate was derided for being a "card-carrying member of the ACLU," and, thereby, for having juridical sensibilities guided by considerations other than a lust for manly vengeance. The concern that a passion for civil liberties is somehow a feminine predisposition may have contributed to what was in December of 2001 a notable gender gap on issues surrounding the secret tribunals. As mentioned in the Introduction, by a margin of 8 percent, men were more likely than women to believe that noncitizens legally residing in the U.S. should not, if arrested, have the same legal rights as a citizen.[34] Right-wing men, it turns out, are the ones anxious about vapors, in particular the toxic effluvium of political effeminacy.

Phallic Terror, Phallic Targets

No discussion of post-9/11 cultural psychology would be adequate without addressing the conscious and unconscious meanings attributed by all parties to the terrorist attacks themselves. "Anyone willing to drive a plane into a building to kill Jews is alright by me. I wish our members had half the testicular fortitude," proclaimed Billy Roper, spokesman for the National Alliance, one of the largest American neo-Nazi organizations.[35] As it turns out, Mr. Roper was not the only person to think about the murderous suicide missions over New York and Washington in terms of male genitals.

To talk about the World Trade Center towers as phallic symbols is to risk reducing the complexity and horror of the events to a pseudo-Freudian cliché. But, as part of a larger and multifaceted analysis, an appreciation of the phallic aspects of the attacks can add to our understanding of the terrorists' psychology, and may give us insights into our own responses to this trauma. The buildings *were* phallic, not just in the crude sense of being towering monoliths that penetrated the sky, but because they, along with the Pentagon, represented (for America as well as its enemies) fantasies and attitudes associated with U.S. global economic, political, and cultural hegemony. The phallic frame of mind held by America's ruling elite did include the fantasy of absolute self-sufficiency, a contemptuous abrogation of international agreements (and the refusal to negotiate others), a thoughtless indifference to the suffering of people in other nations (especially marked in the Bush II regime), a sense of invulnerability, and an unshakable conviction that our wealth could make our arrogance affordable. One particularly destructive consequence of these attitudes has been the American government's longstanding policy of propping up a variety of Middle Eastern dictatorships. While this practice may have stabilized the flow of oil to the West, it brought economic misery and political oppression to the populations of these countries. This process seems to have pro duced among young Arab males, and not just poor ones, a pervasive sense of humiliation and a corresponding envy and hatred of the West. Feeling small, and pumped up with the justifying rhetoric of holy war, some of them decided to bring us down along with the totems of our power.

The two towers, ironically, were leveled, and the Pentagon damaged, after being penetrated by three other symbols of phallic omnipotence—the jets, which ejaculated their incendiary load into the monuments to American economic and political might. Moreover, as described in the Introduction, these missiles were commandeered by terrorists whose leader, Mohammed Atta, was so concerned about feminine pollution that he left a note banning women from attending his funeral. Even after death, he seemed to think, a man must still protect his phallic status. It is important to keep in mind that Atta (whose father, it may be recalled, derided him for being an effeminate mama's boy) and the other hijackers, as well as bin Laden, were already Westernized. Since, in their view, to be Western was to be godless, soft, feminine, and thus impure, we can also understand the attacks as their attempt to kill off the disavowed parts of themselves. What better way to finally leave the feminine and especially the maternal behind than to immolate oneself as a sacrifice to God the Father, and then ascend to his heaven? The dissolution of the self that is both desired and feared in relationships with women can be fulfilled, the holy warrior imagines, through a suicidal merger with the paternal deity—an imagined scenario that psychoanalyst Ruth Stein, who studied Atta's final letter to his comrades, has described as "regression to the father."[36] This could also be thought of as a couvade fantasy from the perspective of the male child. Who needs mothers or their unobtainable wombs, when through a literal baptism of fire one can be "born again" from a male god?

The scene of sanguinary atrocity and ineffable suffering was literally a dream come true for the spiritual mentor of the heaven-bound fundamentalist pilots, Osama bin Laden. In a videotape captured during the war in Afghanistan, bin Laden and his acolytes describe dreams of phallic flight. "I was in a huge plane, long and wide," a sheik recalls about what is supposedly another's dream. Bin Laden, also reluctant to claim ownership of the fantasy/dream, recounts one told to him: "I saw in a dream, we were playing a soccer game against the Americans. When our team showed up in the field, they were all pilots!"[37] Soccer, already a game in which the aim is to penetrate the opponent's defenses, to send one's projectile into the other team's territory, is rendered even more phallic with a home team of pilots whose "long and wide" aircraft carry an apocalyptic payload. In a striking expression of psychological symmetry with the terrorists, the Reverend Fred Phelps of Topeka, Kansas, the infamous homegrown holy warrior of the Christian right, saw in 9/11 a felicitous affirmation of his own cosmology, and deliriously proclaimed, "The Rod of God hath smitten fag America!"[38] Deus ex phallus.

The Phallus Rises from the Ashes

In spite of a new and pervasive sense of vulnerability occasioned by the horrific events of September 11, the phallic associations to the towers were insistently retained by many Americans. In New York City, a flyer was distributed that featured an image of Osama bin Laden being anally raped by the World Trade Center. The accompanying caption read, "You like skyscrapers, bitch?"[39] Even the planned memorial replacement for the destroyed monoliths was referred to by the *New York Post* as the "Power Tower."[40]

There were other, more profound, ways in which the terrorist attacks provided America with an opportunity for cultural remasculinization. First, it facilitated the revivification of "heroic" manhood, by turning altruistic New York firemen, policemen, and assorted male volunteers into iconic rescue-worker hunks, signposts of a new era of defeminized men (who could still, however, be sensitive enough to cry over tragic losses). A month and a half after the attacks, a *New York Times* headline announced, "Heavy Lifting Required: The Return of Manly Men." The article is flanked by a photo of a group of burly male rescue workers and soldiers, studly and uniformed. The caption emphasized the performative aspects of the phenomenon these men supposedly represented: "The attacks of Sept. 11 have brought more than a few good men back into the cultural limelight."[41] Nevertheless, their serious, world-weary expressions and grimy clothing made it clear they were *not* The Village People.

Among the many product tie-ins to this trend was a "2003 Calendar of Heroes," featuring twelve specimens of bare-chested firefighter beefcake. The man on the cover is posed in front of the Empire State Building, now the tallest structure in New York. The photo is framed so as to establish a kind of equivalence between the firefighter and the phallic monument—the former positioned on the left, and the latter on the right, making them appear to be about the same size.[42]

The August 2002 headline for a column penned by conservative pundit James P. Pinkerton proclaimed, "Real Men Back in Style." He quotes grizzled coal miners, whose first request upon being rescued is, "We need some chew." Pinkerton then leaps from this anecdote to a cornball homage to post-9/11 revitalized machismo: "Chewing tobacco? That's men for you, fraternal enough to save lives, macho enough to be jaunty in the face of death, manly enough to be politically incorrect. Male virtues and values have never really changed, but after decades of disdain, Americans are seeing the natural ways of men in a new and more positive light." Even pencil-necked white-collar workers, "those with the softest hands," suffer from that "atavistic yearning to recapture the sweaty, risky ways of the past."[43]

This celebration of recovered masculinity reached all the way to the fashion runways of Milan and Paris, where hulking male models sported the latest in commando chic, camouflage muscle shirts, combat fatigues festooned with cartridge belts, and cowboy clothes. Stefano Tonchi, of *Esquire* magazine, seemed to understand what was at stake in the cowboy designs of Tom Ford, the creative director of Gucci, and a Texan: "For Tom, the western theme is about going back to his roots." Moreover, "with cowboys, there is also less gender confusion. Cowboys are not girly."[44] So, it seems that behind even this festive heralding of the new manhood there lurked the old femiphobic anxiety.

These developments dovetailed perfectly with a pre-9/11 mass culture trend—World War II nostalgia. According to the avalanche of books and films idealizing the "good war" and the men who fought it, this period was supposedly a time of unambivalent and secure masculinity, in which gender and other aspects of cultural life were not plagued by uncertainty and conflict. Such nostalgia was ripe for harvesting by boosters for the new Republican national security state, particularly in its domestic and global war without end against real and imagined terrorist threats. One place where a link was established between the sanitized vision of the past and the present cultural moment was in the variety of soft-focus analyses of George W. Bush's putative transformation from a callow frat boy to a mature leader whose commanding presence now approached the manly gravitas of the "greatest generation." Not surprisingly, such claims were heard frequently on right-wing talk radio. But, even centrist, middle-of-the-road media echoed this perception, though it was expressed with a bit less enthusiasm. For example, a writer for *USA Today* said, "Bush has told advisors that he believes confronting the enemy is a chance for him and his fellow baby boomers to refocus their lives and prove they have the same kind of valor and commitment their fathers showed in WWII."[45] In a *New York Times* op ed column, David Frum, a Republican speechwriter, delivered a expectable piece of partisan puffery on Mr. Bush, chiefly notable for "staying on message" (as political consultants often counsel) regarding the new improved post-9/11 chief executive. "Today," Frum announced, "Mr. Bush is more than a strong president: he dominates his own party in a way that few modern presidents ever have." Should the reader have any difficulty discerning the point, the column is accompanied by a visual aid—a cartoon with a "W" branding iron in the foreground and a herd of elephants bearing the "W" brand on their hindquarters in the background.[46] Domination, for contemporary politicians, no less than for those in ancient Greece, remains the defining criterion for masculinity.

The prize for the most gushing, over-the-top encomium to post-9/11 revivified manhood has to go to the special issue of *The American Enterprise*, entitled "Real Men: They're Back."[47] This delirious right-wing strut-fest defies parody, and contains inspirational articles such as "The Return of Manly Leaders and the Americans Who Love Them," "Why We Need Macho Men," "The Car and the Man," "Me Man, Me Hunt!" and, in case you thought they couldn't get more redundant, "The Manliness of Men." The best feature, however, is surely the "re-search" article, "Indicators," which displays a number of graphs that compare the manliness of Republican and Democratic male members of Congress. Endeavoring to be as scientific as possible, the authors developed objective criteria, such as whether the congressman in question had ever been a hunter ("successfully bagged an animal more than once"), a mechanic ("performed extensive mechanical work on a motor vehicle"), a spy ("operative in any intelligence service"), or an Eagle

Scout. While they grudgingly acknowledge that an equal number of Democrats and Republicans had been firefighters and policemen, those professions are left off the chart titled "GOP=GUY."[48]

It might be instructive to point out an obvious, but never discussed, logical implication of all this talk about a recovered masculinity: where there is a sense of something having been refound, there must have been a prior experience of loss. The search for a feeling of manliness that can never be securely possessed has been a repeating theme throughout this book. As I have argued in various places, male identity will always be an unstable psychological achievement, as long as it is based on re-pression—on the disavowal of whatever is construed as feminine. From my experience as a clinical psychologist, I have learned that repression does not enable people to get rid of anything; it only helps them remain clueless about its presence. Thus, the discourse of the "new" post-9/11 machismo can be read as an indication of something that has felt *ab-sent,* or at least imperiled, as much as it is about something temporar-ily recovered.

The Dawn of the Daddy State

The celebration of the newfound "manly man" (a redundancy that seems to have survived at least three centuries of American public life) has had one particularly curious manifestation. It has enabled certain cold-war dinosaurs, namely Defense Secretary Donald Rumsfeld and Vice President Dick Cheney, to morph into studly septuagenarian pa-terfamiliases, rugged paternal protectors who will keep the barbarians at bay. In one interview, Ann Coulter practically swooned at the thought of Mr. Cheney's reassuring gerontocratic musk, describing him as her "ideal man" and "extremely sexy."[49]

This odd transformation in the public image of two cranky Repub-lican warhorses from another era signals a *second* major dimension of the cultural remasculinization that followed the terrorist attacks: The war on terror, along with its associated domestic security apparatus, has enabled the federal government, at least temporarily, to cast off its

Democratic-era image as an engulfing, infantilizing, and ultimately castrating maternal caretaker, and refashion itself as a stern paternal protector and avenger of the nation's shared trauma. Within three weeks after the September 11 attacks, the *New York Times* was heralding the "muscular new role for government." This assertion was made in a piece entitled "Now, Government Is the Solution, Not the Problem." As if to inaugurate the state's new phallic status, the article is accompanied by a large photo of the Washington monument looming over the capital and its residents, which features the caption, "Monumental government."[50]

Presaging this change in the gendered view of the federal government was a metaphorical distinction drawn ten years earlier by political economist Jude Wanniski. He referred to the Republicans as the "Daddy Party," whereas Democrats belonged to the "Mommy Party." "Republicans represent growth, which results from risk taking, which requires optimism, which father and husband need as they set forth to improve the conditions of the family," asserted Wanniski. They are therefore, he claimed, the party of individualism, harsh discipline, and military aggression. Democrats, on the other hand, belong to the party that "represents security, which must be pessimistic, just as mother and wife as traditional keepers of hearth and home are risk averse."[51] In this view, the Mommies in politics want to give their naughty "children" another chance, and err on the side of permissiveness. They are also more concerned with the collective well-being than with individual self-interest.

A few years after Wanniski's writings appeared, U.C. Berkeley linguistics professor George Lakoff, whose research has focused on the ways metaphors both reflect and shape how we think, developed a much more nuanced political typology, but one uncannily similar to that of Wanniski. In Lakoff's framework, the conservative world-view is based on a "Strict Father Morality," whereas liberalism is founded on a "Nurturant Parent Morality" that is implicitly maternal. Lakoff examined the key phrases and metaphors of conservative and liberal thinkers, which he claimed are derived from two very different models of parenting, to show how each world-view is internally consistent. He revealed the sometimes hidden coherence within each perspective that renders seemingly contradictory positions understandable—for example, how conservatives could simultaneously be "pro-life" (oppose abortion) and favor capital punishment.[52]

It would be a mistake to conclude from the work of Wanniski and Lakoff that it is our sex chromosomes that lead us to view politics or the government through gendered parental metaphors. Clearly, fathers and all males are not preordained to be strict, nor are mothers and all females inevitably nurturing. A more useful way of understanding the tendency of conservatives and liberals to view the role of government in terms of, respectively, paternal or maternal functions is to apply the psychoanalytic concept of *transference*. In a clinical setting, transference refers to the process whereby a patient experiences the therapist as if he or she were a significant person in the patient's past (or sometimes the wished-for antithesis of that person). This process is unconscious, and may involve attributing *(transferring)* to the therapist thoughts, emotions, and motives that are actually conjured from the patient's inner world, and even on occasion attempting to reenact with the therapist a drama from the patient's traumatic history. As most adults can attest from their own experience, transference occurs in many relationships, not just psychotherapeutic ones—the more intimate, the more likely it will occur. In fact, the end of the honeymoon phase of any romance could be defined as that moment when the ghosts from one partner's familial past seem to take up residence in the body of the other partner. A husband expresses mild irritation, or, beyond that, strong resentment, and is suddenly transformed in his wife's mind into her sadistic, rageful, and abusive father. A wife asks for a favor, perhaps in a demanding way, and quickly morphs into the husband's alcoholic mother who required the neglected son to parent *her*.

Governments, like loved ones, tend to evoke transferences that often have at least some foundation in their actual behavior. Since governments are created to set standards, ensure justice, inflict punishment, defend against foreign and domestic threats, implement education, and provide care, it is not hard to see how they could be the objects of parental transference. The transference on the part of any particular individual varies according to the political interest group or party with which he or she identifies, and whether that group is in or out of power. By tuning our ears to the metaphors embedded in political rhetoric, which has been discussed in the earlier chapters, it is easy to see that contemporary Republicans, when out of power, view the government as a malevolent maternal entity. (This transference is shared by those slightly more paranoid conservatives who have traded in their power ties and wing tips for camouflage and combat boots—the various "patriot" groups and antigovernment militias.) Once their party is in power, the federal government, especially when enacting policies that stress vengeance, punishment, discipline, and the withholding of provisions and entitlements, is viewed and interpreted by Republicans as a strong, omniscient, and unaccountable phallic body—a daddy state.

As we have seen throughout this book, conservative men tend to view a government that uses its power to level inequities, protect the public from corporate sociopathy or dangerous products, and monitor and regulate the impact of business on the environment as an intrusive coddling mother. The cover illustration from a 1993 antifeminist manifesto, *Surviving the Feminization of America* (p. 234), condenses in one image many of the features of this political psychodynamic, even though the author, Rich Zubaty, describes himself as a "social conservative and an economic progressive."[53] It pictures a group of men standing in front of the Capitol building in Washington, D.C. Their mouths are agape with horror as they point to the sky. The dome is missing and is about to be replaced with a giant breast, which is being lowered by the cables of an unseen crane onto the building. The only color in this otherwise black-and-white drawing is a vibrant pink, our culture's chromatic signifier of the feminine, and is found in both the large nipple of the breast and the shirt worn by a man in the foreground. Not only does color link the man with the monstrous mammary, but his large open mouth suggests more than fear—the rooting reflex of a nursing infant.

Male ambivalence about the mommy state

The image elegantly, if unconsciously, reveals both sides of a common male ambivalence toward the maternal—that is, the *longing* as well as the dread.[54]

The same conflict can be seen in other manifestations of Republican maternal transferences to the government. Economist Paul Krugman has shown how those states that are the most opposed to "big government," and thus voted for Bush in 2000, are precisely those that have been the most dependent on federal subsidies. But the irony becomes even starker when he points out that it is the tax dollars of the blue states that are disproportionately flowing to the more dependent red states, who receive about ninety billion dollars from their reviled blue American brethren.[55] This not only explodes the fantasy of heartland self-reliance, but mirrors the dependency-denying male electorate in those regions who protest so loudly about the infantilizing services of the "nanny state."

It seems that the more extreme the hatred of a maternally construed government, the greater the disavowed dependency. Ralph E. Clark, the leader of the vehemently antigovernment Montana group the Freemen, posted an angry screed on his land that described the federal government as a "prostitute." But Clark had a little secret. Even though he was armed to the teeth against the threat posed by the malevolent federal bosom, the angry leader of the Freemen was surreptitiously suckling at it. An investigation revealed that he had received $676,082 in government subsidies to make up for agricultural losses on his farm. When the money ran out, his property was foreclosed. He refused to leave and barricaded himself and his associates in for months.[56]

While the administration of George W. Bush relies on a positive paternal transference on the part of the femiphobic Republican "street"—such as the slavering electronic mob that constitutes Michael Savage's growing radio audience—the White House must, on occasion, venture, however cautiously and superficially, into maternal territory. This seems primarily designed to address the Republicans' low level of support among women, to give the appearance that "compassionate conservatism" is more than a useful oxymoron. President Bush's State of the Union Address in January of 2003 was an occasion to throw a few conspicuous federal dollars onto the compassion collection plate.

What was most interesting in all this was how these gestures of "feminine" caring were rationalized by some male members of Mr. Bush's loyal constituency. In February 2003, the Conservative Political Action Conference held its annual meeting on the outskirts of Washington, D.C. While the gathering drew freelance right-wing crackpots from across the country, many White House officials and prominent Republican leaders were in attendance. In fact, Vice President Dick Cheney emerged from his undisclosed location to give the opening

address at the three-day event. (An interesting side note: to avoid embarrassing the vice president, conference officials requested that the
vendor offering bumper stickers reading "No Muslims=No Terrorists"
sell them from under the table, which apparently did not keep him
from doing a brisk business.)[57] Tim Weigel, who ran the Free Republic
booth, dismissed the president's various "compassionate" proposals,
such as the funds he wants to devote to AIDS in Africa, as "Throwaways,
put out there to keep the left quiet while he takes care of Iraq."[58] For
Weigel, it seems as if Bush's "maternal" initiative to send AIDS money
to Africa is only acceptable because it is seen as facilitating the President's true "paternal" agenda of punishing Iraq. Interestingly, behind
Weigel as he spoke hung a computer-generated photomontage of the
face of Hillary Clinton on the body of a pig.[59] Senator Clinton remains
to this day the right wing's nightmare poster child for the evils of maternal government.

Of course Hillary Clinton has long vacated the White House, and
the new regime has stripped the White House of its feminine Democratic associations and any lingering female-driven agenda. The true
nature of its present occupant's concern for women is probably best
symbolized by the response a San Francisco Bay Area woman received
when she wrote to the president early in his term, expressing her wor-
ries about the Middle East, the environment, and the planned national
missile defense system. The envelope from Washington contained only
a card, signed by the first lady, on which was printed the recipe for Cowboy Cookies.[60]

In giving the White House a new butch Republican facade, the Bush
administration has positioned itself to use the terror felt by American
citizens for its own propagandistic benefit, and to facilitate a phallic
agenda of unilateralism and the unaccountable exercise of power. Tax
breaks for the wealthy, harsher discipline for the poor, untrammeled
military expenditures, cold-war style surveillance of citizens (while
wrapping the government in an impenetrable veil of secrecy), erosions
of civil liberties, and invitations to corporate predators to feast on
wilderness areas have all been packaged as essential to fighting terror

and maintaining domestic security. No more national nanny—daddy's in charge now.

While this book is particularly interested in *conservative* transferences—mainly because they generally involve a greater degree of paranoid distortion and aggression, and are more likely to be manifested in men—other political groups deserve at least a brief mention. Democrats, especially those who identify as liberal or progressive, tend to see the "maternal," caretaking functions of government as most important. Thus, when out of power, they have a negative paternal transference to the government, which can be seen as a malevolent, abusive father. For some leftist radicals in the sixties this took the form of identifying the state almost exclusively with its police function—personified as "the Man." Libertarians, on the other hand, seem to attribute both negative maternal and paternal qualities to the government, and insist they need neither love nor the law from those who hold political office.

From Punishment to Politics

Another variable in determining a person's transference to the government is the nature of his or her childhood experience. In chapter 1, I discussed the impact on boys of father absence, physical and/or emotional, and the long-term effect of the pressure from both families and cultures to disidentify with their mothers. The reader may recall that such boys can develop debilitating hypermasculine defenses that, in addition to creating much psychic suffering, predispose them to femiphobic political attitudes. There is another factor associated with child rearing that seems to lead males in a similar direction—the nature of parental discipline. We live in a country in which 65 percent of adults approve of hitting children as a mode of behavioral control. But it is the regional differences that are particularly notable. In Southern states—the most conservative part of the nation—73 percent favor spanking, in contrast with 60 percent elsewhere.[61] Given this regional distinction, we might wonder if there is any causal link between punishment and politics, and if so, which comes first. Two University of Massachusetts research psy-

chologists, Michael A. Milburn and Sheree D. Conrad, found that authoritarian, highly punitive parenting was correlated with later political conservatism, but interestingly, only in men. Their explanation for
the gender difference is that boys and men are socialized to express
anger outwards, either to direct it at someone, or, in the case of anger
generated by punitive parents, to displace their rage and vengeful feelings in the realm of politics once they become adults. Girls and women,
on the other hand, are taught to placate aggressors and use empathy
to manage hostility in others. In fact, Milburn and Conrad found that
women who reported high levels of childhood punishment were more
politically *liberal* than women from low-punishment homes.[62]

Studies of gender differences in the psychophysiology of emotion
are consistent with Milburn and Conrad's explanation for their findings. Under controlled laboratory conditions, in which men and women
were provoked with mild electric shocks, all the subjects showed the
physiological signs of anger, such as increased heart rate and blood pressure. Men chose to respond by retaliating against their "attackers,"
and this response returned them to physiological equilibrium, lower-
ing their heart rate and blood pressure. In contrast, women reacted to
the provocation by being more affable and kind to the aggressors, and
thereby reduced their level of physiological agitation.[63]

The right-wing talk show host Michael Savage, whose many bilious,
femiphobic eructations have provided excellent raw material for analyses in this book, has also made comments that exemplify the work of
Conrad and Milburn. In one interview, he rants against "Turd World
immigration," "left-wing pinko vermin in high places," and "femi-
fascists," all of which have attacked America's "borders, language, and
culture"—Savage's signature mantra, and a slogan that brings to mind
his brown-shirt progenitors. "Only a more savage nation can survive,"
he argues. "Not a more compassionate nation." Nothing evokes his
frothing vitriol more than powerful women. "Today in America we have
a 'she-ocracy,' where a minority of feminist zealots rules the culture," he
insists.[64] In his view, Senator Hillary Clinton and Supreme Court Jus-
tices Sandra Day O'Connor and Ruth Bader Ginsberg have "feminized

and homosexualized much of America, to the point where the nation has become passive, receptive, and masochistic."[65] This concern seems to meld into some sort of white supremacist conspiracy theory: "With the [Latino] population that has emerged, since they breed like rabbits, in many cases the whites will become a minority in their own nation.... The white people don't breed as often for whatever reason. I guess many homosexuals are involved. That is also part of the grand plan, to push homosexuality to cut down on the white race."[66]

A preoccupation with homosexuality characterizes much of Savage's oeuvre. His 1983 novel, *Vital Signs*, is especially revealing. While it is often folly to draw any psychobiographical conclusions about an author based on his or her work of fiction, in this case the central character, Samuel Trueblood, hews astonishingly close to Savage. Both are middle-aged New York Jews who take on rugged-sounding goyish last names (Savage, it may be recalled, replaced Weiner), become herbalists, move to Marin County, California, start a family, and achieve an ambivalent success. Trueblood describes a "childhood beneath tyranny," by which he means the iron rule of a sadistic, brutal, and humiliating father, whose favorite insults were homophobic ones. As a young boy, wearing colorful clothing would elicit comments like, "You're not a fag, are you Sam?" Trueblood would remain haunted by shame and self-doubt. In spite of leading what might look to others like the good life, he continues to be tormented by a variety of unrelenting internal conflicts: "Inner voice screaming at me for years," reads one passage, "first rational, then crazy, telling me to do mad things.... Almost uncontrollable now. Impulses to stab children, strangers, wife, self with scissors." In spite of pursuing the Ladies' Man strategy to manage homophobic anxieties, Trueblood is stirred by "masculine beauty." He nevertheless struggles to maintain his resolve: "I choose to override my desires for men when they swell in me, waiting out the passions like a storm, below deck."[67] The obvious question raised by this material is: Just how close is Savage's history and psychology to that of Youngblood?

There is a passage from Savage's 2003 book, in which he speaks with an uncharacteristic candor. Referring to his childhood, he says, "Things were tough every day of our lives. And we made the best of it. Frankly, that's why I'm driven the way I am. *I was raised on neglect, anger, and hate. I was raised the old-fashioned way*" (emphasis mine).[68] Poet and author Neeli Cherovski, a longtime acquaintance and former close friend of Savage's—back when the latter was a liberal and his homophobia was closeted, if present at all—confirmed in an interview that the portrait of Trueblood's father was based on Savage's own upbringing.[69] His short-lived television show on MSNBC came to a precipitous end after he unleashed a particularly vicious rant at a caller Savage thought might be gay. "Oh, you're one of those sodomites," Savage screamed. "You should only get AIDS and die, you pig.... Go eat a sausage and choke on it!" Protesting a bit too much, he insisted at the end of his tirade, "I don't care about these bums. They mean nothing to me. They're all sausages."[70] Of course, as we have seen, Savage's fictive doppelganger, Youngblood, does indeed fancy bums. All of this brings to mind the announcer's lead-in to the radio version of *Savage Nation,* which warns: "The following program contains adult language, adult content, psychological nudity." The obvious irony is that it is only the *host's* psyche that the program exposes. Taken together, Michael Savage's writings, public persona, and personal history do seem to provide striking confirmation of Milburn and Conrad's research. There are apparently many with whom his politics resonate, and perhaps many share his psychology and authoritarian upbringing; his book *Savage Nation* reached number one on the *New York Times* bestseller list.

Michael Savage is not the only public figure to illustrate the link between male conservatism and the harsh treatment of children. Under the first President George Bush, Jerry Reiger ran the National Office of Juvenile Justice and Delinquency Prevention. In August 2002, Florida governor Jeb Bush decided Reiger would be the best person to head the state's Department of Children and Families, the agency that manages their notoriously troubled child welfare system. The nomination hit a snag when an article surfaced that he had written years earlier for a religious journal. In that essay Reiger insists on the importance of the "manly" discipline of children, by which he means hitting them. Praising the salutary effects of "temporary and superficial bruises and welts,"[71] he quotes the Bible to support his position: "Although you smite him with the rod, he will not die. Smite him with the rod ... save the soul."[72] In addition to the familiar male fundamentalist preoccupation with rods that smite, Reiger also takes a predictable stance on the proper role of women. He writes, "Scripture is clear in stating that women are to be 'helpmates' to their husbands, that they are to bear and nurture, that they are to be 'workers at home.'"[73] Reiger embodies in a single individual the co-occurrence of certain passionately held beliefs and attitudes—authoritarian parenting, political conservatism, the subordination of women, and a fundamentalist phallic sadism that associates manliness with harsh punishment. Also, his nomination is another sign of the creeping theocracy that has come to characterize the current Republican reign.

Conservatism and the Couch

Milburn and Conrad noted another startling finding from their study: men severely punished in childhood who had no experience with psychotherapy were the *most* conservative.[74] There are a number of ways of understanding this correlation. One of the outcomes of psychotherapy, especially with approaches that emphasize insight into unconscious processes, is a diminished tendency on the part of patients to manage painful emotions derived from past trauma by acting out aggressively against others in their present lives. Presumably, this would mean that such "graduates" of therapy would not only avoid attacking, verbally or physically, those in their immediate circle of acquaintances, but would feel less of a need to support politicians or policies that call for punishment, vengeance, military solutions to diplomatic crises, state regulation of private and consensual pleasure (sexual or pharmacological), or cuts in social services. To put it in Lakoff's terms, they would be less likely to advocate a "Strict Father Morality" in their politics. GOP consultant Don Sipple seemed to be expressing an intuitive understanding of this dynamic when he referred to Republicans as the "discipline" party and Democrats as the party of "therapy."[75]

Interestingly, Milburn and Conrad set up another experimental condition as part of a related study in which men with a history of punishment were given the opportunity to recall events and express emotions related to their childhood trauma. As a result of this cathartic intervention, these subjects, compared to those who received no intervention, expressed significantly less support for the death penalty.[76]

There are other ways to think about the correlation between political conservatism and the lack of psychotherapy experience in men raised by highly punitive parents. As described in chapters 1 and 6, respectively, both male gender socialization and conservative ideology view help-seeking behavior, along with the condition of dependency it implies, as something shameful and unmanly. From this perspective, attention to emotion, and especially one's psychological wounds, is seen as a manifestation of weakness and effeminacy in men, and a confirmation of female inferiority when exhibited by women. In other words, men, especially conservative men, are much less likely to seek psychotherapy than women are.

In addition, some men can experience any effort to understand them at a deep level as a kind of threatening homoerotic intrusion, such as was described in the Introduction regarding George H. W. Bush in his first presidential campaign. Finally, though it may seem a bit counterintuitive, the experience of being the victim of extremely punitive parents can make some men even less likely to seek therapy. Their defenses against having felt small, helpless, and humiliated as a child are so brittle that the vulnerability, trust, and transient regressions associated with being in psychotherapy are too unbearable to even contemplate.

Sometimes, when self-reflection seems too threatening, and confronting one's limitations portends intolerable shame, an individual may opt for what psychoanalysts call a "manic defense," an action or a stance that expresses a grandiose denial of weakness, fallibility, and dependency, and that asserts that others are infinitely replaceable. This position can be taken up by governments as well. Like an individual, a regime can jut out its defiant collective chin and bellow, "Who needs the United Nations? Who needs 'Old Europe'? Who needs permission from the rest of the goddamn world to burn fossil fuels and occupy other nations? Not us!"

Flyboys and Action Figures: The Iconography of Gender in the New American Empire

By now, it is old news that the Bush administration had no postwar plans for American-occupied Iraq, that it shunned any advice that failed to comport with its fantasy of a "cakewalk," that there was no sound evidence that Saddam possessed weapons of mass destruction (the putative reason for the invasion), that it had nothing but contempt for the concerns of the majority of America's allies, and that the only scenario it prepared for was one that featured throngs of cheering and grateful Iraqi citizens. Of course, this sort of unilateralist arrogance and grandiose denial of our interdependence with the rest of the world did not begin with the current government.

In spite of the incalculable amount of tax dollars spent on global intelligence operations, a number of U.S. administrations have been oblivious to significant cultural and political developments in other countries. As a result, American officials, civil and military, have been repeatedly blindsided by upheavals around the world. A short list would have to include the surprise victory of the Vietnamese resistance to the American war there, the overthrow of the Shah of Iran, the implosion of the Soviet Union, the rise of Islamic fundamentalist terrorism, the attacks on the World Trade Center towers and the Pentagon, and now, of course, the situation in Iraq. Not that I'm complaining, but the United States seems to have become one of the most ineffectual imperial powers to ever lumber across the globe. And the Bush administration appears to have become the fullest expression of this blundering hubris and indifference to other cultures.

The fantasy that repudiating interdependence and multilateralism would make America stronger should have exploded along with the buildings on 9/11. And what remained should have dissolved in the face of our current bloody quagmire in Iraq. The behavior of the present Republican regime, however, suggests that nothing but spin and the choreography of photo opportunities have been affected by recent events. In sympathy with the manic triumphalism of the Bush administration after the initial military victory in Iraq, country singer Toby Keith recorded a song, "Courtesy of the Red, White and Blue," that quickly went to number one, and became a virtual anthem for the White House architects of permanent war. A few lines say it all: "You'll be sorry that you messed with the U.S. of A. 'Cuz we'll put a boot in your ass—It's the American way."[77] (I will leave it to the reader to ponder what body part the "boot" might be a downward displacement of.) This tune was also the perfect theme song for the president's most glorious, though later regretted, moment of image management, the famous Top Gun landing on the USS *Abraham Lincoln*.

Rarely in the history of political stagecraft has there been a more coherent spectacle, by which I mean a unity of phallic form with phallic content. The famous banner that proclaimed "Mission Accomplished" was a succinct denial of many aspects of reality: the enormity of the military, political, and cultural task that lay ahead for the American occupiers; the missing WMDs; and especially the *real* war on terror that got short shrift while Bush Jr. and company were taking care of some unfinished family business in Iraq. Corresponding to the phallic message on the banner was the flyboy himself. In addition to never having scuffed his snakeskin boots in combat, Bush Jr. appears, by current accounts, to have been AWOL during part of his Viet Nam–era service in the Texas Air National Guard.[78] While evidence may yet refute this widely held impression, many of the records of his service are missing as of this writing. Although the president's military drag performance was in obvious contrast to his history, Bush's photo opportunity became a phallic event primarily because it signified the boot-end of an unstoppable hypermasculine empire. He became, at least for a while, the principal iconic figure of resurrected American manhood. Those who find it improbable that this image of unilateralist swagger was interpreted in specifically phallic terms by the larger American public need only consider some examples of the pervasive media discourse that followed Bush's flight-suit promenade.

In an interview on Christopher Matthews' *Hardball* program, G. Gordon Liddy was not shy about expressing his admiration for the presidential pudenda: "And here comes George Bush. You know, he's in his flight suit, he's striding across the deck, and he's wearing his parachute harness, you know. And I've worn those because I parachute—and it makes the best of his manly characteristic.... You know, all those women who say size doesn't matter—they're all liars. Check that out... what a stud...."[79] Both Salon.com's conservative commentator Andrew Sullivan[80] and leftist culture critic for the *Village Voice* Richard Goldstein[81] wrote articles regarding the authenticity of "Bush's basket." Unlike Sullivan, Goldstein was convinced the Commander in Chief had done a "sock job."[82]

By far the most compelling confirmation of the phallic meaning of the president's aircraft-carrier cakewalk was found on the hot-selling "George W. Bush Top Gun Action Figure" manufactured by Talking Presidents. I originally ordered one to use as part of the cover design for this book. The studly twelve-inch flyboy not only comes with a helmet and visor, goggles, and oxygen mask, but underneath his flight suit is a full "basket"—a genuine fake penis, apparently constructed with life-like silicone. This may not settle the debate between Sullivan and Goldstein, but it makes clear that at least one company realizes the extent to which American males need to know their president is not a Ken doll and is ready for action.

Notes

Fear and the Phallus: An Introduction

1. Corey Robin, "Closet-Case Studies," *New York Times Magazine*, December 16, 2001, 23.
2. "A Portrait of a Terrorist: From Shy Child to Single-Minded Killer," *New York Times*, October 10, 2001, national edition, B9.
3. Bob Armstrong, "The Virgin Suicides," *San Francisco Chronicle*, October 28, 2001, C3.
4. "Suspected Terrorist's Will Details Final Wishes," CNN.com, October 2, 2001, http://www.cnn.com/2001/US/10/02/inv.terrorist.will.
5. This, nevertheless, raises the question of how the phallus has come to be represented by the penis. The answer, I believe, can be found in a rationalization common to nearly all socially dominant groups, regardless of whether that domination is based on class, ethnicity, or gender. To justify its power and privileges, a dominant group will often claim an entitlement based on essential superiority, which is signified by some readily identifiable trait that is shared by all members of that group. For example, some white Americans—most notably in the early years of this nation, especially during times of slavery—have pointed to a relative lack of pigment, "whiteness," as the biological, essential distinction that marked their superiority—that rendered them, in fact, a distinct species relative to the "lower races." Things that erased distinctions, such as literacy, were suppressed. Analogously, for men in a patriarchal order, the penis has served a function similar to that of whiteness. It was and remains a visible signifier of essential difference. Within a structure of gender-based domination, such a difference is used to represent the fantasized superiority of men. Like white skin, the penis then becomes iconic of all that is noble and deservedly triumphant. It becomes the phallus.
6. Will Roscoe, "How to Become a Berdache: A Unified Analysis of Gender Diversity," in *Third Sex, Third Gender: Beyond Sexual Dimorphism in Culture and History*, ed. Gilbert Herdt (New York: Zone Books, 1994), 329–372.
7. Quoted in Lynn Hunt, *The Family Romance of the French Revolution* (Berkeley and Los Angeles: University of California Press, 1992), 158.
8. Stephen J. Ducat, *Taken In: American Gullibility and the Reagan Mythos* (Tacoma, WA: Life Sciences Press, 1988).
9. John J. Winkler, *The Constraints of Desire: The Anthropology of Sex and Gender in Ancient Greece* (New York and London: Routledge, 1990), 45–70.
10. Sidney Blumenthal, *Pledging Allegiance: The Lost Campaign of the Cold War* (New York: Harper-Collins, 1990).
11. *Los Angeles Times*, August 19, 1988.

12. *San Francisco Chronicle*, January 22, 1990, A16.
13. *New York Times*, December 21, 1989, A1.
14. *San Francisco Chronicle*, December 22, 1989.
15. *San Francisco Chronicle*, December 8, 1990.
16. Gary Wills, "The Born-Again Republicans," *New York Review of Books*, September 24, 1992, 9.
17. *San Francisco Chronicle*, August 13, 1992, A1.
18. *The American Spectator*, August, 1992, front cover.
19. Cited in *The Nation*, March 15, 1993, 328.
20. *San Francisco Chronicle*, March 30, 1993, A3.
21. *San Francisco Chronicle*, February 9, 1993, A19.
22. *Newsweek*, February 15, 1993.
23. *San Francisco Chronicle*, May 3, 1993, B3.
24. Ibid.
25. *San Francisco Chronicle*, July 20, 1993, C4.
26. Michael Savage, KSFO, San Francisco, March 16, 1998.
27. A. M. Rosenthal, "Risking the Presidency," *New York Times*, March 17, 1998, A30.
28. *New York Times*, February 24, 1998, A1.
29. *Time*, May 25, 1992, 44.
30. Carolyn Merchant, *The Death of Nature: Women, Ecology and the Scientific Revolu tion* (New York: HarperCollins, 1980).
31. Heard on National Public Radio, February 26, 1992.
32. Ofer Zur and Andrea Morrison, "Gender and War: Re-Examining Attitudes," *American Journal of Orthopsychiatry* 59, no. 4 (1989), 523–533.
33. Rebecca Flourney, research associate, Henry J. Kaiser Foundation, personal communication by e mail regarding unpublished gender cross-tabulations on attitudes toward military tribunals, January 2, 2002.
34. *New York Times*, September 14, 2001, A8.
35. *National Examiner*, 28, no. 11, 4–5.
36. *San Francisco Chronicle*, November 1, 2001, A24.
37. David Talbot, "Andrew Sullivan's Jihad," Salon.com, October 20, 2001, http://www.salon.com/news/feature/2001/10/20/sullivan.
38. *New York Times Magazine*, December 16, 2001, 23.
39. *Chronicle of Higher Education Almanac*, August 26, 1992, 13. Although the magnitude of the homophobia gender gap has decreased a bit since then, contemporary studies echo these findings (*Chronicle of Higher Education Almanac*, August 29, 2003, 17). In addition, as I will show in chapter 7, the right-wing backlash against the increasing clamor to guarantee civil rights for gays and lesbians has only been ratcheted up since the 1990s.
40. Daniel Evan Weiss, *The Great Divide: How Females and Males Really Differ* (New York: Poseidon Press, 1991), 180.
41. Maureen Dowd and Thomas Friedman, "The Fabulous Bush and Baker Boys," *New York Times Magazine*, May 6, 1990, 58.

42. Rush Limbaugh, KNBR, 680 AM, San Francisco, July, 1992.

43. *San Francisco Chronicle,* July 28, 1992, A13.

44. *San Francisco Chronicle,* August 20, 1992.

45. Heard on KGO AM, August 20, 1992.

46. *The American Spectator,* August, 1992, 9.

47. *Mother Jones,* September/October, 1992, 10.

48. Pre- and post-Republican convention polls, The Gallup Organization, Princeton, NJ, August, 1992. There was a twelve-point loss of support from men for Clinton after the convention, and no change in women's support.

49. *USA Today,* March 15, 2000, 1A.

50. *San Francisco Chronicle,* November 9, 2000, A23.

51. *New York Times,* March 12, 2000, WK14.

52. *San Francisco Chronicle,* "Sunday," February 13, 2000, 2.

53. *New York Times,* February 22, 2000, B1.

54. *San Francisco Chronicle,* March 9, 2000, A25.

55. Ibid.

56. *New York Times,* November 18, 2001, B4.

57. *San Francisco Chronicle,* November 9, 2000, A23.

58. *New York Times,* November 19, 2001, B2.

59. Jon Carroll, "Double-u Oh Em Ay En; Say It Again," *San Francisco Chronicle,* November 29, 2001, D14.

60. *New York Times,* November 19, 2001, B2.

61. *New York Times,* November, 18, B4.

62. Heard on National Public Radio, February 27, 2003.

63. Maureen Dowd, "Chest Banging, Here and There," *New York Times,* April 23, 2003, A31.

64. Maureen Dowd, "Perle's Plunder Blunder," *New York Times,* March 23, 2003, WK13.

65. Paul Krugman, "Things to Come," *New York Times,* March 18, 2003, A31.

1. From Mama's Boy to He-Man

1. Theodore Kemper, *Social Structure and Testosterone: Explorations of the Social-Bio-Social Chain* (New Brunswick, NJ: Rutgers University Press, 1990).

2. Ann Fausto-Sterling, "Beyond Difference: A Biologist's Perspective," *Journal of Social Issues* 53, no. 2 (1997), 233–258.

3. Since debates among theorists and researchers have not resolved the definitional confusion between gender and sex, let me just say that I will be using gender to refer to the personal and cultural meanings ascribed to biological sex, and the roles that are derived from those meanings. In a number of cultures, for example, there are three or four genders, even though only two sexes may be recognized. This does not mean that the issue of biological categories is not subject to cultural

influence or that it is without ambiguity—as the existence and cultural invisibility of hermaphroditic or intersex individuals can attest.

4. Carol Lynn Martin, "Attitudes and Expectations about Children with Nontraditional and Traditional Gender Roles," *Sex Roles* 22, no. 3/4 (1990), 151–165.

5. Nicole Crawford, "Understanding Children's Atypical Gender Behavior," *Monitor on Psychology* 34, no. 8 (2003), 41.

6. Eleanor E. Maccoby, *Social Development: Psychological Growth and the Parent-Child Relationship* (New York: HBJ College and School Division, 1980), 238.

7. Denis O'Donovan, "Health and Femiphobia," a paper presented at the 95th annual meeting of the American Psychological Association, 1987.

8. Denis O' Donovan and Sam McFarland, "Femiphobia Measured by Anxiety Increases Following Cross-Gender Behavior Instruction," a paper presented at the 95th annual meeting of the American Psychological Association, 1987.

9. Maccoby, *Social Development*, 145.

10. Robert L. Munroe and Ruth H. Munroe, *Cross-Cultural Human Development* (Prospect Heights, IL: Waveland Press, 1994), 115–133.

11. Scott Coltrane, "Father-Child Relationships and the Status of Women: A Cross-Cultural Study," *American Journal of Sociology* 93 (1988), 1060–1095.

12. Meyer Rabban, "Sex-Role Identification in Young Children in Two Diverse Social Groups," *Genetic Psychology Monographs* 42 (1950), 81–158.

13. Melanie Klein, *Envy and Gratitude and Other Works: 1946–1963* (New York: Delacorte, 1975).

14. Eve Feder Kittay, "Womb Envy: An Explanatory Concept," in *Mothering: Essays in Feminist Theory*, ed. Joyce Trebilcot (Savage, MD: Rowman & Littlefield Publishers, Inc., 1983), 94–128.

15. Munroe and Munroe, 125–131.

16. Ibid.

17. Alan Dundes, *Parsing Through Customs: Essays by a Freudian Folklorist* (Madison: The University of Wisconsin Press, 1987), 145–166; Munroe and Munroe, 125–131.

18. Phillip E. Slater, *The Glory of Hera: Greek Mythology and the Greek Family* (Boston: Beacon Press, 1968).

19. Aeschylus, *The Oresteia*, trans. Douglas Young (Norman: University of Oklahoma Press, 1974), 122.

20. Kittay, 113; Carolyn Merchant, *The Death of Nature: Women, Ecology and the Scientific Revolution* (New York: HarperCollins, 1980), 155–163; Rolf E. Muuss, *Theories of Adolescence*, 4th ed. (New York: Random House, 1982), 16–17.

21. Dundes, 158.

22. Nor Hall and Warren R. Dawson, *Broodmales* (Dallas: Spring Publications, Inc., 1989), 26–27.

23. Gilbert Herdt, *The Sambia: Ritual and Gender in New Guinea* (New York: Holt, Rineholt and Winston, 1987).

24. Numerous cross-cultural studies have found a high correlation between the exis-

tence of male initiation rituals in a culture and the inequality between men and women, the physical and psychological absence of fathers from children care, a high degree of sex segregation, and the disparagement of women. See Munroe and Munroe, 124–133.

25. Ruth Munroe, "Pregnancy Symptoms Among Expectant American Fathers: An Inquiry into the Psychological Meaning" (Doctoral dissertation, Harvard University, 1964).

26. Nancy Chodorow, "The Psychoanalytic Sociology of Gender," in *Advances in Psychoanalytic Sociology*, eds. Jerome Rabow, Gerald M. Platt, and Marion S. Goldman (Malabar, FL: Robert E. Krieger Publishing, Inc., 1987), 113.

27. Dundes, 166.

28. Diane Elise, "Unlawful Entry: Male Fears of Psychic Penetration," *Psychoanalytic Dialogues* 11, no. 4 (2001), 499–531; "Gender Repertoire: Body, Mind, and Bisexuality," *Psychoanalytic Dialogues* 8, no. 3 (1998), 353–371.

29. In research on the effects of subliminal auditory input on the experience of bodily boundaries, females were markedly less threatened than males by the sensation that "some force has gained entry" to their interior. See S. Fisher, "Conditions Affecting Boundary Response to Messages Out of Awareness," *Journal of Nervous and Mental Disease* 162, no. 5, 313–322.

30. Ian Hoffman, "Bush Presses Lab Nuke Research: Memo Asks Scientists at UC Labs to Explore New Types of Nuclear Weapons," Oaklandtribune.com, December 11, 2003.

31. Quoted by Jessica Benjamin, "An Intersubjective View of Gender" (lecture, The Twentieth Professional Conference, Marin Chapter of the California Association of Marriage and Family Therapists, Mill Valley, CA, March 23, 2002).

32. Susan S. Basow, *Gender Stereotypes and Roles*, 3rd ed. (Pacific Grove, CA: Brooks/Cole Publishing Company, 1992), 199.

33. Leonard L. Glass, "Man's Man/Ladies' Man: Motifs of Hypermasculinity," *Psychiatry* 47 (1984), 260–278.

34. *San Francisco Chronicle*, March 29, 1993, A6.

35. *San Francisco Chronicle*, October 15, 1993, A23.

36. *San Francisco Examiner*, May 2, 1993, A15.

37. Cited by Virginia Goldner, "When Love Hurts: Abuse and Victimization in Intimate Relationships," *Psychoanalytic Inquiry* (forthcoming).

38. Stephen A. Mitchell, *Can Love Last? The Fate of Romance over Time* (New York: W. W. Norton and Company, 2002), 135–144.

39. Helen Block Lewis, "The Role of Shame in Depression," in *The Role of Shame in Symptom Formation*, ed. H. B. Lewis (Hillsdale, NJ: Earlbaum, 1987), 11.

40. *New York Times*, January 9, 1993, 1.

41. *San Francisco Chronicle*, March 2, 1994.

42. Gerda Lerner, *The Creation of Patriarchy* (New York and Oxford: Oxford University Press, 1987), 116–117.

43. While masculinity has been defined as dominance for many thousands of years, this in no way naturalizes that definition—nor does it establish its inevitability. Patriarchy, like slavery (a tradition just as ancient), is a social arrangement that can be chosen or refused.

44. Leslie R. Brody, Serra Muderrisoglu, and Ora Nakash-Eisikovits, "Emotions, Defenses, and Gender," in *The Psychodynamics of Gender and Gender Role*, eds. Robert F. Bornstein and Joseph M. Masling (Washington, DC: American Psychological Association, 2002), 225.

45. H. K. Koh et al., *Journal of the American Academy of Dermatology* 267 (1992), 914.

46. Molly Ivins, "Mysteries of the Markets," *San Francisco Chronicle*, April 18, 1994, A19.

47. Promotional material for *Men's Health* received May 1994.

48. *San Francisco Chronicle*, June 27, 1988, A9.

49. Quoted in *Washington Post*, March 11, 1999, A1.

50. John Snavey and Linda Son, "Sex-Identity Development Among Kibbutz-Born Males: A Test of the Whiting Hypothesis," *Ethos* 14, no. 2 (1986), 99–119.

51. The findings of Snavey and Son's study are especially interesting in light of research conducted by an American military psychiatrist, George R. Brown ("Transsexuals in the Military: Flight into Hypermasculinity," *Archives of Sexual Behavior* 17, no. 6 [1988], 527–537) on (presurgical) transsexual men in the military. These were men consciously trying to overcome a cross-gender identity. In other words, they had not come to accept it, viewed it as a shameful pathology, and looked to the military and its hypermasculine milieu to "cure" them. Some of the subjects had completed tours of combat duty, others were veterans, and some were on active duty at the time of the study. However, according to Brown, in 60 percent of the men, their "hypermasculine defenses" broke down, leading to premature discharge. These soldiers seemed to be struggling in a conscious and more dramatic way with dynamics similar to those that drove the kibbutz-born men to volunteer for the most dangerous missions possible.

52. Karen Endicott, "Fathering in an Egalitarian Society," in *Father-Child Relations: Cultural and Biosocial Contexts*, ed. Barry S. Hewlett (New York: Aldine De Gruyter, 1992), 282.

53. Ibid., 286.

54. Ibid., 285.

55. Ibid., 284.

56. Barry S. Hewlett, "Husband-Wife Reciprocity and the Father-Infant Relationship among Aka Pygmies," in *Father-Child Relations: Cultural and Biosocial Contexts*, ed. Barry S. Hewlett (New York: Aldine De Gruyter, 1992), 162.

57. Ibid., 164.

58. Barry Hewlett, "Intimate Fathers: Patterns of Paternal Holding among Aka Pygmies," in *Father's Role in Cross-Cultural Perspective*, ed. Michael E. Lamb (New York: Erlbaum, 1987), 326.

2. The Miss Nancy Man in Nineteenth-century America

1. Lawrence W. Reed, "French Fried by the Welfare State," Pittsburglive.com, November 19, 2003, http://www.pittsburglive.com/x/tribune-review/opinion/guest/s_159204.html; "Beyond Do-Not-Call: the FTC Agenda," Heritage.org, http://www.heritage.org/Press/Events/ev111303a.cfm; Michael D. Tanner, "Do We Really Need a Surgeon General?" The Heartland Institute Web site, November/December 1997, http://www.heartland.org?Article.cfm%3artld'819.

2. David G. Pugh, *Sons of Liberty: The Masculine Mind in Nineteenth-Century America* (Westport, CT: Greenwood Press, 1983), 36.

3. Ibid., 35.

4. Ibid., 28.

5. Mark C. Carnes, *Secret Ritual and Manhood in Victorian America* (New Haven and London: Yale University Press, 1989), 108.

6. E. Anthony Rotundo, *American Manhood: Transformations in Masculinity from the Revolution to the Modern Era* (New York: Basic Books, 1993), 250.

7. Jeffery P. Hantover, "The Boy Scouts and the Validation of Masculinity," *Journal of Social Issues* 34, no. 1 (1978), 188.

8. Gail Bederman, *Manliness and Civilization: A Cultural History of Gender and Race in the United States, 1880–1917* (Chicago and London: University of Chicago Press, 1995), 12.

9. Ibid.

10. Pugh, *Sons of Liberty*, xix.

11. Rotundo, *American Manhood*, 4.

12. Kristin L. Hoganson, *Fighting for American Manhood: How Gender Politics Provoked the Spanish-American and Philippine-American Wars* (New Haven and London: Yale University Press, 1998), 23.

13. Ibid., 23.

14. Ibid., 36–37.

15. Bruce Curtis, "The Wimp Factor," *American Heritage*, November, 1989, 43.

16. Hoganson, *Fighting for American Manhood*, 23.

17. John Winkler, *The Constraints of Desire: The Anthropology of Sex and Gender in Ancient Greece* (New York and London: Routledge, 1990), 45–90.

18. Bederman, *Manliness and Civilization*, 12–13. My discussion of the shift in nineteenth-century notions of manhood draws largely from this excellent historical study of the intersecting discourses of gender, race, and civilization.

19. Ibid., 17.

20. Ibid., 12–14.

21. James D. Norris, *Advertising and the Transformation of American Society, 1865–1920* (New York: Greenwood Press, 1990).

22. Tom Lutz, *American Nervousness, 1903: An Anecdotal History* (Ithaca, NY: Cornell University Press, 1989), 4.

23. Ibid., 4–7.

24. Robert Howland Chase, *Mental Medicine and Nursing* (Philadelphia and London: J.B. Lippincott Company, 1918), 100–101.

25. Lutz, *American Nervousness, 1903*, 20–21.

26. Bederman, *Manliness and Civilization*, 84–88.

27. Ibid., 87.

28. Ibid., 86.

29. Ibid., 77–120.

30. Ibid., 15.

31. Ibid.

32. Rotundo, *American Manhood*, 256.

33. A. E. Willis, *Human Nature or Men and Women Exposed* (Chicago: Globe Book Company, 1892), 60.

34. Rotundo, *American Manhood*, 258–259.

35. Carnes, *Secret Ritual and Manhood in Victorian America*, 1.

36. Ibid., 5.

37. Ibid., 8.

38. Ibid., 100.

39. Ibid., 119.

40. Ibid.

41. Alex Jokay, "Burning Desires: Curing Sexual Maladies the American Way, circa 1900," *Libido* 5, no. 2 (1993), 22–26.

42. Joe L. Dubbert, "Progressivism and the Masculinity Crisis," *The Psychoanalytic Review* 61, no. 3 (1974), 451–452.

43. Hantover, *The Boy Scouts and the Validation of Masculinity*, 186.

44. Rotundo, *American Manhood*, 222–232.

45. Hoganson, *Fighting for American Manhood*, 95.

46. Ibid., 232.

47. Ibid., 224.

48. Ibid., 241.

49. Ibid., 240.

50. Dubbert, "Progressivism and the Masculinity Crisis," 446.

51. Alan Dundes, "Into the Endzone for a Touchdown: A Psychoanalytic Consideration of American Football," *Western Folklore* 37 (1978), 75–88.

52. Alan Dundes, *Parsing through Customs: Essays by a Freudian Folklorist* (Madison: University of Wisconsin Press, 1987), 184.

53. Of course, there is nothing inherently "feminine" about homosexuality. It is in the mind of the homophobe that this link is made.

54. Michael Paul Rogin, *Fathers and Children: Andrew Jackson and the Subjugation of the American Indian* (New Brunswick and London: Transaction Publishers, 1991).

55. Pugh, *Sons of Liberty*, 16.

56. Hoganson, *Fighting for American Manhood*, 16.

57. Ibid., 90.

58. Ibid., 18–19.

59. Ibid., 20.
60. Ibid.
61. Curtis, "The Wimp Factor," 48.
62. Ibid., 44.
63. Rotundo, *American Manhood*, 273.
64. Dubbert, "Progressivism and the Masculinity Crisis," 452–453.
65. Ibid., 448–452.
66. Bederman, *Manliness and Civilization*, 171.
67. Ibid.
68. Ibid., 170–171.
69. Ibid., 175.
70. Ibid.
71. Ibid.
72. Ibid.
73. Ibid., 185.
74. Ibid., 188.
75. Ibid., 187.
76. Ibid., 179.
77. Ibid., 185.
78. Ibid., 189.
79. Ibid., 200–201.
80. Ibid., 203.
81. *San Francisco Chronicle*, December 6, 2003, 1.
82. Rotundo, *American Manhood*, 472–473.
83. Ibid., 274–279.
84. Ibid., 83–84.
85. Leonard Pitt, personal communication.
86. Anne McClintock, *Imperial Leather: Race, Gender, and Sexuality in the Colonial Contest* (New York and London: Routledge, 1995), 25.

3. The Wimp Factor

1. *Newsweek*, September 26, 1988, 19. For the sake of readability, I have taken the liberty of reinserting the missing but obvious few letters in "fucking" that the more squeamish *Newsweek* editors had replaced with asterisks.
2. *Newsweek*, May 23, 1988, 21.
3. Sidney Blumenthal, *Pledging Allegiance: The Last Campaign of the Cold War* (New York: Harper-Collins, 1990), 51.
4. Alan Elms, *Uncovering Lives: The Uneasy Alliance of Biography and Psychology* (New York: Oxford University Press, 1994), 206–219.
5. Blumenthal, *Pledging Allegiance*, 50, 73.
6. *Marin Independent Journal*, September 27, 1988, A1.
7. Ibid.

8. Ibid.
9. *San Francisco Chronicle*, May 10, 1988, A9.
10. Blumenthal, *Pledging Allegiance*, 72.
11. Christopher Matthews column, *San Francisco Examiner*, March 20, 1988.
12. Paul Taylor, *See How They Run: Electing the President in an Age of Mediocracy* (New York: Alfred A. Knopf, 1990), 18.
13. Ibid., 196–201.
14. Blumenthal, *Pledging Allegiance*, 72.
15. *Los Angeles Times*, August 19, 1988.
16. Blumenthal, *Pledging Allegiance*, 284.
17. Ibid.
18. Ibid., 300–301.
19. *San Francisco Chronicle*, September 15, 1988, 1.
20. Ibid.
21. Blumenthal, *Pledging Allegiance*, 312–313.
22. Ibid., 313.
23. Ibid., 315.
24. Taylor, *See How They Run*, 193
25. Ibid., 221–213.
26. Ibid., 213.
27. Ibid., 214–215.
28. As it turned out, reality was a bit more complicated. According to an article in the September 8, 1988, *Houston Chronicle*, Bush had his own prison furlough problem. He had helped to found a Houston halfway house for felons given an early release or parole. The reporter discovered that "one of its residents [had] raped and murdered the wife of a Pasadena minister the year before." While Dukakis did not make an issue out of this event, he did, at the end of the campaign, make mention of two murders committed in the early 1970s by prisoners furloughed in California under then-governor Ronald Reagan, and a rape and murder of a young mother by a federal prisoner furloughed under the auspices of President Reagan. (*San Francisco Chronicle*, September 15, 1988, A10.) But at this point in the campaign, these revelations only warranted a few column inches buried in the back pages of newspapers. The media never conferred official scandal status on these events.
29. Taylor, *See How They Run*, 208.
30. Montague Kern, *30-Second Politics: Political Advertising in the Eighties* (New York: Praeger Publishers, 1989), 30.
31. *San Francisco Chronicle*, September 24, 1988, A1.
32. Ibid.
33. Ibid., A7.
34. Blumenthal, *Pledging Allegiance*, 202.
35. *San Francisco Chronicle*, October 15, 1988, A8.
36. Blumenthal, *Pledging Allegiance*, 308.

37. Taylor, *See How They Run*, 208.
38. *San Francisco Chronicle*, October 15, 1988, A8.
39. *Los Angeles Times*, August 16, 1988, 12.
40. Blumenthal, *Pledging Allegiance*, 292–293.
41. Ibid., 296.
42. *Newsweek*, April 8, 1991, 17.
43. Ibid., 292.
44. *San Francisco Chronicle*, October 18, 1988, A12.
45. *San Francisco Chronicle*, November 9, 1988, 1.
46. *New York Times*, January 21, 10.
47. Paul Erickson, *Reagan Speaks: The Making of an American Myth* (New York: New York University Press, 1985), 100.
48. Lynn Chancer, *Sadomasochism in Everyday Life: The Dynamics of Power and Powerlessness* (New Brunswick, NJ: Rutgers University Press, 1992), 93–124.
49. Of course, the state does perform these functions, but largely as the executor of corporate interests. Even a cursory glance at the powerful economic forces that fund political campaigns can easily confirm the shameless mercenary role of most senators and congresspersons, as well as presidents.
50. Richard Nixon, *No More Vietnams* (New York: Arbor House, 1985), 13, 19; Susan Jeffords, *The Remasculinization of America: Gender and the Vietnam War* (Bloomington and Indianapolis: Indiana University Press, 1989), 43–45.
51. Edwin Diamond and Stephen Bates, *The Spot: The Rise of Political Advertising on Television* (Cambridge, MA: MIT Press, 1984), 286.
52. Lloyd de Mause, *Reagan's America* (New York: Creation Roots, Inc. Publishers, 1984), 29–35.
53. *New York Times*, January 30, 1980, 18.
54. *Time*, January 14, 1980, 32.
55. Lynda E. Boose, "Techno-muscularity and the 'Boy Eternal': From the Quagmire to the Gulf," in *Gendering War Talk*, eds. Miriam Cooke and Angela Woollacott (Princeton, NJ: Princeton University Press, 1993), 67–106; Susan Jeffords, *Hard Bodies: Hollywood Masculinity in the Reagan Era* (New Brunswick, NJ: Rutgers University Press, 1994).
56. Cited in *Extra* 3, no. 8 (1990): 3.
57. *Los Angeles Times*, January 6, 1990, A4.
58. *New York Times*, March 2, 1991, A7.
59. *New York Times*, January 21, 1995, A14; *San Francisco Chronicle*, "Sunday," August 20, 1995, 1; Carol Cohn, "War, Wimps, and Women," in *Gendering War Talk*, eds. Cooke and Woollacott, 243.
60. *Extra* 4, no. 3 (1991).
61. One University of Massachusetts study found that the more respondents watched television, the less they knew about the details of the Gulf War and the issues that underlay it, especially if those facts reflected poorly on the Bush administration (Ibid., 11).

62. "The Best Cartoons of Desert Storm," *National Forum* 4, 1993.

63. Cohn, in *Gendering War Talk*, eds. Cooke and Woollacott, 240–241.

64. "The Best Cartoons of Desert Storm," 37.

65. Ibid., 4.

66. Cohn, in *Gendering War Talk*, eds. Cooke and Woollacott, 236.

67. John M. Broughton, "The Bomb in the Bathroom: Anality in High Tech Warfare," in *Recent Trends in Theoretical Psychology, Volume 4*, eds. I. Lubek, R. van Hezewijk, G. Pheterson, and C. Tolman (New York: Springer, 1994), 7.

68. Ibid.

69. Ibid.

70. *National Examiner* 28, no. 11, 1990, 4–5.

71. Ernest Larsen, "Gulf War TV," *Jump Cut: A Review of Contemporary Media* 36, 1991, 8.

72. *San Francisco Chronicle*, March 21, 1991, A8.

73. Ibid.

74. Ibid., 34.

75. The conflation of warfare and football reached its ultimate expression in a joint venture between National Football League Films and the U.S. Defense Department to produce a "Highlights of Desert Storm" video. Apparently oblivious to the psychosexual links between the two manly endeavors, the president of NFL films, Steve Sabol, explained the reason for his special covenant with the Defense Department: "The same spirit and ideology that football glorifies and inspires— discipline, devotion, commitment to a cause—is also the spirit necessary for a successful military endeavor." (Larsen, "Gulf War TV," 9.)

76. *San Francisco Chronicle*, September 27, 1991, A26.

77. *Newsweek*, March 25, 1991, 39.

78. *New York Times*, June, 29, 1993, A5.

79. *Pacific Sun*, June 30, 1993, 9.

80. *San Francisco Chronicle*, November 15, 1991, A31.

81. Garry Wills, "The Born-Again Republicans," *New York Review of Books*, September 24, 1992, 9.

82. *San Francisco Chronicle*, February 19, 1992, A2.

83. *San Francisco Chronicle*, February 20, 1992, A20.

84. Ibid., A18.

85. *San Francisco Chronicle*, July 28, 1992, A13.

86. *The New York Times*, August 26, 1992, A17.

87. *The American Spectator*, August, 1992, 65. Interestingly, the same ad promoted T-shirts that said "Pave the Rainforest," illustrating the link between misogyny and antienvironmental attitudes that will be explored further in chapter 6.

88. *Time*, September 14, 1992, 30.

89. Garry Wills, "The Born-Again Republicans," 13.

90. *San Francisco Chronicle*, August 24, 1992, A16.

91. *Newsweek*, July 13, 1992, 47.

92. *San Francisco Chronicle,* June 22, 1992, 2.
93. Ibid.
94. *McNeil/Lehrer News Hour,* PBS, July 10, 1992.
95. Maureen Dowd, "Bush vs. the 'Billionaire Bubba,'" *San Francisco Chronicle,* June 10, 1992, D3.
96. Ibid.
97. *San Francisco Chronicle,* January 23, 1992, A11; February 18, 1992, A16; March 10, 1992, A16; *New York Times,* September 13, 1992, E6.
98. *Saturday Night Live,* NBC TV, October 10, 1992.
99. *San Francisco Chronicle,* August 5, 1992, A4.
100. *San Francisco Examiner,* October 25, 1992, A16.
101. *New York Times,* September 19, 1992, 6.
102. *San Francisco Chronicle,* August 20, 1992, A4.
103. *New York Times,* October 10, 1992, 1.
104. *New York Times,* November 29, 1992, 1.
105. *New York Times,* November 5, 1992, B9.
106. Ibid.

4. Vaginas with Teeth and Castrating First Ladies

1. It should be noted that while the dialogue in the clinical vignettes recounted in this chapter are verbatim, I've disguised other aspects of these cases to protect the patients' anonymity.
2. Merry E. Wiesner, *Women and Gender in Early Modern Europe* (Cambridge: Cambridge University Press, 1993), 218–238.
3. Heinrich Kramer and James Sprenger, *The Malleus Maleficarum* (New York: Dover Publications, 1971), 43.
4. Ibid., viii.
5. Erich Neuman, *The Great Mother: An Analysis of the Archetype* (Princeton, NJ: Princeton University Press, 1955), 168.
6. Wolfgang Lederer, *The Fear of Women* (New York: Harcourt Brace Jovanovich, Inc., 1968), 46.
7. Ibid., 44.
8. Ibid., 45–46.
9. Ibid., 49.
10. Ibid. 46.
11. Jill Raitt, "The Vagina Dentata and the Immaculatus Uterus Divini Fontis," *The Journal of the American Academy of Religion* XLVII, no. 3 (1979), 415–431.
12. Bram Dijkstra, *Idols of Perversity: Fantasies of Feminine Evil in Fin-de-Siècle Culture* (New York: Oxford University Press, 1986), 294.
13. Carol Clover, *Men, Women and Chainsaws: Gender in the Modern Horror Film* (Princeton, NJ: Princeton University Press, 1992), 6–7.

14. Barbara Creed, *The Monstrous Feminine: Film, Feminism, Psychoanalysis* (London and New York: Routledge, 1993).
15. Clover, *Men, Women, and Chainsaws*, 234.
16. Ibid., 26–27.
17. Creed, *The Monstrous Feminine*, 107.
18. Ibid.
19. Kramer and Sprenger, *The Malleus Maleficarum*, 47.
20. Ibid., 121.
21. Klaus Theweleit, *Male Fantasies, Volume 1: Women, Floods, Bodies, History* (Minneapolis: University of Minnesota Press, 1987), 43.
22. *People*, December 13, 1993.
23. Ibid., 94.
24. *Marin Independent Journal*, November 26, 1993, D2.
25. *People*, 95.
26. Ibid., 96.
27. *New York Times*, January 23, 1994, 13.
28. *Pacific Sun*, June 22, 1994, 7.
29. *San Francisco Chronicle*, June 19, 2003, A2.
30. Robert Crumb, *HUP: The Comic for Modern Guys*, no. 4, 1992.
31. Howard Eilberg-Schwartz and Wendy Doniger, eds. *Off with Her Head: The Denial of Women's Identity in Myth, Religion, and Culture* (Berkeley and Los Angeles: University of California Press, 1995).
32. Howard Eilberg-Schwartz, "The Nakedness of a Woman's Voice, the Pleasure in a Man's Mouth: An Oral History of Ancient Judaism," in Eilberg-Schwartz and Doniger, eds., *Off with Her Head*, 167.
33. Ibid., 168.
34. Ibid., 169.
35. Ibid., 173–174.
36. Molly Myerwitz Levine, "The Gendered Grammar of Ancient Mediterranean Hair," in Eilberg-Schwartz and Doniger, eds., *Off with Her Head*, 77–79.
37. Ibid., 92–95.
38. Ibid., 93.
39. Phillip Slater, *The Glory of Hera: Greek Mythology and the Greek Family* (Boston: Beacon Press, 1968), 309.
40. Ibid., 331.
41. Sigmund Freud, "Medusa's Head," in *Collected Papers, Volume V* (New York: Basic Books, 1959), 105–106.
42. Creed, *The Monstrous Feminine*, 111. This oversight on Freud's part seems like a kind of repression, an unconsciously motivated undertheorizing akin to his picture of psychosexual development, in which he locates the young boy's castration fears entirely in the image of the oedipal father, and ignores the likely ambivalence toward the powerful, sexualized mother, even when his clinical data suggest other-

wise. Barbara Creed elaborates on this conceptual problem in her compelling reinterpretation of Freud's case study of "Little Hans" (Creed, *The Monstrous Feminine*, 88–104).

43. Carol Delaney, "Untangling the Meanings of Hair in a Turkish Society," in Eilberg-Schwartz and Doniger, eds., *Off with Her Head*, 53–75.

44. Ibid., 60.

45. Ibid., 68.

46. Ibid., 68–69.

47. Mary Rose D'Angelo, "Veils, Virgins, and the Tongues of Men and Angels: Women's Heads in Early Christianity," in Eilberg-Schwartz and Doniger, eds., *Off with Her Head*, 134.

48. Susan Faludi, "The Power Laugh," *The New York Times*, December 20, 1992, E13.

49. Barbara Burrell, *Public Opinion, the First Ladyship and Hillary Rodham Clinton* (New York and London: Garland Publishing, Inc., 1997), 21.

50. *New York Times*, August 25, 1996, 1.

51. *New York Times Magazine*, November 12, 1995, 37.

52. *New York Times*, July 14, 1996, Section 4, 7.

53. *New York Times*, September 27, 2000, A1.

54. *New York Times*, December 20, 1992, 13.

55. Heard on *Politically Incorrect*, Comedy Central, May 28, 1997.

56. *Newsweek*, January 10, 1994, 19.

57. Fred Barnes, "What Health-Care Crisis?" *The American Spectator*, May 1993, 20–23.

58. *The American Spectator*, May 1993, 73.

59. Ibid.

60. Ibid., 75.

61. Garry Wills, "A Doll's House?" *The New York Review of Books*, September 22, 1992, 6–10.

62. Burrell, *Public Opinion, the First Ladyship, and Hillary Rodham Clinton*, 13–17.

63. Garry Wills, "A Doll's House?" 10.

64. Susan Jeffords, *Hard Bodies: Hollywood Masculinity in the Reagan Era* (New Brunswick, NJ: Rutgers University Press, 1994), 10.

65. Ibid.

66. Burrell, *Public Opinion, the First Ladyship, and Hillary Rodham Clinton*, 54.

67. Ibid., 100.

68. Ibid., 37.

69. Ibid., 66–70.

70. Ibid.

71. Ibid., 132.

72. Ibid.

73. *Time*, September 14, 1992, 28.

74. Burrell, *Public Opinion, the First Ladyship, and Hillary Rodham Clinton*, 101.

75. Ibid.

76. Ibid., 133.

77. *New York Times,* July, 16, 1996, C18.
78. Burrell, *Public Opinion, the First Ladyship, and Hillary Rodham Clinton,* 41.
79. David Brock, *Blinded by the Right: The Conscience of an Ex-Conservative* (New York: Crown Publishers, 2002), 87–120.
80. Daniel Wattenberg, "The Lady Macbeth of Little Rock," *The American Spectator,* August 1992, 25–32.
81. Ibid., 28.
82. Ibid., 26.
83. Ibid., 30.
84. Ibid.
85. Ibid., 31.
86. Vera L. Bullough, Brenda Shelton, and Sarah Slavin, *The Subordinated Sex: A History of Attitudes Toward Women* (Athens, GA: University of Georgia Press, 1988), 259.
87. Henry Louis Gates, "Hating Hillary," *The New Yorker,* February 26 and March 4, 1996, 124.
88. *Time,* May 23, 1994.
89. Burrell, *Public Opinion, the First Ladyship, and Hillary Rodham Clinton,* 114.
90. *The Hillary Clinton Quarterly,* Winter 1994, 11.
91. Burrell, *Public Opinion, the First Ladyship, and Hillary Rodham Clinton,* 30.
92. The Norman verb "fornicate" eventually came to replace the more crude Saxon term "fuck," which itself came from the Old English word *fokken,* meaning "to beat against." (Charles Panati, *The Extraordinary Origins of Everyday Things* [New York: Harper and Row, 1987], 347.) Thus, even in its origins, sexual and violent connotations were blurred. Interestingly, *fock* in Swedish means penis. (*The Random House Dictionary of the English Language,* 2nd Edition Unabridged, [New York: Random House, 1987], 773.) Regardless of the above, it might be argued that "fuck" is a gender-neutral word. While this is true in a literal sense, when viewed in the historical and cultural contexts of male dominance, wherein sexual agency and agency in general are often seen as masculine prerogatives, "fuck" seems to be a decidedly phallic verb, even when describing women's actions.
93. Mark Ebner and Jim Mauro, "How to Win Friends and Influence Politicians," *Spy,* October, 1995, 42–49.
94. Linda Williams, *Hard Core: Power, Pleasure, and the Frenzy of the Visible* (Berkeley and Los Angeles: University of California Press, 1989), 100–103.
95. *Slick Times,* September/October 1994, 22.
96. Ibid., 35.
97. *Slick Times,* Spring 1994, 21.
98. *The Big Clinton Joke Book* (Valley Center, CA: Slick Times, 1995), January 1995, 23, 26.
99. *San Francisco Chronicle,* May 26, 1994, A30; *Newsweek,* December 26, 1994, 52; *San Francisco Chronicle,* October 4, 1993, A19; *New York Times,* November 29, 1992, 6.
100. *The American Spectator,* June 1994.

101. Sigmund Freud, "Fetishism," *The Standard Edition of the Complete Psychological Works of Sigmund Freud*, Volume 21, James Strachey, ed. and trans. (London: Hogarth, 1953–1966), 147–158. For a feminist reading of Freud's theory of fetishism as applied to popular culture, see Laura Mulvey, *Visual and Other Pleasures* (Bloomington and Indianapolis: Indiana University Press, 1989), 6–13.

102. Molly Ivins, "Gummed by Rush," *San Francisco Chronicle*, October 14, 1993. A24.

103. Leah Garchik, "Personals," *San Francisco Chronicle*, February 22, 1995, E8.

104. *New York Times*, January 15, 1995, 2; Burrell, *Public Opinion, the First Ladyship, and Hillary Rodham Clinton*, 25.

105. Ibid., 26.

106. Ibid., 27.

107. *New York Times*, January 10, 1995, 1.

108. *New York Times*, February 18, 1995, 8.

109. *New York Times*, April 6, 1995, 1.

110. *New York Times*, October 15, 1996, 16.

111. Ibid.

112. *New York Times*, August 25, 1996, 1.

113. David Brock, *The Seduction of Hillary Clinton* (New York: The Free Press, 1996).

114. *New York Times Magazine*, November 12, 1995, 37.

115. *New York Times*, September 16, 1998, A1.

116. Maureen Dowd, "Her Brute Strength," *New York Times*, September 17, 2000, WK19.

117. John M. Broder, "The Devil and Political Fund-Raising," *New York Times*, December 10, 2000, WK4.

118. Ibid.

119. Ibid.

5. Permutations of the Presidential Phallus

1. *Slick Times*, Spring 1994, 21.

2. *New York Times*, March 1, 1998, WK5.

3. Maureen Dowd, "About Last Night," *New York Times*, May 28, 2000, WK11.

4. *New York Times*, July 15, 2000, A9.

5. Richard Berke, "Who's a Liberal! Is Clinton One? Was Nixon?" *New York Times*, September 29, 1996, Section 4, 1.

6. Ibid.

7. *New York Times*, November 23, 1994, 11.

8. *The Big Clinton Joke Book* (Valley Center, CA: Slick Times, 1995).

9. Ibid., 4.

10. Ibid., 76, 106, 143.

11. Ibid., 6.

12. *San Francisco Chronicle*, March 30, 1993, A3.

13. *San Francisco Chronicle,* March 16, 1996, E3.

14. Rush Limbaugh, KNBR, 680 AM, San Francisco, January 10, 1994.

15. Frank Rich column, *New York Times,* January 22, 1997, A19.

16. *San Francisco Chronicle,* August 27, 1993, A2.

17. With the various Clinton sex scandals obviously in mind, Christopher Hitchens said of the president's "don't ask, don't tell" policy, "Has there ever been a Chief Executive who stood to gain more by such an injunction?" (*The Nation,* July 7, 1997, 8).

18. David Corn, "CPAC Comeback?" *The Nation,* March 15, 1993, 328.

19. *San Francisco Chronicle,* March 19, 1993, A6.

20. *New York Times,* May 11, 1993, 1; *San Francisco Chronicle,* May 11, 1993, A1.

21. Jeffrey Schmalz, "From Midshipman to Gay-Rights Advocate," *New York Times,* February 4, 1993, B1.

22. *New York Times,* February 1, 1993, A8.

23. *New York Times,* February 14, 1995, A6.

24. *San Francisco Chronicle,* February 2, 1993, A4; *New York Times,* February 4, 1993, A8; *San Francisco Examiner,* August 8, 1993, A4.

25. *San Francisco Chronicle,* February 26, 1997, A3.

26. *Slick Times,* Spring 1994.

27. *New York Times,* February 14, 1995, A6.

28. *National Gallery of Cartoons,* November 27, 1994, 3; *National Gallery of Cartoons,* December 4, 1994, 16; *Newsweek,* December 26, 1994–January 2, 1995, 105.

29. Jeffrey Klein, "Newt's War on Clinton Is Just Beginning," *San Francisco Chronicle,* December 23, 1994, A27.

30. Jules Feiffer, "Newt the Brute," "Sunday," *San Francisco Chronicle,* January 22, 1995, 6.

31. *Gallery of Cartoons,* February 26, 1995, 6.

32. "Sunday Punch," *San Francisco Chronicle,* June 19, 1994, 1.

33. *San Francisco Examiner,* October 3, 1993, A16.

34. *New York Times,* June 8, 1996, 8.

35. Michael Savage, KSFO, 560 AM, San Francisco, July 18, 1996.

36. Christopher Matthews, "Clinton Courts Angry White Males," *San Francisco Examiner,* January, 15, 1995, A2.

37. *New York Times,* January 10, 1996, A7.

38. *San Francisco Chronicle,* January 1, 1999, A4.

39. Maureen Dowd, "Father's Little Helper," *New York Times,* April 26, 1998, WK15.

40. Shann Nix, "King of Schwing," *San Francisco Examiner Magazine,* June 14, 1998, 20.

41. Leah Garchick, "Personals," *San Francisco Chronicle,* December 2, 1998, E8.

42. Maureen Dowd, "1600 Madison Avenue," *New York Times,* August 16, 1998, WK15.

43. Michael Savage, KSFO, 560 AM, San Francisco, March 16, 1998.

44. George Will, "A Problem of Asterisks," *Newsweek,* February 2, 1998, 72.

45. A. M. Rosenthal, "Risking the Presidency," *New York Times,* March 17, 1998, A30.

46. *60 Minutes,* CBS, March 15, 1998.

47. *New York Times,* June 11, 1998, A11.

48. *New York Times,* January 24, 1998, A11.

49. *Newsweek,* February 8, 1998, 17.

50. *Newsweek,* March 23, 1998, 21.

51. *Slick Times,* May/June 1998, 8.

52. Ibid., 2.

53. Maureen Dowd, "In All His Feathered Glory," *New York Times,* July 8, 1998, A21.

54. Ibid.

55. Ibid.

56. Maureen Dowd, "Maladroit Du Seigneur," *New York Times,* September 30, 1998, A23.

57. Jane Gallop with Lauren Berlant, "Loose Lips," in *Our Monica, Ourselves: The Clinton Affair and the National Interest,* eds. Lauren Berlant and Lisa Duggan (New York and London: New York University Press, 2001), 248. My thoughts here owe much to the provocative and fruitful dialogue between Gallop and Berlant.

58. John J. Winkler, *The Constraints of Desire: The Anthropology of Sex and Gender in Ancient Greece* (New York and London: Routledge, 1990), 45–70.

59. Christopher Hitchens, "Deep in the Heart of Texas," *The Nation,* February 5, 2001, 9.

60. Ibid.

6. Voting Like a Man

1. Steven Stark, "Gap Politics," theatlantic.com, July 1996, http://www.theatlantic.com/issues/96jul/gender/gender.htm.

2. Arlie Hochschild, "Let Them Eat War," alternet.org, October 2, 2003, http://www.alternet.org/story.html?StoryID=16885.

3. Ibid.

4. "Democrats, Unions Blast GOP as House Backs Bush Rules on Overtime," usatoday.com, July 11, 2003, http://www.commondreams.org/headlines03/0711-09.htm.

5. Ibid.

6. David Barstow, "U.S. Rarely Seeks Charges for Deaths in Workplace," *New York Times,* December 22, 2003, A1.

7. Ronald Brownstein, "For 2004, Bush Has Strength in the White Male Numbers," latimes.com, December 28, 2003, http://www.latimes.com/news/politics/la-na-men28dec28,1,6148891.story?coll'la-home-headlines.

8. Ibid.

9. Ibid.

10. Arlie Hochschild, "Let Them Eat War."

11. Ibid.

12. Ibid.
13. Ibid.
14. Marjorie Connelly, "Who Voted: A Portrait of American Politics, 1976–2000," *New York Times*, November 12, 2000, WK4.
15. Susan Page, " 'Til Politics Do Us Part: Gender Gap Widens," USATODAY .com, December 19, 2003, http://www.usatoday.com/news/nation/ 2003-12-17-gendergap-cover_x.htm.
16. Ibid.
17. Ronald Brownstein, "Campaign 2000: Education Surfacing as Key Issue for Bush," *Los Angeles Times*, March 24, 2000, A34.
18. Connelly, "Who Voted: A Portrait of American Politics, 1976–2000."
19. Katherine Q. Seelye, "Marital Status Is Shaping Women's Leanings, Surveys Find," *New York Times*, September 20, 2000, A19.
20. Christopher Matthews, "Why Liberals Get Little Respect," *San Francisco Examiner*, April 2, 1995, C17.
21. Senator Trent Lott, *All Things Considered*, National Public Radio, June 6, 1995.
22. Ronald Brownstein, "For 2004, Bush Has Strength in the White Male Numbers."
23. Stark, "Gap Politics."
24. Hector Tobar, "For White Males, Bush Is Their Guy," *Los Angeles Times*, September 11, 2000, A12.
25. "Attitudes and Characteristics of Freshmen," *The Chronicle of Higher Education*, August 29, 2003, 17.
26. Ronald Brownstein, "Gender Mathematics Adding Up to Unusual Factor for Both Parties," http://pqasb.pqarchiver.com/latimes/46600873.html?did= 46600873&FMT =ABS&FMTS=FT&date=Nov+22,+1999&desc=National+ Perspective%3b+Gender+Mathematics+Adding+Up+to+Unusual+Factor+ for+Both+Parties.
27. Deborah Tannen, "Bush's Sweet Talk," *New York Times*, January 20, 2000, A23.
28. Maureen Dowd, "The Erin Factor," *New York Times*, April 5, 2000, A31.
29. Tannen, "Bush's Sweet Talk."
30. Bo Ekehammar and James Sidanius, "Sex Differences in Sociopolitical Attitudes: A Replication and Extension," *British Journal of Social Psychology* 21 (1982), 249–257.
31. Stark, "Gap Politics."
32. Michael Adams, *Fire and Ice: The United States, Canada, and The Myth of Converging Values* (Toronto, Canada: Penguin Canada, 2003), 98.
33. Daniel Evan Weiss, *The Great Divide: How Females and Males Really Differ* (New York: Poseidon Press, 1991), 119.
34. Anne Fausto-Sterling, *Sexing the Body: Gender Politics and the Construction of Sexuality* (New York: Basic Books, 2000), 147.
35. Anne Fausto-Sterling, *Myths of Gender: Biological Theories About Men and Women*, 2nd ed. (New York: Basic Books, 1992), 127.
36. Ibid., 126.

37. Ibid.
38. Ibid., 130.
39. Ibid., 147.
40. Ibid., 146.
41. Theodore D. Kemper, *Social Structure and Testosterone: Explorations of the Social-Bio-Social Chain* (New Brunswick, NJ: Rutgers University Press, 1990).
42. Ibid., 23.
43. Ibid., 111–166.
44. Ibid., 167–206.
45. Nance W. Gallagher, "The Gender Gap in Popular Attitudes toward the Use of Force," in *Women and the Use of Force*, eds. Ruth R. Howes and Michael R. Stevenson (Boulder, CO: Lynne Rienner Publishers, 1993), 23–38.
46. Brian D'Agostino, "Self-Images of Hawks and Doves: A Control Systems Model of Militarism," *Political Psychology* 16, no. 2 (1995), 279.
47. Ibid.
48. *New York Times*, January 14, 2004, A1.
49. James Sidanius and Felicia Pratto, "Racism and Support for Free-Market Capitalism: A Cross-Cultural Analysis," *Political Psychology* 14, no. 3 (1993), 381–401.
50. John Kifner, "Extremist Army Group Wages War with U.S. Policy," *New York Times*, December 15, 1995, A17.
51. Ibid.
52. Ibid.
53. *New York Times*, December 14, 1995, A10.
54. *San Francisco Examiner*, September 13, 1994, A1.
55. *San Francisco Chronicle*, September 14, 1994, A1.
56. These data were sent to the author by The Gallup Organization, Princeton, NJ, September 1994.
57. Barbara Ehrenreich, *The Hearts of Men: American Dreams and the Flight from Commitment* (New York: Doubleday, 1983), 106.
58. Paul Krassner, *Whole Earth Review*, Fall 1986, 72.
59. Weiss, *The Great Divide*, 122.
60. These data were sent to the author by Mark Decamillo at Field Research, November 1994.
61. Spencer Hughes, KFSO 560 AM, October 30, 1995.
62. *New York Times*, January 5, 2003, WK11.
63. *San Francisco Chronicle*, November 22, 1995, A12.
64. Douglas J. Besharov, "Orphanages Aren't Welfare Reform," *New York Times*, December 20, 1994, A19.
65. Bob Herbert, "A Nation of Nitwits," *New York Times*, March 1, 1995, A15.
66. Ruth Sidel, "The Welfare Scam," *The Nation*, December 12, 1994, 712–713.
67. *San Francisco Chronicle*, June 7, 1994, A6.

68. Robert Pear, "Welfare Debate Will Re-Examine Core Assumptions," *New York Times*, January 2, 1995, 1.

69. David Frum, *Dead Right* (New York: Basic Books, 1994), 45.

70. Nancy Fraser and Linda Gordon, "A Genealogy of *Dependency*: Tracing a Keyword of the U.S. Welfare State," *Signs*, Winter (1994), 320.

71. Ibid., 317.

72. Ibid., 320–321.

73. Ibid., 319, 322.

74. Arlie Russell Hochschild, *The Second Shift* (New York: HarperCollins, 1990).

75. Richard L. Berke, "This Candidate Isn't Quite His Daddy's Boy," *New York Times*, September 2, 1994, 1.

76. Ibid.

77. George Gilder, "The Roots of Black Poverty," *The Wall Street Journal*, October 30, 1995, A18.

78. John H. Cushman, "House Debate Turns to Slurs and Venom," *New York Times*, May 12, 1995, A15.

79. Bob Herbert, "Behind the Smile," *New York Times*, November 11, 2002, A21.

80. George R. Brown, "Transexuals in the Military: Flight into Hypermasculinity," *Archives of Sexual Behavior* 17, no. 6 (1988), 529.

81. *Public Eye*, Fall 2002, 23.

82. Garry Wills, "The Born-Again Republicans," *New York Review of Books*, September 24, 1992, 10.

83. *Newsweek*, October 2, 1995, 44.

84. Ibid.

85. Paul Krugman, "At Long Last," *New York Times*, April 5, 2002. A23.

86. Patricia Holt, "Scars on the Earth," *San Francisco Chronicle Review*, March 13, 1994, 1.

87. *San Francisco Chronicle*, August 1, 1990, A7.

88. Richard L. Berke, "In a Reversal, G.O.P. Courts the 'Greens,'" *New York Times*, July 2, 1997, A1.

89. Todd S. Purdum, "Suburban 'Sprawl' Takes Its Place on the Political Landscape," *New York Times*, February 6, 1999, A1.

90. Paul McHugh, "Attack of the Martian Machiavellis on Earth's Environment," *San Francisco Chronicle*, December 29, 2002, D4.

91. Marla Cone, "Animal Feminization Reported Spreading," *San Francisco Chronicle*, September 22, 1998, A4.

92. Carl T. Hall, "Field Study Finds Deformed Frogs," *San Francisco Chronicle*, October 31, 2002, A6.

93. Geoffrey Lean, "Low Sperm Counts May Be Due to Pesticides," *San Francisco Examiner*, June 30, 1996, A11.

94. Doug Ireland, "Republicans Relaunch the Antigay Culture Wars," *The Nation*, October 20, 2003, 18.

95. Elaine Herscher, "Furor over Montana Sex Bill," *San Francisco Chronicle*, March 23, 1995, A4.

96. *San Francisco Chronicle*, August, 31, 1996, A4.

97. *San Francisco Chronicle*, January, 31, 2004, A2.

98. Ireland, "Republicans Relaunch the Antigay Culture Wars," 18–23.

99. Carol Ness, "Big Jump in Gay Bias among Top Students," *San Francisco Examiner*, November 12, 1998, A1.

100. Ibid.

101. Karen Franklin, "Antigay Behaviors among Young Adults: Prevalence, Patterns, and Motivators in a Noncriminal Population," *Journal of Interpersonal Violence* 15, no. 4 (2000), 339–362.

102. Frank Rich, "Family Values Stalkers," *New York Times*, January 13, 1999, A25.

103. David Dunlap, "Survey on Slayings of Homosexuals Finds High Violence and Low Arrest Rate," *New York Times*, December 21, 1994, A10.

104. *San Francisco Examiner*, June 27, 1999, D2.

105. Elisabeth Young-Bruehl, *The Anatomy of Prejudices* (Cambridge, MA: Harvard University Press, 1996), 143–153.

106. Carole A. Beere, *Sex and Gender Issues: A Handbook of Tests and Measures* (New York: Greenwood Press, 1990), 335.

107. Gregory M. Herek and John P. Capitanio, "Black Heterosexuals' Attitudes toward Lesbian and Gay Men in the United States," *The Journal of Sex Research* 32, no. 2 (1995), 95–105.

108. Beere, *Sex and Gender Issues*, 338, 352, 354.

109. Ibid., 354.

110. Ibid.

111. Ibid., 342.

112. Ibid., 338.

113. Ibid., 351.

114. Ibid., 354.

115. Patty K. Devlin and Gloria A. Cowan, "Homophobia, Perceived Fathering, and Male Intimate Relationships," *Journal of Personality Assessment* 49, no. 5 (1985), 467–473.

116. *New York Times*, December 14, 2002, A14.

117. Stephen E. Kilianski, "Explaining Heterosexual Men's Attitudes toward Women and Gay Men: The Theory of Exclusively Masculine Identity," *Psychology of Men and Masculinity* 4, no. 1 (2003), 37–56.

118. Ibid.

119. Karen Franklin, online interview with PBS in conjunction with the *Frontline* program "Assault on Gay America," February, 2000, http://www.pbs.org/wgbh/pages/frontline/shows/assault/interviews/franklin.html.

120. Henry E. Adams, Lester W. Wright, and Bethany A. Lohr, "Is Homophobia Associated with Homosexual Arousal?" *Journal of Abnormal Psychology* 105, no. 3 (1996), 440–445.

121. Sigmund Freud, "Psychoanalytic Notes on an Autobiographical Account of a Case of Paranoia (Dementia Paranoids)," *The Standard Edition of the Complete Psychological Works of Sigmund Freud,* Volume 12, ed. James Strachey (London: Hogarth, 1953–1973), 1–82.

122. Seymour Fisher and Roger P. Greenberg, *Freud Scientifically Reappraised: Testing the Theories and Therapy* (New York: John Wiley and Sons, Inc., 1996), 71.

123. Young-Bruehl, *The Anatomy of Prejudices,* 150–151.

124. Gregory M. Herek, "Beyond 'Homophobia': A Social Psychological Perspective on Attitudes toward Lesbians and Gay Men," *Journal of Homosexuality* 10, nos. 1, 2 (1984), 1–15.

125. *San Francisco Chronicle,* February 10, 1999, A3.

126. In addition to a political gender-gap scale that I developed for this research, other measures used were: the Avoiding Femininity subscale of the Brannon Masculinity Scale, developed by Robert Brannon (Robert Brannon and S. Juni, "A Scale for Measuring Attitudes about Masculinity," *Psychological Documents* 14, no. 1 [1984], 6); the Gender Role Conflict Scale, developed by James M. O'Neil (James M. O'Neil, B. J. Helms, R. K. Gable, L. David, and L. S. Wrightsman, "Gender Role Conflict Scale: College Men's Fear of Femininity," *Sex Roles* 14 [1986], 335–350); and the Attitudes toward Lesbians and Gay Men scale, developed by Gregory M. Herek (Gregory M. Herek, "Heterosexuals' Attitudes toward Lesbians and Gay Men: Correlates and Gender Differences," *Journal of Sex Research* 25 [1988], 451–477).

127. James M. O'Neil, Glen E. Good, and Sarah Holmes, "Fifteen Years of Theory and Research on Men's Gender Role Conflict: New Paradigms for Empirical Research," in *A New Psychology of Men,* eds. Ron Levant and William Pollack (New York: Basic Books, 1995).

128. John T. Jost, Jack Glaser, Arie W. Kruglanski, and Frank J. Sulloway, "Political Conservatism as Motivated Social Cognition," *Psychological Bulletin* 129, no. 3 (2003), 339–375.

129. Ibid.

130. Ibid.

7. Gender in a Time of Holy War

1. Laurie Goodstein, "Falwell's Finger-Pointing Inappropriate, Bush Says," *New York Times,* September 15, 2001, A16.

2. Seth Mydans, "In Pakistan, Rape Victims Are the 'Criminals,'" *New York Times,* May 17, 2002, A3.

3. Ibid.

4. Ibid.

5. Maureen Dowd, "Father Knows Worst," *New York Times,* March 20, 2002, A27.

6. Vicki Haddock, "Son of a Preacher Man: How John Ashcroft's Religion Shapes His Public Service," *San Francisco Chronicle,* August 4, 2002, D6.

7. Nick Madigan, "Professor's Snub of Creationists Prompts U.S. Inquiry," *New York Times*, February 3, 2003, A11.

8. Paul Krugman, "Gotta Have Faith," *New York Times*, December, 17, 2002, A35.

9. Nicholas D. Kristof, "Women's Rights: Why Not?" *New York Times*, June 18, 2002, A25.

10. Michelle Goldberg, "Yes to the Bible, No to the Treaty," Salon.com, June 22, 2002, http://www.salon.com/news/feature/2002/06/22/women/index_np.html.

11. Ibid.

12. Ibid.

13. Colum Lynch, "Islamic Bloc, Christian Right Team Up to Lobby U.N.," *The Washington Post*, June 17, 2002, A1.

14. Ibid.

15. Ibid.

16. Jennifer Block, "Christian Soldiers on the March," *The Nation*, February 3, 2003, 19.

17. Bill Maher, *Real Time*, HBO, January 23, 2004.

18. Charles Taylor, "When Right-Wing Fembots Attack," Salon.com, June 27, 2002, http://salon.com/books/feature/2002/06/27/coulter.

19. Ibid.

20. Caryl Rivers, " 'Crazed Foes' of Women's Rights Are Advancing," *San Francisco Chronicle*, January 9, 1995, A25.

21. "The Promise Keepettes," *New York Times Magazine*, April 27, 1997, 15.

22. Ibid.

23. Nicholas D. Kristof, "The Veiled Resource," *New York Times*, December 11, 2001, A27.

24. Lynsey Addario, "Jihad's Women," *New York Times Magazine*, October 21, 2001, 40.

25. Mary Douglas, *Purity and Danger* (London: Frederick A. Praeger, 1966), 35–36.

26. Kristof, "The Veiled Resource."

27. Karen Houppert, "Wanted: A Few Good Girls," *The Nation*, November 25, 2002, 13.

28. Don Lattin, "Baptists Say Wives Must Submit," *San Francisco Chronicle*, June 10, 1998, A1.

29. Mark S. Hamm, *In Bad Company: America's Terrorist Underground* (Boston: Northeastern University Press, 2002), 12.

30. Ibid., 36.

31. "Soldiers in the Army of God," *America Undercover Sundays*, HBO, April 1, 2001.

32. Robert L. Munroe and Ruth H. Munroe, *Cross-Cultural Human Development* (Prospect Heights, IL: Waveland Press, 1994), 115–133.

33. William Safire, "Kangaroo Courts," *New York Times*, November 26, 2001, A19.

34. Rebecca Flourney, research associate, Henry J. Kaiser Foundation, personal communication by e-mail regarding unpublished gender cross-tabulations on attitudes toward military tribunals, January 2, 2002.

35. Joe Conason, "The Real 'Fifth' Column," Salon.com, November 1, 2001, http://archive.salon.com/news/col/cona/2001/11/01/fifth_column/index_np.html.

36. Ruth Stein, "Evil as Love and as Liberation," *Psychoanalytic Dialogues* 12, no. 3 (2002), 393–420.

37. Sarah Boxer, "Dreams of Holy War Over a Quiet Evening," *New York Times*, December 16, 2001, Section 4, 1.

38. Daniel Levitas, "The Radical Right after 9/11," *The Nation*, July 22/29, 2002, 19.

39. Nancy Ehrenreich, "Masculinity and American Militarism," Tikkun.org, November/December 2002, http://www.tikkun.org/magazine/index.cfm/action/ tikkun/issue/tiko211/article/021113d.html.

40. Richard Goldstein, "Butching Up for Victory," thenation.com, January 26, 2004, http://www.thenation.com/doc.mhtml?i=20040126&s=goldstein.

41. Patricia Leigh Brown, "Heavy Lifting Required: The Return of Manly Men," *New York Times*, October 28, 2001, WK5.

42. Suzanne Herel, "The Latest Superhero––U.S. Firefighters," *San Francisco Chronicle*, August 18, 2002, A1.

43. James Pinkerton, "Real Men Back in Style," *San Francisco Chronicle*, August 4, 2002, D4.

44. Cathy Horyn, "Macho America Storms Europe's Runways," *New York Times*, July 3, 2003, A1.

45. Katha Pollit, "Victory Gardens," *The Nation*, November 19, 2001, 10.

46. David Frum, "It's His Party," *New York Times*, January 5, 2003, WK11.

47. *The American Enterprise*, September 2003.

48. Karl Zinsmeister and Eli Lehrer, "Indicators," *The American Enterprise*, September 2003, 12–13.

49. *The New York Observer*, August 26, 2002, A1.

50. Robin Toner, "Now Government Is the Solution, Not the Problem," *New York Times*, September 30, 2001, WK14.

51. Jude Wanniski, "Mommy Party, Daddy Party," January 19, 1999, http:// www.polyconomics.com/searchbase/01-19-99.html.

52. George Lakoff, *Moral Politics: What Conservatives Know That Liberals Don't* (Chicago: University of Chicago Press, 1996).

53. Rich Zubaty, personal e-mail communication.

54. Rich Zubaty, *Surviving the Feminization of America* (Chicago: Panther Press, 1993).

55. Paul Krugman, "The Blue Americans," *New York Times*, May 7, 2002, A33.

56. James Brooke, "Freeman Depended on Subsidies," *New York Times*, April 30, 1996, A8.

57. Michelle Goldberg, "Shock Troops for Bush," Salon.com, February 4, 2003, http://archive.salon.com/news/feature/2003/02/04/cpac/index_np.html.

58. Ibid.

59. Ibid.

60. Leah Garchick, "The In Crowd," *San Francisco Chronicle*, August 28, 2001, C10.

61. Julie Crandall, "Support for Spanking," ABCNEWS.com, November 8, 2002, http://abcnews.go.com/sections/us/DailyNews/spanking_poll021108.html.

62. Michael A. Milburn and Sheree D. Conrad, *The Politics of Denial* (Cambridge, MA: The MIT Press, 1996), 1–71.

63. Ibid., 66.

64. Ben Fritz, "Savage with the Truth," Salon.com, February 19, 2003, http://archive .salon.com/books/review/2003/02/19/savage/index_np.html.

65. Fair.org, http://www.fair.org/activism/msnbc-savage.html.

66. Ibid.

67. David Gilson, "Michael Savage's Long, Strange Trip," Salon.com, March 5, 2003, http://archive.salon.com/news/feature/2003/03/05/savage/index_np.html.

68. Dan Fost, "Savage Talk," *San Francisco Chronicle*, February 6, 2003, E11.

69. Gilson, "Michael Savage's Long, Strange Trip."

70. GLAAD transcript of MSNBC's *Savage Nation*, airing July 5, 2003, http://www.glaad.org/publications/resource_doc_detail.php?id=3281&.

71. Dana Canedy, "Florida Child Welfare Appointee under Fire for View on Spanking," *San Francisco Chronicle*, August 17, 2002, A2.

72. *New York Times*, August 24, 2002, A6.

73. Ibid.

74. Milburn and Conrad, *The Politics of Denial*, 69.

75. Thomas B. Edsall, "Women's Political Muscle Shapes 2000 Race," *Washington Post*, March 11, 1999, A1.

76. Milburn and Conrad, *The Politics of Denial*, 69.

77. James MacKinnon, "Brand America," *New York Times*, January 27, 2003, B7.

78. David Corn, "Bush's Top Gun Photo-Op," Alternet.org, May 2, 2003, http://www.alternet.org/story.html?StoryID=15806.

79. G. Gordon Liddy, interviewed on *Hardball*, MSNBC, May 8, 2003.

80. Andrew Sullivan, "Idiocy of the Week," Salon.com, May 23, 2003, http://archive.salon.com/opinion/sullivan/2003/05/23/goldstein/index_np.html.

81. Richard Goldstein, "Bush's Basket: Why the President Had to Show His Balls," *The Village Voice*, http://www.villagevoice.com/issues/0321/goldstein.php.

82. Ibid.

Acknowledgments

Whatever phallic delusions of self-sufficiency I may have labored under prior to undertaking this book have not withstood the challenge of needing and using the generous help of so many. My wife, Susan, was always my first and most demanding reader. Her vigilant attention to lapses in logic, inelegant phrasing, and glib interpretations was indispensable. Only I, however, am responsible for those blunders that may have escaped her discerning eye. My friend and comrade Iain Boal provided invaluable editorial and intellectual feedback on numerous incarnations of this book. His wide-ranging critical sensibilities have been essential in sharpening my thinking and apprising me of valuable references. Neil Altman graciously agreed to do the work of giving a close reading to the manuscript of someone he scarcely knew. His comments and supportive response helped me push through to the end. Lisa Buchberg also contributed significantly to whatever coherence the final version achieved. Her thoughtfulness and interest in my ideas were an enormous buoy to my spirits. I am also grateful for the diligence with which my agent, Anna Ghosh, approached the challenge of finding me a publisher, and for the unrelenting faith she demonstrated in this project. Gayatri Patnaik, my editor at Beacon Press, has been extremely helpful in shepherding the manuscript through the convolutions of the publishing process. Most important was the palpable excitement she had for my book, which engendered the enthusiasm of all the others at Beacon who have worked so hard to bring *The Wimp Factor* to fruition. The grandiose fantasy that I have not entirely given up is that this book may somehow affect how Americans think about masculinity and politics, such that the impediments to a more democratic and egalitarian world can be understood with more clarity. Whatever the extent to which this fantasy is realized, I will have many people to thank, not just those mentioned here, but the countless others—teachers, students, and colleagues—who have helped shape my thinking over the years, and who have provided unceasing encouragement for my writing.

Index

Afterword to the Paperback Edition

As we have seen throughout the preceding chapters, anxious masculinity in public life has taken many forms. While I wrote much about the demonization of powerful women, I focused less on the deification of *powerless* women. Since the 2004 edition of this book, Hillary Clinton has remained the paleoconservative fundraising poster child for feminine danger. But for a number of months in the spring of 2005, another woman's image, one that had a decidedly different emotional valence for Republicans, monopolized attention in the media spectacle and revealed something about the femiphobic political unconscious.

Brian H. Darling, a former gun industry lobbyist and, until his resignation, legal counsel to Republican senator Mel Martinez of Florida, eventually admitted authoring the memo that declared Terri Schiavo's tragic predicament "a great political issue" for his party. As we have seen, this turned out to be an assessment shared by many of his colleagues, including those in the White House. How can we make sense of the right-wing view that the debate over whether to keep a feeding tube tethered to the living ghost of Ms. Schiavo was a situation ripe for political exploitation? There are some obvious explanations that come immediately to mind. As the infamous memo openly stated, Republican lawmakers saw her case as an opportunity to shore up their Christian Right base—fundamentalist pro-lifers who viewed the dispute between Ms. Schiavo's parents and her husband as a surrogate for the debate over whether the state should intervene in *other* private medical decisions, namely abortion. For one GOP representative, Tom Delay, the family's anguished and bitter conflict was a coveted chance to play a brazen ethical shell game—directing the public eye away from ongoing investigations into his own sociopathic conduct. For Bush there was the prospect of reversing his sliding approval ratings—the worst of any second term president in seventy years—by striking his most heroic pose since the infamous aircraft carrier "victory" swagger.

Then there is the obvious hypocrisy of the claim by Ms. Schiavo's would-be Republican rescuers that they were driven by a "reverence for life." Some may recall that George W. Bush, when he was governor of Texas, signed legislation allowing hospitals to discontinue a patient's life support against the wishes of the family, and permitting them to cite inability to pay as an acceptable rationale. This was the same state politician whose administration made the death penalty a virtual sacrament. He couldn't kill people fast enough—whether the condemned were mentally retarded, schizophrenic, juveniles, or represented by ineffectual, drunken attorneys widely observed to have slept through trials. Now, as CEO of a neoconservative federal regime, he has presided over the deaths of tens of thousands of Iraqi civilians and an ever mounting toll of American soldiers, all in a quixotic and manic pursuit of global domination spurred on by a grudge match with his daddy's nemesis, Saddam. This is the same White House that has officially sanctioned the torture of prisoners of war and promoted those whose policy memos gave the green light to the actual perpetrators. Last but not least in this curriculum vitae of hypocrisy is the Republicans' slavering enthusiasm for developing a new generation of nuclear weaponry.

While all of the above are clearly true, they still leave one question unanswered: why was a *woman* in a persistent vegetative state cast as the main character in this histrionic morality play? Why couldn't a man in the same condition play such a role? A moment's reflection tells us that, except in the days of slavery, a male's value is rarely reduced to his limbs and torso. Without a functioning brain, the physiological locus of selfhood, a man is regarded as already dead—just as Tom Delay's father was when the life-revering congressman elected to pull the plug on his brain-dead progenitor.

A woman's value, on the other hand, seems to be assessed by other criteria. More specifically, conservative and misogynistic men, especially of the fundamentalist variety, have always had a special affection for women without minds. The history of patriarchal cultures is saturated with ambivalence about the talking, thinking, and self-authorizing female head—women who can speak and act for themselves. In Chapter 4, I traced this back to one of the earliest feminine images of cephalic malevolence, Medusa. And, as numerous examples throughout this book attest, men's fear of women who have a head on their shoulders has not been confined to mythic worlds. We have seen how fundamentalist versions of most patriarchal religious traditions mandate that women cover their heads, mute their voices, forsake their autonomy, and trammel their sexuality to the imperatives of men.

Terri Schiavo was the paradigmatic example of a woman who "knew" her proper place and stayed there—in bed, without agency or any sense of self. She had no will to interfere with the desires and plans the men in her life, and especially her would-be saviors in Washington, had for her. Their efforts to sacralize vegetative femininity could not be challenged by the one they tried to beatify. Forever voiceless, she could put up no resistance to those who sought to hitch their ideological and political wagons to her pale star, a star in which the light of personhood had faded into oblivion fifteen years earlier.

By way of conclusion, it might be illuminating to look at an example of how conservative males show their concern for women *not yet* in intensive care. As I was preparing this afterword, I came across an interesting news item, one that emanated from the statehouse in Columbia, South Carolina. The House Judiciary Committee approved a Republican-sponsored bill that made cockfighting a felony, while they deliberately left on the books a law that defined domestic violence, even after multiple convictions, as a misdemeanor. Of course, this simply confirms what we have come to know about right-wing patriarchs of all persuasions: they can be counted on to privilege their cocks over the welfare of women.